D1474961

HUD SCANDALS

HUD SCANDALS

Howling Headlines and Silent Fiascoes

HD
7293
. W372
1992
West

Irving Welfeld

Transaction Publishers
New Brunswick (U.S.A.) and London (U.K.)

Copyright © 1992 by Transaction Publishers.
New Brunswick, New Jersey 08903

All rights reserved under International and Pan-American Copyright Conventions. No part of this book may be reproduced or transmitted in any form or by any means, electronic or mechanical, including photocopy, recording, or any information storage and retrieval system, without prior permission in writing from the publisher. All inquiries should be addressed to Transaction Publishers, Rutgers-The State University, New Brunswick, New Jersey 08903.

Library of Congress Catalog Number: 91–32042
ISBN: 1-56000-042-2
Printed in the United States of America

Library of Congress Cataloging-in-Publication-Data
Welfeld, Irving
HUD scandals : howling headlines and silent fiascoes / Irving Welfeld.
    p. cm.
    ISBN 1-56000-042-2
    1. United States. Dept. of Housing and Urban Development. 2. Political corruption—United States. 3. Waste in government spending—United States. I. Title.
HD7293.W372 1992
364. 1'68—dc20

91–32042
CIP

The views expressed in this book are those of the author, who in no way purports to speak for his employer, the Department of Housing and Urban Development.

To all those people who cared enough to counsel me that I should not
be writing this book.

I would like to thank:

Robert Haveman for offering a change of climate and Secretary Jack Kemp for deciding I was expendable.

The staff at the LaFollete Institute of Public Affairs at the University of Wisconsin for putting up with my hard returns.

Alice Honeywell for being my English maven.

The people in Orem, Utah, who produce WordPerfect.

Jim Matheny and Mary McMullen for providing me with reading material during the long cold winter.

Those who helped but whose careers will not be furthered by mentioning their names.

Chuck Lamb whose publishing campaign came at the expense of his tennis game.

My brother for showing me how health leads to wealth.

Hilbert Fefferman for holding me to the rigorous clarity standard, "Even a Harvard graduate student should be able to understand it." If I failed, it's not because he didn't try.

Contents

Introduction   1

PART I - HISTORY IN A POLICY CONTEXT

1. The 1954 FHA Investigations   5
2. From Mike Wallace to the Moratorium   27
3. Robin Hook and His Holy Band   51
4. Circles of Shame   71

PART II - THE MANAGERS AND THE OVERSEERS

5. The Circle of Neglect   113
6. Good Management of Bad Programs   125
7. No Better People and No Greater Honesty   143

PART III - HUD IN THE MARKETPLACE

8. HUD in the Marketplace   157
    Bibliography   179
    Index   185

Introduction

It was the summer and Trump was in the headlines. The headlines were neither about Ivana nor Marla nor about the difficulty of staying on top. In fact, they were not about the Donald. They were about his father, Fred.

It was the summer of 1954 and the media were concerned with a nondescript apartment house in what then were the far reaches of Brooklyn. He was explaining and complaining. Fred Trump was explaining how he made his fortune—not to a group of eager bookbuyers or even to a group of creditors—but rather to the Senate Committee on Banking and Currency. He was complaining about the bad publicity. The headline on the front page of the hometown paper *The Brooklyn Eagle*

CHARGE $4 MILLION WINDFALL TO BUILDER OF BEACHHAVEN

Federal investigators checking the housing loan scandals have accused Fred C. Trump, Jamaica, Long Island, builder of pocketing $4,070,000 windfall on the Beach Haven Apartments in Brooklyn....

Congress was investigating the Federal Housing Administration (FHA, which was then a part of the Housing and Home Finance Agency [HHFA], which in 1965 would achieve cabinet status as the Department of Housing and Urban Development [HUD]). What they found would not have come as a surprise to the Government Operations Committee, headed by Representative Tom Lantos, that in the late 1980s and early 1990s has been investigating the "Abuses, Favoritism, and Mismanagement in HUD Programs."

There is a well-known Yiddish proverb that when a poor man eats a chicken, one of them is sick. When HUD appears in a headline, or is even noticed by the media, it is usually engrossed in a scandal. In the main, these headline grabbers are examples of mismanagement or nonmanagement and in recent history they border on parody:

Imagine: a cabinet Secretary . . . sleeps through his eight-year tenure . . . at his multi-billion dollar agency and watching soap operas. Filling the vacuum is the best-connected bar maid in Georgetown (Debbie Dean), who takes control of the department and doles out contracts for questionable projects to her pals. A host of get-the-government-off-the-peoples-back conservatives pocket huge fees for lobbying the agency. In seeking greater efficiency through "privatization," the agency hands its programs over to private companies who leave the government saddled with

1

$5 billion worth of loan liabilities. . . . Enter "Robin HUD" (Marilyn Louise Harrell) who steals more than $5 million before anyone notices. It's about as far-fetched as the coup plot in *Seven Days in May*.[1]

What is more interesting, although not as funny, are the silent fiascoes - the major policy mistakes that have occurred while HUD was paying dutiful attention to managing its misshapen programs. As an article entitled "Why We Need More Waste, Fraud, and Mismanagement in the Pentagon" put the matter:

> [T]here is indeed something wrong with our defense policy . . . and what is wrong is very serious indeed. The obsessive attention now being devoted to micro-manage-ment is the root cause of an evil far greater than any marginal inefficiency or any thievery could possibly be. Our . . . leaders . . . are systematically distracted from the pursuit that should be their dominant business by a wrong-headed quest for paper efficiencies and marginal savings.[2]

In the first part of the book I will narrate and analyze seven scandals and fiascoes that have occurred since World War II. The first will be the Section 608 rental housing program in which developers were able to reap huge profits and the last will be the administrative porkbarreling of the Pierce Administration during the 1980s.

The second part of the book deals with more general questions. Why did the media, the Congress, the General Accounting Office, the Office of Management and Budget and the Office of the Inspector General do such a poor job in their oversight functions? To what extent is poor management the root cause of the failures in the past? To what extent are these failures likely to be reformed by better people and tighter administrative procedures?

The third part of the book describes a set of programs that would minimize discretion on the part of administrators and the temptation to misuse and abuse the public trust. Hopefully, these programs will also enable HUD to more effectively fulfill its missions to see to it that there is a sufficient supply of decent housing and there is assistance available to all Americans who at present cannot afford such housing.

Notes

1.   DeParle, Jason, "What the Smartest Man in Washington Doesn't Understand. And Why it Will Hurt You," *The Washington Monthly*, November 1989, 34.
2.   Luttwak, Edward, *Commentary*, February 1982, 20.

I

History in a Policy Context

1

The 1954 FHA Investigations

There was a time, long ago, when the Federal Housing Administration could do almost no wrong. It was one of the New Deal's most respected creations. It had made homeownership easier for millions of American families—having insured 20 million home loan mortgages covering $30.8 billion in borrowing. It had repaid the last $85 million that the U.S. Treasury had advanced to get it started. It was netting a substantial profit. FHA was sailing merrily along and then the ship hit the shoals.

On the evening of 11 April 1954 James Hagerty the White House press secretary announced, much to the surprise of the FHA Commissioner, Guy Hollyday, (described by one and all as a "good Christian gentleman"), that the President would accept his resignation—that is, he was fired. At dusk of 12 April 1954, the HHFA Administrator, acting on President Eisenhower's orders, impounded all FHA files and records of the Title I property improvement loan insurance program and the section 608 rental housing insurance program.

Two reports touched off the investigations. The Commissioner of Internal Revenue had reported that the income tax return of corporations sponsoring 608 projects revealed large windfall profits in hundreds of projects; and a report by the Federal Bureau of Investigation had pointed to evidence of extensive victimization of property owners by unscrupulous dealers and salesmen negotiating property improvement loans.

The combination of fat cats making millions and thousands of little people being swindled made great political theater. The Senate Committee on Banking and Currency's "FHA Investigation" ran from June to

5

November and the four thick volumes of testimony and cross-examination ran to 3,749 pages.[1]

Loose Lips Sink Ships — Loose Laws Build Houses

Section 608 (of the "National Housing Act")[2] had rather modest beginnings. It was enacted in 1942, to provide mortgage insurance for rental housing designed for occupancy by defense workers. At the end of 1946, 513 projects containing 38,419 apartments had been insured. The program was amended to cover housing for veterans in 1946, after which it became very successful. After 1946 over 425,000 rental apartments were built, for a grand total of 465,603 units in 7,065 projects. In 1989 dollars, over 44 billion dollars worth of housing were constructed under the program which ended in 1950.[3]

Why it Grew?

The program grew up in an era of near panic about the housing shortage facing the country and near awe at the power of the profit motive. The former can be seen in the name of the key legislation expanding the Section 608 program and its first two sentences. The "Veterans' Emergency Housing Act of 1946"[4] began with the following words: "The long-term housing shortage and the war have combined to create an unprecedented emergency shortage of housing, particularly for veterans of World War II and their families. This requires during the next two years a housing construction program larger than ever before."

Almost 3 million veterans returned to America's crowded shores in 1946. In addition, the rural-to-urban migration to (wo)man the war industries further complicated the matter. In Los Angeles, for example, 85 percent of the defense workers did not return to their farms and towns. In the spring of 1948, there were nearly 2.5 million married couples who lacked separate homes of their own, an increase of over half a million over the 2 million such families in 1940.[5] The shortage produced the following results:

> Throughout the nation many veterans and their families lived in attics, basements, chicken coops and boxcars. Washington D.C. . . . reported 25,000 homeless veterans. Chicago had four times the number . . . . In Atlanta, 2,000 persons answered one advertisement of a vacancy, and a want ad in an Omaha newspaper read, "Big Ice Box, 7 by 17 feet. Could be fixed up to live in."[6]

Builders were slow in responding. It was reported that President Harry S.Truman called Ray Foley, then head of the FHA, pounded the table and wanted to know, "Why more builders were failing to take advantage of the golden opportunities that were available under the liberal terms of the new legislation."[7] In January 1947, FHA sent its minions far and wide across the nation with the message that it was the patriotic duty of the builders to relieve the housing conditions of the returning veterans and the FHA was ready to make it easy. The messengers were instructed to tell their audiences, "Remember that every suitable site is the basis of a rental-housing project. If you have the site you have a deal."[8]

Senator Russell Long, a major supporter of the program, entwined private profit to the public weal:

> I want to say right here and now that frankly I believe this project was intended to be extremely profitable to builders and the purpose was based on the American tradition that if you want to get the job done, if you will show the American businessmen where they can make a hefty profit, they will go out there and do you a job. That has caused this country to grow the way it has.[9]

The conventional wisdom about bureaucracies is that they are slow, cumbersome, and unresponsive. This is usually the case when the message from on high is unclear. In the case of Section 608, the message was loud and clear—the business of government was business. Field offices were rated on the basis of the volume of housing produced. The salary of the local director and his staff depended directly on the volume of business they could generate.

The Housing and Home Finance Agency's investigation makes this point abundantly clear:

> FHA officials tended to measure success in terms of the volume of the business. FHA files are studded with examples of this point of view. When in 1948 an underwriting supervisor remonstrated with the chief underwriter in the Des Moines office because of the frequent waiver of items of noncompliance and deficiencies in the inspection system, the reply was: "Well, you know we're hungry for business."[10]

And, if competition makes business run faster, the FHA would run for glory. As the HHFA reported:

> Another reason for the emphasis on volume was the desire of FHA officials to keep their place in the sun in the relation to the volume of credit available conventionally and through the Veteran's Administration. In particular, the active competition between FHA and VA undoubtedly sharpened volume consciousness.[11]

The FHA would also run for presents and for money. When Christmas came to the District of Columbia field office in 1947, Santa and kind and considerate developers brought bottles of liquor, fruit, hams, cigars, turkeys, and ties for the men and nylons, scarves, candy, and fruit for the women; and to keep everyone abreast of the finest of literature, subscriptions to the *Readers Digest*. The more important officials received gifts more appropriate to their rank—wristwatches, portable radios, and Philco console television sets.[12]

Christmas was not the only party time. To celebrate the groundbreaking of a project in New Mexico, the FHA director for the state, suggested to the contractor that he deserved a party in his honor. The party was held at the Motel Almogordo with three party girls furnished by the contractor—the $500 charge for the services of the girls was charged to the construction job.[13]

The conflict between the public purse and the private pocketbook and the gift for graft reached the highest places. The director of the New York office Thomas Grace was also a partner in a law firm whose client list included sponsors, brokers, or counsel for the mortgagee. The firm was so skilled that it filed sixty-four applications and received $85 million in mortgage insurance commitments.[14] The assistant commissioner for multifamily housing, Clyde L. Powell, who was in charge of the 608 program, had excellent credentials. He was a thief and a liar. He had passed bogus checks, embezzled and had been confined to hard labor for being AWOL while in the Army. At FHA, he had a reputation as a high-stakes gambler. He, however, rarely gambled away his salary, which in 1946 was $9,742.20. The total of payments stated to have been paid to Powell by various promoters went comfortably into six figures for the years, 1946-50.[15]

A Rich Cake

The graft and the corruption was only the icing on the cake. The "hefty profit" to which Senator Russell Long had referred had become a "scandalous windfall". Many developers had "mortgaged out" of their Section 608 projects. They had built the projects for less than the FHA insured mortgage and pocketed substantial sums of money. The camel, whose nose was let in to smell and taste the honey had ripped through the tent and devoured the honey and a whole lot more.

To understand what had occurred it is necessary to first look at the original legislation and its subsequent modifications. The legislation in 1942 creating the program had four basic limitations on the amount of the mortgage. The mortgage could not exceed:

a. $5 million;

b. 90 percent of the Administrator's *estimate* of the *reasonable* replacement cost of the completed project including the land, architect fees, taxes and interest during construction and miscellaneous charges;

c. the Administrator's *estimate* of the completed project cost exclusive of land, legal expense and off-site streets and public utilities;

d. $1,350 per room attributable to dwelling use.

In 1946, when the program was directed at veterans, the Congress was concerned with the "serious shortages and bottle-necks with respects to building materials"; the legislation was amended to delete the term "reasonable replacement cost" and replace it by the term "necessary current cost." The purpose of the change was to permit recognition of the need to pay premium prices to obtain scarce materials or high wages to obtain scarce labor, or to provide a bigger or better appliance than called for in the specifications when the cheaper appliance was not available. The per room cost limitation was also raised to $1,500.

In 1947, concerned that the terms were too favorable the legislation instructed FHA:

> In estimating necessary cost . . . the Federal Housing Commissioner shall . . . use every feasible means to assure such estimates will approximate as closely as possible actual costs of efficient building operations.[16]

Finally in 1948, the limit per room was replaced by $8,100 per apartment unit and the estimate of replacement costs was to be made "on the basis of costs on December 31, 1947, for properties or projects of comparable quality in the area where such property was located."[17] In spite of all the legislative tinkering, the project costs were limited by such mushy terms as "estimates," "reasonable," "comparable," and "estimates will approximate." Given these terms, a gap between the FHA's estimate and the developers' cost is almost guaranteed. The architectural fee is a perfect example.

The FHA allowed a 5 percent fee of its estimate of building costs to pay for architectural services. However, an experienced architect who has a set of garden apartment plans, specifications, and blueprints that in the past had met the FHA's "Minimum Property Requirements for Multi-Family Dwelling" is willing to sell his services at far below the standard fee. He has less work than if he were starting from scratch and the smaller profit on each unit is made up by the greater volume of business. In addition, he brings to the FHA architectural reviewer, who is usually at best overworked and underpaid and at worst either inexperienced or had spent his whole career reviewing single family housing, a set of plans according to the "Bible" and safe to approve. Since time is money for the developer the experienced architect is a bargain. Throw in a fee at 30 percent of the going rate, usually 1½ percent, the average developer would be crazy not to hire him.

It is not surprising that the first major article on "mortgaging out" appeared in the *Architectural Forum* in 1950 entitled, "FHA Impact on the Financing and Design of Apartments." The article not only detailed the mortgaging out process, but also scathingly attacked FHA's architectural viewpoint:

> One of the most fascinating aspects of FHA's underwriting . . . is its strange mixture of financial radicalism . . . and design conservatism . . . [I]t is far more conservative than the average banker in its refusal to take a chance on any new architectural solutions for the problem of rental building.
>
> With both FHA and the sponsor lined up solidly against any departure from exactly what was done yesterday, the architect is helpless. If he wants to keep his 608 clients he soon learns not to start any arguments with FHA processors. Some local FHA offices actually go so far as to suggest that the architect simply make use of FHA's stock site or building plans, which it is happy to take off the shelf . . . [I]ts rigid insistence on routine . . . has reduced the architect to the status of draftsman . . . . Its indifference to what the builder actually pays in architectural and engineering fees is enough in itself to make sure that top-rate firms will have little to do with apartment buildings.[18]

While in the 1980s and 1990s the financing of a project involves the payments of points and fees to the lender to provide the mortgage loan, from the late forties through the sixties, the shoe was often on the other foot. FHA allowed a financing fee in the mortgage, but it was the mortgagees who were paying the fee to the developer. Banks would pay premiums to the builder for the privilege of lending him government-insured money. The mortgage premium in most places was 1 or 2 percent.

However, with the advent of New York and Massachusetts savings banks into the national market the competition was keener and many a developer received premiums of 3 or 4 percent.

The drain off of the fees was minor compared to the funds that could flow from the construction process. If the developer had his own organization he would collect the builder's fee and the overhead costs. The actual cost of the overhead could be quite lean. Senator Frederick Payne of Maine probing for the actual cost of maintaining an office received the following response from Fred C. Trump of Queens: "Our offices are very meager. It was built right on the project as part of the storage sheds . . . it is just an office to get out of the rain."[19] What a difference a generation makes.

There is also the matter of luck. When Congress changed the law in 1946 and introduced the phrase "necessary current costs" it expected a very tight market and an inflationary construction industry. But as luck would have it, there was a sharp decline in the building material cost due to a recession in the late forties. Thus, any developer who was building in 1948 and just prior to the Korean War would have lower costs than those estimated by FHA—given the long lag between the time of the estimate and the time of the expenditure.

The change in the law in 1948 was also a boon to builders. When the law changed to an apartment-based dollar limitation of $8,100, developers built smaller apartments. They had the converse experience from that of the public housing program. When the program started the cost limits were based on apartments. In 1949, Congress changed the legislation to base the dollar limits by room counts and all of a sudden Public Housing Authorities were building large apartments.

Competence paid well in the 608 program. Since the FHA was basing construction costs on the average in the locality, the costs of the better than average builder would be substantially below the FHA estimate. There is a pot of gold for the builder who can build speedily. He can, on a large project, save hundreds of thousands of dollars in interest, real estate taxes, insurance premiums, and general overhead during construction that was included in the mortgage *and* collect rents.

Although there were no rewards for innovative architects, there were substantial rewards for innovative builders. A developer from Norfolk, Bertram Bonner, explained to the committee why the total left over from mortgage proceeds was $858,000. After providing the Committee a schedule which showed $469,000 in savings from lower fees, interest and land costs, he went on to account how he saved the other $389,000:

> [T]he balance can be accounted for by savings effected by the corporations in performing much of the work performed by subcontractors. This applied to a great deal of the heavy work such as masonry and carpentry. In connection with the carpentry work methods entirely new to the builders in the area as well as the local FHA office, were employed. For the first time in the area, roof trusses with a split-ring design [were used] which resulted in an economy of labor and materials. Plumbing systems were also prefabricated for the first time in the area, and . . . resulted in substantial economies.[20]

The bottom layer of the rich cake of profit available to the developers was the difference between their cost for the land and FHA's valuation of the land, although FHA rarely valued the land at more than 10 percent of the total cost of land and buildings. Even when FHA valued the land at a much lower percentage there were often substantial gains. The Bonner list of savings included $85,000 representing the difference between his cost and the FHA appraisal equal to 4.13 percent of the total cost.[21]

Some of the developers were a little more clever. Instead of including the land in the mortgage, the land was placed in a trust which would rent the land to the corporation that owned the project. The use of the leasehold permitted the entire $8,100 maximum to be applied to costs other than land leaving more room for savings or the construction of larger units. Not taking money for the land did not involve a hardship for the developer. In case of the Trump project, the land was purchased for $180,000 and put in a trust to make sure that his kids would have a kitty for the future. The rent was $60,000 a year for ninety nine years. Since the lease took precedence over the FHA mortgage, FHA agreed that if it were to foreclose and repossess the project it would pay the trust $1.5 million.[22]

Was There a Windfall?

HHFA's Special Investigation Office identified 1,410 projects where the proceeds of the mortgage was greater than the costs. As of September of 1954 the excess was $110 million. The "windfall" profits ranged from $2,833 for Audubon Park Apartments in Jersey City, New Jersey to $4.3 million in Glen Oaks Village in Bellerose, New York.[23]

The traditional view of the 608 affair was set forth in a HUD report that was produced in the wake of scandals in the early seventies that resulted in a shutdown of HUD programs. *Housing in the Seventies: A Report of the National Housing Policy Review* in recounting HUD's earlier history stated:

> The frauds under the Section 608 War and Veterans Housing program consisted primarily of "mortgaging out" on the basis of greatly excessive costs that determined the mortgage amount. The sponsor simply kept the money under the mortgage to the extent it was not needed for development. This was prevented in future programs by the "cost certification" requirement, which obligates the sponsor to certify costs after development, and requires FHA to limit the mortgage amount accordingly.[24]

At what point, does a "hefty profit" become fraud? In fact, is the term "windfall" an accurate characterization? A "windfall" has been defined in a HUD funded study by Donald Hagman and Dean Misczynski, entitled *Windfall For Wipeouts,* "as any increase in the value of real estate—other than that caused by the owner—or general inflation." For example,

> Mr. A bought a lot on Elm Street for $5,000 in 1965 that was zoned for single-family use. He did nothing with the lot for 10 years, during which there was considerable high-class private development in the area. A millionaire who owned 20 acres of land adjoining Mr. A's lot died, his will leaving the acreage to the Horticultural Society of America with an endowment to establish a formal garden. A's lot thus received the enhancement of a park-like setting. The formal garden being the diadem of the city's aesthetic resources, it decided to enhance the approaches to it by downzoning the property around the formal garden for space use. The downzoning did not include Mr. A's lot, which the city rezoned for 100-story commercial-residential uses to serve the needs of city dwellers who came seeking quiet in the garden. To minimize automobile congestion, the city also rerouted a planned subway, opening a station near the gardens and adjacent to Mr. A's lot. Mr. A sold his lot for $5,000,000. Five thousand dollars to $5,000,000 . . .[25]

That is a windfall! Mr. A did nothing except smile on the way to the bank. Compare the case of Mr. Bonner and his land:

> I had to begin with a careful selection of land, which involved foresight and courage on my part in converting to residential use property in an industrial area . . . . This property was lying dormant and was viewed by real estate people as probably suitable for industrial development . . . .

> We saw the possibility of using the property for a sound 608 development with housing. . . . After many weeks of negotiation we obtained the option. . . . In that time we made a very careful study of the area, a survey of the various industries and

concluded that housing with a shelter rent of $61.50 a month would serve the need and would be successful.[26]

He didn't wait for the wind to make the apple fall into his lap. The profit was the fruit of his labor.

Construction work is never risk free. In spite of the use of corporations, bonding companies required personal guarantees. Strikes by the teamsters, accidents, or even a war in a far-off country can shatter the most carefully constructed timetable and budget. In late 1949, the price of lumber was $70 for a thousand board feet. North Korea invaded South Korea and the United Nations decided to enter the fray and the price jumped to $110 a thousand. For a large project that is using millions of board feet, the price jump can turn a profitable job into a financial disaster.

The "windfall" characterization also failed to distinguish between cost and value. The following tête-à-tête between the Committee's Chairman Homer Capehart of Indiana, the Committee counsel William Simon, and, our old acquaintance, Mr. Trump illustrates the gulf:

THE CHAIRMAN: Your actual costs we want . . .
MR. SIMON: Did you pay any builder's fee?
MR. TRUMP: [W]e did the work you would ordinarily pay a builders's fee . . . we performed the service.
MR. SIMON: When you mow your own lawn, does anyone pay you a fee for it?
MR. TRUMP: If a tailor has one of his own men make a suit of clothes, that suit will cost x dollars. If the boss tailor makes a suit of clothes, he can't sell that suit cheaper. that suit is worth just as much as though he paid a man to make that suit . . . when he sells his suit he will be compensated for his services but the suit is worth exactly what the other suit was worth that he had made. Now whether we supervised the work ourselves or paid someone to do it we are entitled to the builder's fee.
MR. CHAIRMAN: What was your cost, Mr. Trump . . .?[27]

Mr. Trump was a better businessman and a better economist than his inquisitors. As Wallace Smith has noted:

[T]he real costs incurred in constructing a building must be considered "sunk" for business and economic purposes. If the building does not earn rent, the costs cannot be withdrawn. . . . The level of rents has no necessary relation to the historical costs incurred. An extravagantly constructed building may represent costs far greater than the capitalized value of . . . rents, and buildings constructed just before an inflation may produce rents greatly in excess of its historical course.[28]

Only the Winners

Cases considered by investigating committees are comparable to the cases reported by race track bettors and stock market players. We hear about the winners. No one speaks about the losers. We only see developments that have succeeded where everything has worked out.

In the real world, for every winner there are usually one or more losers. There is no guarantee when the land is bought (options cost money) or the plans are developed that a success will follow. In the typical case 15 percent of the mortgage amount is at risk if the mortgage is not approved or if the program ends before the developer has a chance to put his project before the processors—a not unlikely event in the case of emergency legislation.

What is ironic is that when the 608 program was about to finish its emergency run in 1950, even bitter opponents of the program fought to bring their constituents in from the cold and appropriated money to assure everyone on line that their loan would be approved:

MR. LONG: I wonder if the Senator is aware that under Section 608 loans may be actually unsound and represent loans for housing development in amounts far greater that the cost of building the houses.

MR. WHERRY: Whether the provisions are right or wrong are completely besides the point . . . . A constituent of mine worked 5 1/2 months to develop one project; he put up the money; he made the survey; he got his loan; he put up his 1 1/2 percent; and his application has never been looked at by the Department . . . that is not fair and just.

MR. LONG: [who had offered an amendment to keep 608 alive but to drop the maximum loan to 80 percent of cost] If . . . this [were a] wonderful project would it not be logical that he would have enough confidence to put up a little of his own money.

MR. WHERRY: He put in [the] money that the . . . act required . . . . [I]f we wrote in 80 percent, he would be one of the first to comply. He is one of the most honorable men I have ever known. He is merely doing what the legislation itself provides. If there is anything wrong, it should have been amended long ago.

Where Was Congress?

The annual changes in the legislation and the program's demise in 1950 would seem to indicate that Congress (or at least the committees) did deliberate on the matter and tried to align the twin goals of volume and profit. Nevertheless, when the chips were down, the necessity to produce carried the day.

New rental projects in any sort of volume had not been built since the 1920s. After World War II, new rental projects had to face the competition of mass-produced single-family housing and the low rents on older apartments reflecting the lingering affect of rent control. The price differential between the old apartment and a new apartment was greater than the differential between the old apartment and new single-family housing.

Lenders were not standing in the wings to minimize the developer's risk by providing high loan-to-value loans. In many states they could not, since they were by law prohibited from making loans in excess of 70 percent of the value of the project. And even if they could, they wouldn't. The Depression experience was fresh in their minds—35 percent of the loans made by life insurance companies between 1925 and 1929 were foreclosed.

If builders were going to come out of the woodwork, the government would need to entice them out. The *Architectural Forum* quoted anonymously, the excellent, indispensable man in our society—the man who gets things done: "Sure we're gambling with the Government's money. Any man who would gamble with his own money under rent control would be a fool."[30]

The large loopholes that were sewn into the fabric of the legislation were done in the sunlight of Congressional hearings. The same committee that did the investigating in 1954, did the drafting in 1942. The representatives of public housing strongly objected to 608. Coleman Woodbury, representing the National Association of Housing and Redevelopment Officials, testified, "It is bound to stimulate irresponsible fly-by-night operations because a speculative builder with . . . insurance does not have to put up a cent of cash of his own. . . . The promoter is in about the same position he occupied in the free and easy financing days of the 20's. . . . "[31] The sentiments where echoed by representative of the American Federation of Labor and of the Congress of Industrial Organizations.

These objections could not overcome the need for production. The homebuilders, admitting that the legislation might not be economically sound, but no more so than loans to tank factories when there was an emergency, correctly read the mood of Congress.

In 1946, when the emergency shifted from defense workers to veterans, Senator Robert Taft, a sponsor, was willing to overcome his conservative sensitivities:

The only sign of some kind of rental housing occurred under section 608 . . ., which is I think, perhaps somewhat too liberal for builders, but under that [there is] some building of rental housing rather than the building of housing for sale, the sale of which is forced on many veterans who should not have to buy them, and who would prefer to live in rental housing.[32]

His sentiments were echoed by Bill Levitt whose name is synonymous with single-family sales housing. As a witness before the investigating committee he pointed out to the Chairman:

The Title VI program . . . was a program of desperation. You had no building for 5 solid years and you had a tremendous amount of people who needed to be housed.In all common sense you would never have gotten any builder over the age 16, to go in and venture either time, trouble, money, or anything else and get the volume of housing that had to be gotten.

Certain evils had to be experienced. And as you know, the section 608 program expired in 1950.

I think it should be borne out that while section 603 and 608 were moneymakers, and that if the housing had not been produced you gentlemen might have greater troubles on your hands now.

Loose lips sink ships; loose laws build houses!

Benign Neglect and Callous Disregard

Title I was part of the original National Housing Act of 1934. The loans insured under this provision were aimed at home improvements. The loans were for short terms (3 years) and the maximum loan was $2,500. They, originally during the Depression years, financed repairs and preservation work. With the onset of prosperity in the post-war years, the use shifted to modernization and improvements. Most of the initial loans were for the basics—roof repairs, exterior walls, heating and plumbing systems and for structural changes. They gradually shifted to cover amenities such as interior decorating and patios.

The loan application was made directly to the private lending institution by the contractor or dealer. The lender had full responsibility for approving the homeowner's credit. Lenders were expected to use "prudent business judgment" in making the loans. The FHA insured any loan the bank approved. The only check on the lenders was after the fact. FHA would cease to insure if 10 percent of the lender's portfolio were in default.

Unlike the Section 608 program, the small amounts of the loans didn't justify major review. Despite its role as an insurer, the FHA did not intrude itself into the processing of the loans. The *Sixteenth Annual Report of the Federal Housing Administration* for the year ending 31 December 1949 noted:

> *No review of these loans is made by FHA* other than the verifications that the loans comply with the regulations. . . . Unlike the Title II mortgage insurance procedure where each individual transaction is reviewed and approved by FHA prior to insurance, under Title I each loan is reported . . . and accepted . . . for insurance . . . in reliance upon the certification of the institution . . . . (My emphasis)[34]

The View from the Top

By the end of the 1952, over 14 million borrowers had used the program. The typical loan was $400 and was amortized over thirty six months. The monthly payment of principal and interest was $12.78. In spite of the small dollar amounts of the loans, the volume was so large that it represented a significant portion of the FHA insurance program— one-fifth of the total amount of loans and mortgages during the 18+ years of FHA operations were home improvement loans.[35]

1952 was a very good year. One and a half million home improvement loans were insured. The number understates the demand for the loans since the program was limited under the law to $1.25 billion in insurance. FHA had to limit its insurance to the amount of repayments of prior year loans. At the end of the year there was a backlog of 260,000 property insurance loans waiting for insurance.[36]

At the same time that the volume of loans was increasing, the ratio of claims paid to insured loans was declining. The ratio of claims to loans of 1.0 percent was the lowest reported for any full year since the program's enactment. In addition, as a result of intensified collection efforts, cash recoveries and proceeds from the disposal of real properties received by FHA in payment of defaulted loans were at an all time high.[37]

The premiums and fees collected by FHA more than covered its modest losses. Title I was self-supporting and had built up substantial reserves. Everything smelled like roses from a business point of view.

The Smell from the Bottom

The United States was (and probably still is) a land of dissatisfied consumers. The Association of American Business Bureaus, surveying its contacts with the public in the years 1949–53, found that inquiries were dropping and complaints were rising. And, nowhere were they rising more quickly than in the home improvements area. Although the overwhelming number of contractors were honest, when the volume of business is a million loans, a "crook factor" of 5 percent provides 50,000 cases of fraud.

Disgruntled homeowner and New York City Department of Sanitation employee, Anthony D'Aquila of Flushing, New York told this unhappy tale to the committee:

A fellow approached me and he told me about his new product that was out, this Protex-Wall, and they were looking for a home to display this product on. And he thought that my house was the ideal home to display it because it was a cedar single-home. . . . And he also told me that my job would be at cost. And I was to receive $50 for every job that was done in the vicinity of Long Island. . . . He told me also that the product was guaranteed for a period of ten years. There were two insurance policies to go with the product. One was from the manufacturer of the product and the other was from North American Indemnity Program . . . .

About 7 o'clock that evening he came back . . . with a fellow he introduced as Jack Lee. He was a fast-talking salesmen . . . He showed me a number of pictures of homes they had done throughout Jersey and they had all been approved by the FHA. He also showed me a [insurance] policy with a seal . . . then he told me . . . [that] the United States Testing Laboratory had tested it for a period of ten years against the weather, against dust, stains, acid, and as insulation. Well it sounded good and he drew up a contract and I didn't see anything in the contract he told me about. I asked him how come he was using a regular contract instead of a special contract . . . and he said, since there were only two homes we were going to display, it doesn't pay for us to have a special contract printed. . . . I also asked him about the $50. He told me that he had seven salesmen working in the vicinity and every time one of his salesmen brought a client, . . . they were to give me a card with the people's name on so I could go over and look at it.

[The work did not proceed well at Mr. D'Aquila's home. The work went "oh so slowly." The product was sprayed on too thinly. Sealer wasn't put on and the material started to stain. The work was never finished and no one was quite sure who Jack Lee was?]

A couple of months after this it started to peel. About 2 weeks after, I got a note from the bank . . . saying that I owed them $1,500 for the job . . . . I never remembered signing the note . . . I got an attorney and went over to see the note. There was a fellow by the name of Rude . . . . He said "Well, that's your signature." . . . So I explained to him about the product and he said to me, " We are not concerned about the product, we are concerned about this note.". . . [T]hey sued and they got a judgement against me. We had a trial about it and the jury gave me the decision. . . . Mr. Furst [the bank president] . . . said "D'Aquila, this case is going right up to the Supreme Court. . . . "

So I told him, I says, "I spent 2½ years in the frontlines, and I am going to spend 5 years fighting . . . . thieves like you . . ."[38]

The "Jack Lees" selling home improvements were known in the parlance of the trade as "dynamiters." They could generate sales pressure that would blast homeowners into signing sales contracts. They were also known as "suede shoe boys" because of their flashy attire and fancy cars. We are dealing with Danny De Vito and Richard Dreyfuss and their Baltimore cohorts in the movie *Tin Men.*

They most often operated on a "par" basis with local dealers. Under this arrangement the dealer would set his price for the job at a fixed amount which included his cost and profit. The salesmen would be free to sell at what the traffic would bear, taking as profit any excess over par.

In a typical case, a homeowner obligated himself for $1,600. If par were $800, the dealer would receive $800 and the other $800 would be divided among the two or three salesmen who put the deal together. The dealers were in the main part honest businessmen. As even Mr. D'Aqila admitted, "There have been a dozen homes in a radius of my homes. One thing I will admit, mine is the only one that has peeled as bad as it has."

Groups of salesmen who sold mastic paints, aluminum siding, patios, and other home improvements often moved across the country, flying by night like a band of locusts stripping the pockets of the gullible. At one time there were as many as sixty five out-of-town home improvement salesmen staying at one hotel in Dayton, Ohio. At the same time another 200 were reported as living in two hotels in Oakland, California. They often had garnered so much work that they would auction the work off to legitimate dealers, with the dealers setting the lowest "par" and therefore the highest profit for the salesmen receiving the work.

The methods used by the salesmen were varied and imaginative:

Model homes. The sales method in Mr. D'Aquila's case. The discount and the ability to obtain commissions from the use of his home as an advertising sample is sufficient bait to bring in the fish.

"Life Magazine." The one used in the *Tin Men,* in which the homeowner is led to believe that her home will be the "before" in an article to appear in *Life Magazine* showing the beautification resulting from aluminum siding. She implores the photographer-salesman to put her in touch with a siding company and have her home become an "after." He is happy to oblige.

Free siding. In this *Tin Men* scam, Danny De Vito enters into a contract for $4,000 worth of siding but assures the owner and marks across the contract that "it will be done at no cost to the homeowner." Danny's associate immediately comes back and explains that Danny has had a nervous breakdown and they both would be fired if they bring back a "for free" contract. The contract is renegotiated and the price of the work is set at $2,500.

Consolidation of debt. The salesman offers the customer the opportunity to raise the price set in the home improvement loan to a level that would enable the consumer to pay off all of his installment debts. The "shrewd" consumer agrees to raise the amount of the loan. After the job is completed, the salesman has disappeared and the dealer has no knowledge that the price included a "kickback" to the homeowner. The consumer is left with a very expensive home improvement.

False completion certificates. The object of the salesman is to get his money and move on. However, the proceeds of a dealer originated loan—one in which the loan has been negotiated directly between the salesman and the borrower—will not be disbursed by the bank until it has received a completion certificate signed by the borrower. To expedite payment, unscrupulous salesmen forged completion certificates or used fraudulent means to get the borrower to sign before the work was completed.

False credit applications. This method involved the falsification of the borrower's credit application so as to make the loan acceptable to a credit institution. A more elaborate swindle involved a group of salesmen who set up a phony credit company and manufactured credit reports which they passed off on lending institutions.

The Structural Fault.

The dealer (and the salesman as his agent) was in a unique position in business life when he participated in the Title I program. As a go-between between the homeowner and the lender, he acted both as a contractor and a credit interviewer for the lender. The contractor is furnished with credit application forms and completion certificates. The homeowner never sees the cash since it is paid directly to the contractor by the bank. It did not take too long for some contractors to realize that a false credit applications and phony completion slip can be transformed into a ticket for immediate payment.

The lenders were also in a unique position. Aside from the moral responsibility of the institution to ascertain the true nature of the loans, there was no legal or business reason to look behind the paper. The home improvement loans were very good business deals. In addition to fees, the banks received a high return on the loans. Although, the documents carried a 5 percent interest rate, the 5 percent was taken as an up-front discount. Since the debt was paid off in installments the average debt outstanding was about half of the initial loan amount. The 5 percent taken initially was the equivalent of a 9.6 percent interest rate on the outstanding balance.

The notes were negotiable. The banks were, therefore, protected by the "holder-in-due-course" doctrine. Fraud cannot be used as a defense against the holder of the note. The homeowner cannot claim that he was fooled or fouled. If it is his signature the bank can collect. Had the bank taken Mr. D'Aqila to the Supreme Court, the decision of the trial court would have been reversed. There was, thus, no reason for lending institutions to "use prudent business judgment" when they stood to lose nothing in the case of default. FHA was waiting to insure every loan as long as the number that went bad did not exceed 10 percent of the bank's portfolio of Title I loans. The FHA had cast its safety net to protect the lender, the dealer and the salesman and let the homeowner with a hole in his pocketbook fall through the net. If the homeowner defaulted on his loan, the bank turns it over to the Federal Government for collection and the lender is indemnified. All the vast law-enforcement powers of the United States are now directed at the hapless victims of fraud.

This anomaly was the straw that broke the camel's back. As the Housing and Home Finance Agency (FHA's parent organization) internal investigation reported:

> Also, in 1953, new United States attorneys, coming in with the change of adminis-
> trations . . . were surprised and distressed at the unexpected duty thrust upon them.
> In taking the office of United States District Attorneys, they had expected to prosecute
> criminals . . . and defend civil actions against the United States. They had not expected
> to sue Mrs. Jones on behalf of the United States in an action in which Mrs. Jones had
> been defrauded. They complained to the Department of Justice, which caused the
> Federal Bureau of Investigation to make a survey of the situation.[39]

Who Was Watching the Store?

The great share of Title I work was legitimate. Most of the work was done by such large organizations as Sears Roebuck and Montgomery Ward and a host of smaller dealers and salesmen (granted that there is often a fine line between "puffery" and misrepresentation). What brought the FHA administrators to grief was that they had lost sight of the program's beneficiaries. When in the 1930s, the repairs were for basic necessities there was little room and even less money to rouse the interest of the hustlers. With post war prosperity, the extra pocket money and the yearning for a better life—be it a patio with a barbecue pit or a house protected and beautified by aluminum siding—brought out the fly-by-nighters. At this point, FHA had the obligation to do more than count its profits. It should have understood that times had changed and the new times required that some of the money be used to hire monitors.

Operating in the marketplace in which the rule is *caveat emptor* (let the buyer beware) FHA administered the program on the honor system. The fraud that was occurring was viewed as a local police matter. The FHA had great faith in the integrity of the bankers and of local law enforcement to keep the program clean. FHA was oblivious to the fact that many bankers are unlikely to do the right thing if more money and no risk is the other choice. Local police work will inevitably be one step behind traveling salesmen who rarely unpacked their bags and hydra-headed corporations constantly changing names.

Understaffed FHA offices across the country were able to do little to arrest the influx of crooks into Title I territory. For example, the San Francisco office's jurisdiction covered twenty one counties in Northern California. The area stretched to more than 400 miles and included the entire San Francisco Bay area. FHA had one person assigned to monitor Title I *and* all of its multifamily programs. On the other hand, it had three claim collectors assigned solely to the Title I program.[40]

In any large program there will be some chiseling (the *Tin Men* scams were in 1963 well after Title I was tightened up). In some cases more red tape and policing may be enough. Title I, however, had become so flabby and full of holes there was a need to go beyond these steps in order to tighten it. The result of the investigation was legislation that limited FHA's liability on default to 90 percent of *each* loan and limited the types of loans that could be insured.[41] Having a little money of their own in the insurance pot, made the lending institutions far more eager to exercise prudent judgement.

Out of Control

The scandals of the early fifties were in programs that were out of control. Section 608 enacted to lift up the sagging rental housing sector inflated it to the point of exceeding the bounds of the market place and in the process filled the pockets of many developers. Title I was designed to help bring the nation out of the Depression doldrums. Home improvements meant improved homes, jobs, and markets for materials. It was not designed to make anyone rich. When the program came to life after the war, the loopholes in the law opened the door to living room racketeers aided and abetted by FHA's attitude of benign neglect when it came to prosecuting swindlers and a "callous disregard" to the plight of defrauded homeowners.[42]

In the 608 program, FHA was overly involved to the point of corruption. In the Title I program FHA was totally disengaged in the face of corruption. Averaging out is not a defense.

Notes

1. FHA Investigation, *Hearings before the Senate Committee on Banking and Currency, 83rd Cong. 2d sess.* (1954) (herein cited as FHA Investigations). The House Hearings in 1989 and 1990 contained 6 volumes and 3,756 pages.
2. National Housing Act, P.L. 73-749; 49 Stat. 1246.
3. Frederick Kaiser, "Past Program Breakdowns in HUD-FHA: Section 608 Multifamily Rental Mortgage Insurance Programs of the 1940s", n. 4 (Congressional Research Service, The Library of Congress; 19 March 1990).
4. Veterans, Emergency Housing Act, P.L. 79-388, 60 Stat. 207, 214.
5. HHFA, *The Housing Situation - A Factual Background,* 10. (June 1949).
6. Richard Davies, *Housing Reform During the Truman Administration,* 42.
7. *House and Home,* 14 May 1954, I-h.
8. FHA Investigations, 3683.
9. Ibid. 710.
10. Ibid. 2089.
11. Ibid.
12. Ibid. 32.
13. Ibid. 256.
14. Ibid. 2087.
15. Ibid. 2087-8.
16. P.L. 80-394, 61 Stat. 945.
17. Housing Act of 1948, P.L. 80-901, 62 Stat. 945.

18. "FHA Impact on the Financing and Design of Apartments," 100.
19. FHA Investigation, 413-4.
20. Ibid. 711.
21. Ibid.
22. Ibid. 416-18\7.
23. Ibid. 3581-7.
24. The conclusion is based on ignorance. Even after cost certification a sponsor could "mortgage-out" due to the spread between allowed and actual fees and the difference between the cost and the FHA estimate of the value of land. Cost certification will prevent "mortgaging-out" resulting from deflation. In the 1960s, there was rarely a case in which the cost certification process reduced the mortgage to an amount less than the initial estimate.
25. Donald Hagman, "Windfalls and their Recapture," in *Windfalls and Wipeouts*, 15.
26. FHA Investigations, 712.
27. FHA Investigations, 402-3.
28. *Housing: The Social and Economic Element*, 19-20. (1970)
29. Ibid. 971-72.
30. "FHA Impact on Design," 101.
31. "FHA Investigation," *Journal of Housing*, May 1954, 154.
32. Quoted in FHA Investigations, 970.
33. Ibid.
34. P. 102.
35. *19th Annual Report of the FHA*, 123-28.
36. Ibid.
37. Ibid.
38. FHA Investigations, 671-74.
39. Ibid. 2082-84.
40. *House and Home*, May 1954, I-M.
41. Section 101 (a) "Housing Act of 1954", PL 569 83rd Cong., 68 Stat. 590. 41.
42. The phrase was used in a memorandum to the FHA General Counsel that gave him notice of the reasons he should be removed from the office. FHA Investigations, 276.

2

From Mike Wallace
to the Moratorium

In the 1960s, the FHA was given new worlds to conquer. In the previous quarter of a century, responsibility for subsidized housing for low-income families was in the hands of local public housing authorities. Public housing had a sorry record. Public housing starts represented less than 2 percent of all housing starts in the 1950s—the government was destroying (under the highway and urban renewal program) more housing than it was building. And what it was building left much to be desired. The projects were poorly located, economically and racially segregated, badly designed, and very expensive.

Given the success of private enterprise in meeting the need of middle-income households, it seemed obvious (or at least plausible) that what was missing in America was subsidized FHA-insured private production of housing for poor people. This idea mobilized traditionally conservative housing industry groups in support of a liberal housing program.

The first steps were modest ones. Remembering how greedy developers could be, Congress restricted access to the subsidized kingdom (in which loans equal to 90 percent of the cost of the development were being offered) to nonprofit organizations and private entities that would agree to limit their profit to 6 percent of their 10 percent investment. Since the HHFA wanted to achieve a large volume (a higher income group needs a smaller subsidy) the initial group targeted was composed of those too well off to qualify for public housing and yet not quite middle-income—the moderate income folks.

The subsidy vehicle was the Section 221(d)(3) program. FHA agreed to insure private loans to private developers. During construction, the loans would bear a market rate of interest. When construction was finished and FHA gave its stamp of approval (final endorsement of the mortgage), the interest rate would drop to approximately 3 percent. Since lenders were not interested in making long term below-market interest rate loans, the loans were immediately sold to a government agency (initially Fannie Mae and subsequently Ginnie Mae)[1] for par (the face value of the loan, not taking any discount to reflect the low-interest rate). Eligibility for residence in these projects was generally restricted to families and individuals with incomes that were below the median income level in the particular locality.

In 1965, a replacement was sought for the program. The program was not providing enough of a production bang for the buck. The problem was that every time Fannie Mae would purchase the loan, HUD's budget would be charged for the full amount of the loan rather than for the subsidy. HUD sought a program in which only the subsidy was recorded on the budget (akin to leasing a post office rather than building one). The rent supplement proposal that FHA introduced to Congress was such a program. The private developer would obtain market-rate mortgages and a subsidy would be paid to the landlord to cover the difference between the rent and 20 percent of the tenant's income.

In spite of an overwhelming Democratic majority that rode in on the tail of the Johnson landslide, the proposal ran into a buzzsaw of opposition. Poverty had been discovered earlier in the decade and liberals attacked the program as being unfair in failing to address the needs of those at the bottom of the income scale. The income limits were, therefore, reduced to public housing levels. It was a pyrrhic victory. Conservatives couldn't understand why poor peoples deserved new housing. A policy of taxing Peter to provide adequate housing for Paul they could understand. They couldn't fathom a policy that taxed Peter to provide better housing than his own for Paul.

Congress tinkered with this dilemma and ultimately crippled the program. New construction was permitted but the monthly rent for a new two-bedroom apartment could not exceed $120 a month. Although the program could be used to build housing in low cost hamlets in the rural south, it was useless in the cities.

HUD came on the scene in the fall of 1965, without any workable housing subsidy program and without any idea how to get a volume low-income production program through the Congressional gauntlet. HUD's major initiative, undertaken in the early months of 1967, was an anti-rat program.

In 1968, a miracle occurred. The Johnson Administration prodded by a homeownership-for-the-poor proposal from the Republican side of the aisle, produced one of its own. And either as an act of one-upmanship or an attempt at legislative symmetry, it was accompanied by a rental proposal. With almost the same cast of characters in the Congress and with little change in basic attitudes, two programs were enacted—Section 235 and Section 236—that unleashed private enterprise. The homeownership subsidy program (section 235) resulted in 116,000 starts in 1970 and 150,000 starts in 1971. The rental subsidy program (Section 236) reached 105,000 starts in 1970 and 130,000 starts in 1971.

Alas, the headlong rush was to the cliff. The homeownership program, when it was directed to poor families, was an instant failure and the program was marked by scandal. The buildings constructed under the rental subsidy program had their foundations in financial quicksand and by the mid-1970s were in the need of a thickly bound rope of additional subsidy to keep them from sinking.

Borrowers and Buildings on the Brink

Homeownership was not the be all and end all of housing policy after World War II. Remembering the wave of foreclosures that accompanied the Depression, there was a certain wariness about homeownership. A key reason for support of the Section 608 rental housing program, at both ends of the political spectrum was to give veterans a choice. They shouldn't be forced to buy because of the absence of rental housing.

By the mid-sixties, homeownership was viewed as a panacea rather than as a potential problem. Homeownership was associated with the middle class and suburbia. On the Republican side of the halls of Congress, in the far reaches of the Great Society (at the Office of Economic Opportunity), and in academia, homeownership was being viewed as a way out of poverty and as a way to improve the condition of the slums and its tenements (two nearly archaic words).

In January of 1967, the ranking Republican member of the House Banking and Currency Committee William Widnall welcomed a low-income homeownership proposal from the junior senator from Illinois, Charles Percy:

> The promise of homeownership provides a meaningful incentive to the initially lower income family to spur its efforts to climb the ladder of economic security and responsible citizenship.[2]

George Sternlieb in his classic housing study, *The Tenement Landlord* wrote,

> *There is no question of the significance of landlord residence, particularly of single parcel landlords, as insurance of proper maintenance of slum tenements . . . . No one shotwave of maintenance and paint-up sweep-up campaign can provide the day-to-day maintenance which is required in slum areas . . . .* [T]his can only be accomplished by a resident landlord . . . .
>
> By making it feasible for more residents to become owners, we further encourage the development of local leadership which is so sorely lacking in most slums. The role of resident owners as guides and creators of life patterns for the youth of the slums to follow is clearly evident.(Emphasis in the original)[3]

Although HUD was skeptical about the values of homeownership for low and moderate income families, rioting in the streets and the upcoming election, had begun to erode their doubts. HUD and Congress's first steps across the threshold involved the liberalization of underwriting standards. In 1966, Section 221(d)(2) was amended to waive the "economic soundness" test in riot corridor areas. In 1968, Section 223 (e) was enacted to provide mortgage insurance for housing located in older declining urban areas without regard to the normal requirements that the area be "reasonably viable". Instead the FHA should give consideration to the need for providing adequate housing for families of low-and-moderate income in the area and that the property is an "acceptable risk" in view of this Federal interest.

In direct response to the Percy proposal, HUD came up with its own subsidized homeownership program for lower income families - Section 235. HUD would make up the difference between 20 percent of families' income and the required payment under the mortgage for principal, interest, taxes, insurance, and the mortgage insurance payment. In no case, however, could the subsidy exceed the difference between the required payment under the mortgage at the prevailing interest rate and the payment that would be required if the mortgage bore an interest rate of 1 percent. The minimum downpayment was $200.

Eligibility was limited to families whose income at the time of initial occupancy was not in excess of 135 percent of the local public housing limit. Although primarily intended to build new houses, up to 25 percent of the contracts authorized to be made under the program during its first year were to go to existing housing, 15 percent in the following year, and 10 percent in the third year.

Trouble was not long in coming in the existing segment of the program. The FHA Commissioner, Eugene Gulledge, was hauled before the cameras of "Sixty Minutes" and in an interview with Mike Wallace mauled before tens of million viewers. The staff report to the House Committee of Banking and Currency "Investigation and Hearing of Abuses in Federal Low-And Moderate-Income Housing Programs," issued in December 1970, opened with the following statement:

> The Department of Housing and Urban Development and its Federal Housing Administration may be well on its way toward insuring itself into a national housing scandal. This conclusion has been reached because of the role that FHA has played in the operation of the section 235 and other programs.[4]

In January 1971, HUD Secretary George Romney held an extraordinary series of meetings in Washington and Denver in which each field office director was grilled as to how the program was working. Prior to the meeting, the director, the chief underwriter, and chief appraiser were instructed to visit at least five existing inner-city projects. After the first meeting, Secretary Romney suspended the Section 235 home mortgage program as it applied to existing houses until, as he told a House committee, "we could strengthen our procedures, properly evaluate our capabilities, and assure satisfactory performance."[5]

Crashing on Takeoff

Unlike the prior programs, in which the bad news followed a long period of good news, in the case of insuring existing homes the news was all bad from the beginning. The Section 608 and Title I programs got into trouble in part because they flew too fast and too high; the existing housing programs for poor people crashed on takeoff.

The most telegenic and financially shameful disaster was the Paterson Tavern case. The "house" at 471 Graham Street in Paterson, New Jersey had been built around 1900 and was located in a rapidly deteriorating neighborhood. It had been previously used as a tavern. In October 1969, the owner was ordered by the city to board-up the building. In November, the house was sold for $1,800. A permit was obtained for electrical repairs at an estimated cost of $450. In March of 1970, the house was sold to a "235" purchaser for $20,000.

The house wasn't quite a home. The tavern bar covered one side of the living room. In order to enter the rest of the house, one had to go up two steps to the area where the tables had been in the tavern. The walls were rough and unevenly covered by fresh paint that had been sloppily applied. The bedroom floors were warped and buckling.[6]

The tavern was only one of the 200 FHA-owned overappraised houses that were standing vacant in Patterson. In the winter of 1971, the appraiser from the Newark FHA office (which had jurisdiction over the area) was indicted for taking bribes for giving high appraisals. He was only one of eleven indicted employees of the Newark office.

The Patterson Tavern was not the typical case and Newark was not the typical office. HUD reviewing 92 cases cited in the Staff Report presented a more balanced, but equally bleak, report of the extent of the problem:

a. One third of the properties were overappraised.

b. There were 289 omissions of requirements: (1) 84 major defects including sagging floors, inoperable furnaces, rotted siding, fallen plaster in 39 units; (2) 119 items of deferred maintenance including leaky faucets and peeling paint; (3) 86 instances in 37 properties that lacked certifications concerning the operability of the plumbing, heating, or electrical systems, absence of termites, and weather tightness of the roof.

c. Three-fifths of the cases involved speculators.

d. Instructions with regard to code inspection were not being carried out.

e. False and improper certifications that required repairs were completed.

f. Utility and maintenance expenses were underestimated in order to qualify purchasers.

g. Over 60 percent of the households were female-headed and in many cases there were "many children, poor housekeeping, and no maintenance."[7]

The Charge of the Light Brigade

HUD had run headlong into an area of operations in which the organization had little experience or expertise. This urgency was engendered by the crisis in the ghettos which led to rioting in the streets. Until 1964, FHA had a redlining policy and only 3 percent of FHA-insured mortgages were in low-income central city areas. FHA standards had been developed to reflect the construction standards of newly built suburban homes and a clientele that was decidedly middle-income.

Tacking to the winds of the Great Society and bowing to the criticism of Congress, the FHA propelled its policy towards the use of mortgage insurance in older inner-city areas. The temper of the times can be seen in a speech by the Assistant Secretary of HUD and FHA Commissioner Phillip N. Brownstein to the troops. It was inserted in the *Congressional Record* by Senator Walter Mondale on 27 October 1967:

> The principal reason for the existence of the FHA in 1967 is to enlist and encourage private enterprise to play a leading role in providing decent housing for families of low and moderate income, and in providing housing and related human conditions in the inner city—especially in the slums and blighted portions . . . . I am asking you and every employee of FHA to enter into a new crusade . . . . This means making our home programs available for the purchase sale and improvement of properties throughout the inner city . . . . Everyone should carry away from here . . . a sense of urgency . . . and a determination to take steps, reach decisions, and make the sacrifices necessary . . . . I have given a number of reasons why I believe FHA must mount a major effort . . . Let me give you one more reason. You should work at this task as though your job depended on it—because it may.[8]

Congress echoed the theme. The Declaration of Policy of the Housing and Urban Development Act of 1968, instructed the Secretary "that in the administration of those housing programs authorized by this act . . . designed to assist families with incomes so low that they could not otherwise decently house themselves . . . the highest priority and emphasis should be given to meeting the housing needs of those families for which the national goal has not become a reality."

As in the case of previous crusades excessive zeal could wreak havoc on the environment. The following tale of the affect of the program on Sunset Park, a low-income neighborhood in Brooklyn, depicts the damage:

[T]he Section 235 difficulties between 1969 and 1972 owed something to the fact
that it evolved into something very nearly the reverse of redlining: It provided more
mortgage money to the poor than the poor could beneficially absorb. The origin of
the problem was in lax lending standards compounded by outright fraud. The scam,
in Sunset Park as elsewhere, was a combination of panic selling, blatant over-apprais-
als, and shoddy merchandise. Typically, speculators contrived the purchase of a house
from a distressed owner for $5,000 or less. After cosmetic touch-ups, the property
was sold for $20,000 to be provided by an FHA-approved mortgage of nearly
equivalent amount. The buyers of these overpriced and overmortgaged houses were
usually the new Puerto Ricans, unwary families who lacked the means to meet
monthly financial charges plus the cost of keeping oft-defective homes in good repair.
Substantial numbers of properties went into default, turned back to the mortgagees
and eventually to FHA. In Sunset Park, nearly 100 were boarded up, to become prey
of vandals, drug dealers, and weather.[9]

The words of the FHA Commissioner may well be the origin of a
comment that made the rounds in the FHA Field offices, "If we don't
make the program work, we lose our jobs. If we make the program work,
we go to jail."

Worthless Paper

The main direction of HUD efforts to revise the existing program was to
devise procedures to avoid a repetition of the "Paterson Tavern" incident.
New instructions were written and new circulars were issued and promises
were made that more staff would be assigned to monitor the program.

One of the administrative problems uncovered was the worthlessness of
certifications on the condition of the property and that the instructions to the
code inspections were not being carried out. Certifications concerning the
condition of mechanical equipment had been accepted from nonexistent
companies and from persons having an interest in the property.

How worthwhile was an honest certification? A certification as to the
present satisfactory condition of a ten-year-old roof or a twenty five-year-
old heating system is no guarantee that a costly repair will not hit the
homeowner. As for code compliance, FHA's circular dealing with the
requirement stated in part: "In areas where codes are in effect and are
being actively enforced the FHA should require code compliance."

What is the honest electrician supposed to certify in a city in which
the code has many archaic provisions and in an area in which the
inspectors rarely visits (or where those who visit are looking for payoffs
rather than violations)? Should FHA require compliance with the archaic
requirements and thereby disqualify the low-income buyer?

Other regulations required large increase in staff. The need to limit speculation requires the tracking of transactions and numerous visits to the recording office. Property repair inspection is not a skill all appraisers have. The appraisal staff would have to be supported by property inspectors. The FHA Commissioner promised there would be 900 new bodies in the field. He never made good on his promise.

Reasonably Viable or Scarcely Breathing

The difficulties with the building were simple compared to the conundrums involving the location. It was generally agreed that the initial instructions (both written and oral) that accompanied the loosening of underwriting standards went too far. The impression was spread in the field that the property and location standards were abandoned. The FHA "Mortgage Letter" issued in 1968 stated that:

> FHA insurance programs are to be used everywhere, provided only that the individual property meets eligibility requirements which have been sufficiently broadened by the new act to limit rejection only to those instances where a property has so deteriorated or is subject to such hazards, noxious odors, grossly offensive sites or excessive noises that the physical improvements are endangered or the livability of the property or the health or the safety of its occupants are seriously affected. A property will be deemed an acceptable risk when a market exists and the property is free of the above cited dangers.[10]

FHA produced a new circular on 31 December 1970, *Identification of Areas Ineligible for FHA Mortgage Insurance*. It is a masterpiece in the art of mumbling through:

> Section 223 (e) is not intended as a complete abandonment of location eligibility criteria. . . . [I]f the property is located in an area that has deterioration or blight to the extent that rejection is proper the application should be rejected ... [However] care must be exercised to limit rejection to the actual blocks that are affected.[11]

In response to a question as to exactly what types of locations were meant to be excluded, an FHA official indicated that "An AFDC mother with 7 daughters should not be put into a house on a block that has a large number of abandoned buildings."

Would six daughters make the location suitable?

The Maintenance Dilemma

To the extent it was providing ownership opportunities to marginal mortgagors in marginal buildings and neighborhoods, the program had serious deficiencies that could not be overcome. The limitation of the subsidy to a portion of the mortgage payment meant that the stock of housing that fit the parameters of the program were old buildings that would need repairs. The repairs, however, could not be so extensive as to raise the cost of the house to a level that the family could not afford. The FHA *Underwriting Manual for Home Mortgages* was quite clear on this point:

> Required repairs will be limited to those necessary to preserve the property and to protect the health and safety of the occupants.

The problem was pinpointed by Lawrence Katz, a Director of the FHA Office in Milwaukee and then a personal consultant to Secretary Romney:

> Predictably, this program too will fail, because no provision is being made for the dollars necessary to spend for significant major repairs and maintenance that will inevitably occur, no matter how well the older home is currently rehabilitated . . . .

Money could theoretically be replaced by do-it-yourself skills, but as Mr. Katz continued:

> I taught a graduate course in the University of Wisconsin . . . one black [student with 3 children] reported that he had been going around looking for a 235 home . . . and he saw 20 homes occupied by white families for sale. He said "Mr. Katz, one of the outstanding things I saw which epitomizes the difference between a white community and the black community is that in everyone of these homes I saw a workbench in the garage or basement . . . . We have never seen this in a black home, the best we had was a rusty tool pail . . . ." [D]o-it-yourself skills are significantly absent among the poor and low . . . income buyer in the central city. Budget skills are also absent, and even if present, it becomes most difficult on meager earnings to put sufficient dollars aside . . . to make major carpenter repairs . . . that . . . will be necessary; a new roof, or a new furnace in due time . . . . The result is that today's well rehabilitated homes will come back to HUD in spite of all its precautions currently to do the best underwriting job. Unless we solve this problem which involves major counseling efforts and more, we will be confronted with acquisitions and massive financial losses.[12]

The homeowners walking away from their Section 235 homes did not need economic counseling. The rational economic response, when faced with a major repair in a house that was bought with a tiny downpayment and that has a mortgage that exceeded the value of the property, is to pack up one's belongings, checkout, and leave the key in the mailbox.

There was no way (except through increased subsidy) to avoid exposing the homeowner to the danger of unexpected majorcatastrophe without pricing the buyer out of the market initially. Adopting a metaphor from the automobile market of the early 1970s, the low income buyer could not afford a new Ford Pinto. The program offered a ten-year-old gas guzzling lower priced Mercury Marauder. As in the used car business, there was a very clear trade-off between lower debt service and higher maintenances costs. The failure to take into account the latter costs, shattered hearts, turned buildings into rubble, and killed the inner-city segment of the program. It would take HUD two decades to come back to the idea of homeownership for the poor and attempt by a massive infusion of subsidy to resuscitate the hope. The jury is still out.

Production Triumphs and Management Disasters

A Congress of Innocents

The rental subsidy program introduced in 1968 attempted to achieve the best of both worlds—a very low interest rate and a minimum budget impact. In the initial legislative proposal, the interest rate was dropped to one percent and the secretary was left with the discretion as to which income group would be served by the program. HUD was seeking a high volume production program. As Secretary Weaver testified:

> We have, on the one hand, the problem of families most in need, and this represents the lowest income families having the priorities. But we also have the need . . . of having something produced quickly in large volume. And to achieve this volume . . . . you have to do not only the most difficult . . . but also the less difficult, as long as it contributes to the objective of providing housing for those for whom housing is not available in the marketplace.[13]

Congress had its own desires. It wanted to serve lower income families. The Senate set the income limits at 70 percent of the local median income for 80 percent of the funds. The remaining 20 percent could be used for higher-income families. The house came up with its own limitation—an amount representing 130 percent of the income that would allow for continued occupancy in public housing in the locality, plus $300 for each minor child. The Conference Committee finally settled at 135 percent of the local public housing limit for admission for

80 percent of the funds and 90 percent of the local median for the remaining 20 percent plus $300 for each minor child.

To assure that the households affected were genuinely interested in housing, and to reduce the level of the subsidy, the minimum rent was raised from 20 percent to 25 percent of income. The number was plucked from the air. In fact, it was meant to cut the wings of the program before it took flight as the following colloquy involving the author of the amendment, Representative William Brock, (who had unsuccessfully attempted to impose a minimum 25 percent ratio in the homeownership program) indicates:

MR. ECKHARDT: If the . . . first amendment had been passed, would he offer this amendment at 30 percent . . .?
MR. BROCK: I think that probably I would and maybe at 40 percent . . . . I honestly hope we could reduce the program.[14]

The program that emerged from Congress as Section 236 provided for the development, ownership, and management of rental housing by private, limited distribution, and nonprofit sponsors. The projects would be financed by private lending institutions at a market interest rate and the mortgages would be insured by FHA. The owner's interest payments to the lender were made as if the mortgage rate were equal to one percent. HUD would pay the difference between market rate and one percent. Each tenant had to pay the greater of the basic rental (calculated on the basis of a one percent mortgage) or 25 percent of adjusted (a reduction of income of $300 for each child and an overall reduction of 5 percent) income not to exceed the rent based on a marked rate of interest. Rents collected by the mortgagor in excess of basic charges were to be returned to HUD.

The net result of the congressional action left many of the proponents of the original Administration proposal despondent. In the words of Representative Henry Reuss, the program would serve only "paupers plus 30 percent." Representative William Barrett, the chairman of the Housing Subcommittee thought the changes crippled the program. Both the proponents and opponents didn't understand what had actually occurred. The main result of the arcane game of income limits and rent/income ratios, contrary to everyone's expectations, was to prime the program for production and price the poor out of the projects.

Quality and Quantity

The basic problem that had faced the developer in the prior FHA subsidized programs was getting enough mortgage money to build the project. The renting of the apartments was deemed the easy part since the subsidy provided the owner with a safe haven from the turmoil of the marketplace. The key test that a mortgage must meet is that there be sufficient income (after deducting the expenses of operation) to service (pay the principal and interest) the mortgage.

The one percent rate meant that a small amount of net income could support a large debt. In the Section 236 program, which provided for forty-year loans, every $1 supported $27 of mortgage principal (in contrast, in the Section 221 (d)(3) below-market interest rate program in which every dollar supported $21). The problem was how to generate the net income from a project geared to lower income households. It turned out to be no problem.

In the case of estimating rental income, Congress's attempts to deflate the program inflated the mortgages. The "lower" income levels of the Section 236 program—135 percent of income limits for public housing admission—were surprisingly high. Congress didn't realize that the income of the actual tenants was significantly below the level of the locally determined public housing limits. The income limit in the Section 236 program was quite close to the local median income in representative areas of the country. In Boston it was $8,020 (90 percent of the median), in Concord, New Hampshire $8,730 (89 percent), in New Orleans, $7,460 (91 percent), in San Antonio, $7,310 (100+ percent, in Dallas, $6,600 (83 percent), and in Seattle $8,060 (90 percent).

The attempt to clip the program by raising the rent-to-income ratio backfired. Instead of projecting gross income of the project by assuming a family at the income limit was paying 20 percent of its income for rent, FHA now could assume that the tenant was being clipped for 25 percent of its income. This raised gross income projections by 25 percent.

To move from gross income to the amount available for debt service there is a need to estimate future expenses. If legislators are attuned to the voice of their constituents, government employees are attuned to the voice of their leaders. This is especially so when the Congress and the leaders of the Department are on the same wavelength. Congress had set a goal in the 1968 legislation of six million subsidized units for the decade. The secretary, George Romney, who had gained reknown for getting Ramblers on the road, and the head of FHA, Eugene Gulledge, a former head of the National Association of Home Builders, were ready to demonstrate that if Democrats could start up the engine, the Republicans could move the program into high gear. The new team reorganized FHA so that there was a clear division between production and management and there was no question of which, as in the case of children, (from the perspective of the male dominated FHA) was more fun doing.

After the split, the mortgage processors lacked the expertise when dealing with operating expenses. They were also aware that high cost estimates for operating expenses would fly in the face of their leader's emphasis on production. Since, in any event, future operating expenses were "guesstimates," the developer invariably guessed low and received the benefit of the doubt.

The ability to build high-cost units also overcame the objection of localities that had always equated subsidized housing with drab and dreary public housing. Neighbors could be convinced that these new developments did not pose a threat to the equity in their houses. The developer could show the neighbors that low-income housing was quality housing. Although the HUD Handbook on the program required the units that were produced be "modest but attractive," in many areas they were anything but modest. In Dallas, for example, the typical two-bedroom unit contained over 1,000 square feet of living area, 1 ½ bathrooms, was fully air-conditioned and carpeted. It also contained a range, refrigerator, kitchen exhaust fan, disposal, drapes in the living room and master bedroom (venetian blinds in the other rooms) and an antenna system.

The fact that the developers were limited-distribution-entities did not mean that they were not interested in profit. All the cards were stacked in favor of higher-cost units. There was little difference in time and talent (the developer's most precious commodities)in developing a 100-unit project with a unit cost of $16,000 rather than $14,000. Moreover:

1. if the mortgagor is also a builder, the size of the builder's fee is directly related to the size of the project;

2. the size of the permitted equity return was also directly dependent on the cost of the project (the 6 percent return was not based on a cash investment—it was calculated as 6 percent of 11.11 percent of the mortgage);

3. the management fee was directly related to the project's gross income (before deducting operating expense and debt service); and

4. the value of the project as a tax shelter varied directly with the size of the mortgage.

Depreciation and Tax Shelters

It is time to follow the rabbit into the Wonderland of taxes to meet the queen—depreciation—which is based on the metaphysical notion that nothing material lasts forever. Ever since the Revenue Act of 1913, the wear and tear of property used in a trade or business that will necessitate its replacement has been recognized as a legitimate cost of doing business. The classical method of depreciation is "straight line" - in which the amount to be deducted is determined by dividing the cost of the property by its "useful life" (determined by the Internal Revenue Service). What the tax law allows should not be confused with either business or economic reality. As Paul Taubman, a professor at the University of Pennsylvania wrote, in regard to rental real estate, "[F]or each of the first 40 years of useful life—the average tax life of the shell and equipment—the true loss is less than that allowed by the straight line formula ." In addition, in inflationary times, the building, if properly maintained will increase in value. Taking these two factors into account, Taubman concluded, "[I]t seems that not only are the permissible tax depreciation rules . . . a subsidy, but so is straight line depreciation."[15]

What are these more liberal rules and why were they enacted? The rules permit the owners of new rental housing to adopt liberal depreciation formulas: the declining balance method allows depreciation at up to twice the straight line method in the initial years and the sum-of-the-years-digit method at only a slightly slower top speed.[16] Its not a question of more, but rather of faster. The total remains the same, the methods speed up the deductions in the initial years. Table 2.1 illustrates the different results during the first eight years. The application of the rapid depreciation provisions to real estate was a result of the invisible mind. Stanley Surrey, a former assistant secretary of the Treasury for Tax Policy and a professor of tax law at Harvard Law School noted:

> The present accelerated methods were initially adopted . . . with industrial machinery and equipment . . . in mind. Acceleration in buildings . . . appears to have been a happenstance . . . . No conscious decision was made to adopt the present system as a

useful device to stimulate building or to provide us with more or better housing, let alone lower-income housing.[17]

The tax system that was created broke the bonds between cash flow and profit. The real estate industry moved from double-entry bookkeeping to double-sets of books. A simple example (see Table 2.2) shows the double benefit available to the investor; he not only gets cash flow but also "losses" as an offset against income. At a time when the tax rate was as high as 70 percent this meant real money.

TABLE 2.1
Comparison of Annual Depreciation Allowances
(First 8 Years)

End of Year	Straight-Line	Declining Balance	Sum of the Year's digits (5%)
1	$25,000	$50,000	$48,780
2	25,000	47,500	47,561
3	25,000	45,125	46,341
4	25,000	42,869	45,122
5	25,000	40,725	43,902
6	25,000	38,685	42,683
7	25,000	36,755	41,463
8	25,000	34,917	40,244

Cost and Equity vs. Production

Of course, higher costs and rents would reduce the number of potential tenants. This worry was washed away by the subsidy that shrank rents by 35 percent. And just as the market restraints were attenuated so were the usual FHA constraints. A $1,000 increase in mortgage amount resulted in only a few dollars of extra monthly subsidy. The increase in cost need not even result in increased expense if the project attracted higher income tenants who would pay higher rents than those projected.

TABLE 2.2
Sample Statement of Taxable Income (Loss) and Cash Flow

	Tax	Cash
Income	$230,000	$230,000
Less: Operating expenses	86,300	86,300
Interest on mortgage	89,500	89,500
Mortgage amortization	—	11,200
Replacement reserve	—	5,700
Depreciation	64,500	—
Taxable Income (Loss)	(10,300)	
Cash Flow		37,300

Source: Ross Touche, *Study of Tax Consideration in Multi-family Investments*, 18. (HUD:1972)

Improving the economic soundness of the project was also a justification for higher costs. The insured mortgage was to be amortized over forty years. The building if it were to contain its marketability in the future would require many features that may be considered "luxuries" today but "necessities" tomorrow.

A final reason for not being strict on cost was the embarrassment that HUD had faced over the overly modest units in the Section 235 homeownership scandal. The underwriter who failed to allow the construction of an attractive project could be accused of violating the oral law of the department. FHA Commissioner Gulledge had continually emphasized in the meetings with field personnel in Washington and Denver that "quality is remembered long after cost is forgotten."

How wrong he was! The high volume of costly units that looked like heaven to the developers, looked like hell to those concerned with the budget. The program was also caught on the horns of the cost and equity dilemma. It was not a new dilemma. In the debate over the public housing authorization, in 1949, the following colloquy occurred between Senator A. Willis Robertson and Senator John Sparkman:

MR. ROBERTSON: If we commit ourselves to a $15 million which takes care of only 810,000 families . . . what provisions would the Senator recommend for the remainder of the 6 million similarly situated families?

MR. SPARKMAN:I realize the problem we are up against in providing only 810,000 units. . . .

MR. ROBERTSON: The Senator agrees that this start is inadequate . . . will cost $15 million . . . and that if we do a fair and just job for the more than 7 million families the cost will be more than $200 million. Is not this the time to consider what we are starting?[18]

Within months after Commissioner Gulledge spoke, President Richard Nixon (who had voted against the authorization of public housing in 1949) in his *Third Annual Report on National Housing Goals* gored the programs on the horns of the same dilemma. The goal was only 6 million but the cost was now $200 billion. And the higher income limits and the inability of poor families to afford the programs had sharpened the equity horn:

Under present law, as many as 25 million American households - 40 percent of the total population - are eligible for the major subsidy programs. If all eligible families were subsidized the cost would be astronomical.

The other serious problem is that too often the present housing subsidy programs cannot help the very poor . . . The typical family moving into a new home subsidized HUD's section 235 program . . . had an income of nearly $6,200 [the equivalent of $20,000 in 1989 dollars] . . . . Poor families earning under $4,000 are not common beneficiaries . . . . In late 1969, 13.3 percent of the families assisted under the section 235 program had incomes of less than $4,000. A year later . . . the ratio was down to 6 percent.[19]

Unable to find a way out of the cost and equity dilemma, President Nixon upon reelection decided to get off the horse in midstream. Halfway in the decade long schedule laid out in the Housing and Urban Development Act of 1968, he suspended the subsidy programs in January of 1973.

Post Moratorium Scandals

It was a good thing that the president got off the horse since it was a beast that could not make it across the river. In city after city, subsidized projects would move into serious financial difficulty. By 1978, of 6,000 HUD-subsidized projects, 2,750 were in dire financial straits. Of the 115 projects in Boston, HUD had foreclosed or assumed ownership in forty seven of the developments. It was projected by Senator Edward Brooke that HUD would become the owner of most of the housing projects in the inner city.[20]

Showcase projects had turned into "jungles." The following on-
-the-scene report was filed from the South Bronx in 1978:

> Welcome to Jose de Diego-Beekman housing project where upwards of 6,000 people
> live in the largest government-subsidized effort at rehabilitated housing in the country.
>
> Five short years ago, Diego-Beekman was billed as a showcase project, with fancy
> graphic numerals, outside each of the five and six story tenement. It was nationally
> celebrated as a model for urban renewal.
>
> There is not much disagreement that the showcase has become a jungle. The
> hallways are dark, muggings and burglaries are frequent. Small children found
> playing in the rubble of burned-out buildings that surround the project and provide
> its playing area tick off accounts of the latest rape, child molestation or knifing.
>
> The promised recreation area - a community center - is shut down, a security
> problem, management says. The washers and dryers tenants say were promised for
> each unit never materialized. . . .
>
> [O]ne could find no trace of social services to deal with [the] . . . problems in this
> garbage-strewn Calcutta of the Bronx, which certainly looks different than the original
> proposal. . . .
>
> Most of the people in Diego-Beekman originally came with hope. The first 600
> families were screened, prepped and enthusiastic. Tenant patrols were established and
> order maintained. It went down rapidly after that and the causes for the decline are
> open for debate. It was, management says, rising operating costs and . . . 300
> unscreened welfare cases foisted on them by the city. The tenants blame management
> for not providing effective security, janitorial supplies, or the staff necessary to
> maintain the building.[21]

Many reasons have been put forth for the problems. Too many it was
merely bad luck. As Senator William Proxmire stated, "At bottom, the
problem appears to be uncontrollable and rapidly increasing operating
expenses — primarily utilities and property taxes."[22] The increase in oil
prices by OPEC in 1974 would support this viewpoint. HUD had submitted to the Senate, in 1968, an estimate of the future costs of the
program that made the blithe assumption that the operating costs in the
program would stay constant.[23] Nevertheless, there was ample evidence
in the late 1960s that operating expenses would rise. The utility sector in
the public housing program was rising in the late 1960s at a rate of close
to 7 percent.[24] The increase in environmental concern and the prospect
of a fuel shortage had arrived by 1970. The fact that utilities were paid

by the owner in most section 236 projects meant that the tenants would be rather liberal in their use of a "free" item.

The tax shelter aspect of the program and the fact that the owners were not concerned with long-term management was also trotted out as a reason for the sudden demise. Although there is truth in the statement there are also countering truths. If an owner's project were successful he could expect a continuing flow of projects—a foreclosure poisons the well. Even worse, an early foreclosure would allow the government to recapture the tax benefits of the investors.

A third reason given for the trouble was that the staff at HUD had not done a good job in reviewing projects. When problems began to surface HUD did try to reform itself and move to "quality processing." Anthony Downs writing for the National Association of Home Builders supported this position: "HUD should review estimated projects with far more care and more emphasis upon actual local experiences with existing section 236 projects. This is necessary to avoid cost underestimation . . . and to prevent requests for rent increases arising very soon after a project is occupied."

An Early Death or Permanent Disability

The troubles were actually predictable. Before the shovel hit the dirt for the first project, the Kaiser Committee reported to President Johnson:

> Congress has often unwittingly undermined the feasibility of programs by impos-
> ing income limits for eligibility which are too low given the amount of subsidy
> provided. If only a small subsidy is provided, but eligibility is restricted to poor
> families, the program will not work . . . The Congressional motivation for
> imposing low limits . . . is apparently to make sure that the most needy families
> receive priority. This is indeed a worthy goal. But lowering eligibility limits
> without at the same time increasing the depth of the subsidy, in effect, squeezes
> the life out of the program by narrowing the target population. It is possible, for
> example, that Congress has seriously damaged the . . . 236 rental program by
> imposing limits too low for the subsidy available.[26]

They almost had the right problem. However, it was not that the program limits were too low, but that the income of the actual occupants of the projects were too low. There were, however, other warnings. At the 1977 hearings, Max Kargman, who was president of the National Association of Housing Managers and Owners, stated that:

[I]n 1971, HUD did a study . . . [I]n March 1971, which was little more than 2 years after the law was passed. This study said: The section 236 program may be simultaneously building a large number of units and massive future problems."[27]

As the author of the study, let me explain the reason for the conclusion. Quality processing would have killed the goose that was laying the golden eggs. If there had been realistic processing, few projects would have been built. Had the projects been processed using the likely income of the residents (rather than the maximum income limits) and had realistic estimates of expenses been made, the later problems would have been avoided because very few projects would have been built.

This can be seen by retracing the FHA underwriting process using real rather than hypothetical numbers. In 1972, the gross income of the average tenant was under $6,000. If we assume we are dealing with a 4 person household (2 children) that income after adjustment of $6,000 would equal $5,100 ([$6,000 x .95] − [$300 x 2]). A rent based on 25 percent of that amount would equal $1,275. This amount would be reduced by 5 percent to account for a vacancy rate. The effective gross income would be $1,211. If we deduct $1,000 for operating expenses we are left with $211 to service the debt. Even at a 1 percent rate and an amortization period of forty years, $211 could support only a $6,330 loan. There were very few places where a $6,000 apartment could be built that would have met FHA's architectural and property standards.

Fortunately or unfortunately, FHA proceeded blissfully, ignorant of the implications of building projects that could not be supported with the likely available income. To support the $15,000 per unit projects that were being built, the net income of the project would have to be 150 percent higher. Unfortunately, the underestimation of operating expenses meant that a project was lucky if it had any net income. When developers began to look at what they would have to manage, many came (even before their buildings were finished) to HUD with requests to approve rent increases to cover the operating expenses. This, however, was a difficult proposition since the tenants with incomes of $6,000 were already paying more than 25 percent of their income. In the case of projects serving the inner-city poor many built by non-profits, even before any rent increase, welfare tenants were paying between 40 and 100 percent of their income (in one case, in San Antonio, the $107 monthly rent exceeded the less than generous Texas welfare monthly payment of $102). The request for rent increases put HUD between a rock and a hard place. If the developer's request were granted, the rent would rise to a level that would be crushing to the tenants. If the request were denied, the owner would have to cut back on maintenance and services and that would lead to a real accelerated deterioration of the project.

Not all the projects were doomed. Projects worked where low income was either not synonymous with poor or where the tenants' income were higher than the average. For example, projects serving the elderly (who could rely on assets or children), the military (who could rely on off-base allowances), graduate students (who could rely on parents), or blue collar and service workers. In a city like Brockton, Massachusetts, there was the irony of the shoe worker who can afford to live in the project while he is working. However, when the shoe plant closes and he really needs the assistance, he is forced to move because he cannot afford the rent.

Congress would grapple with the problem with a series of patchwork devices. In 1978, a decade after the legislation was enacted, by HUD's own admission, 4,833 projects, more than two-thirds, of the 6,725 projects in the subsidized universe, were troubled or were going to potentially have problems. And in the 1990s, as the next chapter will indicate Secretary Kemp continues to grapple with the patchwork devices.

To reverse the lawyer's dictum, "Bad law makes hard cases!

Notes

1. Fannie Mae-The Federal Mortgage Association, Ginnie Mae-The Government National Mortgage Association.
2. 113 *Cong. Rec.*, H. 90th Cong., 1st sess., 1967, pt. 1:163.
3. George Sternlieb, *Tenement Landlord*, 228.
4. "Staff Report and Recommendations," 1.
5. "HUD Investigation of Low- and Moderate-Income Housing Report", *Hearing Before House Banking and Currency Comm. 92nd Cong., 1st sess., 7.*
6. "Staff Report," 11-12.
7. "HUD Investigation," 9.
8. 113 *Cong. Rec.*, S., 90th Cong., 1st sess., 1967, pt. 22 30, 351-53.
9. Louis Winnick, *New People in Old Neighborhoods*, 98-99. (1990).
10. Quoted in "Prepared Statement of C. Travis Taylor, Vice Chairman, Legislative Committee, Mortgage Bankers Assoc. of America," in *Hearings on Mortgage Servicing and HUD Property Management before a House Subcommittee of the Committee on Government Operations, 94th Cong., 1st sess., (1975), 137.*
11. "FHA Circular 4035.9."

12. *Joint Economic Committee, Hearings on Housing Subsidies and Housing Policy, 92nd Cong., sess., 226.* (December 1972).
13. *Hearings on the Housing and Urban Development Legislation of 1968 before the Senate Subcommittee of Housing and Urban Affairs, 91st Cong., 2nd sess.,* part 1, 62.
14. 114 *Cong. Rec.,* H. 90th Cong., 2nd sess., 1968, pt. 15:20,321.
15. "Housing and Income Tax Subsidies," *National Housing Policy Review Housing in the Seventies Working Papers 2,* 983.
16. These methods could be speeded by breaking the building into its components. The landscaping and equipment in the building would have much shorter lives than the building envelope.
17. Quoted in M. Schefler, "Study of Legislative History of the Rapid Depreciation Provisions," 120 *Cong. Rec.* H., 93rd Cong., 2nd sess., 1974, E, 1974.
18. 95 *Cong. Rec.,* S. 81st Cong., 1st sess., 1949, pt. 4:4808-11.
19. 23-24.
20. *Hearings on Distressed HUD-Subsidized Multifamily Projects before the Senate Banking, Housing and Urban Affairs Comm. 95th Cong., 1st sess.,* 2.
21. Robert Scheer, "Rehabilitated Housing a Costly Failure", *Los Angeles Times,* 7 August 1978.
22. *Distressed Housing Hearings,* 1.
23. *1968 Legislation Hearings,* Part 2, 1320-1409.
24. Frank de Leeuw, *Operation Costs in Public Housing: A Financial Crisis* (Urban Institute, 1970).
25. *Summary Report, Federal Housing Subsidies: Their Nature and Effectiveness and What We Should Do About Them.* (NAHB, 1972).
26. *The Report of the President's Committee on Urban Housing* (1968).
27. *Distressed Housing Hearings,* 75.
28. *House Appropriations Comm. Hearings on HUD-Independent Agencies Appropriations for 1979, 95th Cong., 2nd sess.,* 168.

3

Robin Hook and His Holy Band

The moratorium led to the termination of the subsidized rental housing programs of the Great Society. HUD was left to pick up the pieces—the distressing number of troubled projects. No group of projects was more troubled than the ones owned by non-profit organizations, many of which were black church groups. The subsidized programs had seemingly offered the opportunity to extend their good works beyond the preaching of the gospel. The availability of 100 percent loans meant they could go forward without a need to increase collections from their pious, but on the whole, poor parishioners.

Unfortunately, a large number of the sponsors were totally inexperienced. In the words of George Sternlieb, "A non-profit usually consisted of six bewildered bishops and a slick lawyer." Being community based, they built in their neighborhood and for their constituents. This meant they were tackling the most difficult job of serving the very poor in less than neighborly areas. Many rehabilitated or built projects for very low-income families in acutely distressed neighborhoods. Often they were in Model Cities areas where planned improvements never materialized.[1]

The development and the management aspects involved on-the-job training. The project was usually their first venture in the field of housing. In New York City, for example, 65 percent of the subsidized projects

51

were managed by individuals or firms that managed only that single development.

What further distinguished the non-profits were that they were under-capitalized. They wanted to do good, but they did not have the where-withal to weather the bad times. Unlike the limited distribution projects in which the tax benefits far outweighed the cash flow losses, there were no partners to contribute funds to tide the projects over. As expenses swept over income, non-profits were facing two equally unpleasant choices: becoming slumlords by holding on to their undermaintained projects or giving up by defaulting on their mortgage and eventually have the project foreclosed by HUD.

"Tar Baby" Projects

In HUD's hands these project were "tar babies." The normal procedure in a nonsubsidized project would have been to sell the project as quickly as possible in order to replenish the insurance fund. The new owner would use the property for what he deemed was its best use. It is unlikely that the use would have been housing for poor families given the inadequate subsidy structure of the Section 236 program.

The foreclosure would have been a hard bullet to bite for HUD managers. The overcapitalization of the project meant that the 100 percent of cost mortgages were based on bloated values. The foreclosure of many project loans in which there would be large losses was a frightening prospect. The insurance fund was deep in the red and Con-gress is never in a good mood when its comes to appropriating money for an item that has no constituency—an insurance fund. In addition, unlike a private entrepreneur, HUD had to consider the general welfare of its clients as well as its profit and loss statement.

In 1974, Carla Hills, the secretary of HUD, after meeting with leaders of various church and non-profit groups declared a moratorium on foreclosures of non-profit multifamily subsidized projects. HUD funded PUSH, a Chicago-based organization headed by Reverend Jesse Jackson, to study the matter. The study concluded that the issue involved pride and the probability of violence:

> Non-profit organizations . . . have demonstrated concern and pride about retaining ownership in the housing units. Any proposal for assistance which rings of "foreclo-

sure" to an "absentee slum landlord" would meet with considerable social and political resistance.[2]

Free Enterprise for the Poor; Social Justice for the Rich

HUD could have granted the ministers their wish by tinkering with the programs. If the income limits are too low for the subsidy, the limits could be raised. Congress took that course in the Housing and Community Development Act of 1974 with respect to public housing. The law instructed the secretary to instruct local housing agencies to obtain a better cross section of income for their projects—a euphemism for higher-income families. A variation on that theme had been tried with respect to the Section 236 program. HUD, on its own, worried that many eligible tenants would not be able to afford the rent and in the early 1970s, instructed project owners not to take in any tenants whose rent represented more than 35 percent of their income. The courts had rejected that approach since it would have deprived the poor of the "benefits" of the program. A solution that involves directing the program to higher-income tenants would save the projects and the investment of the landlords. Unfortunately, it would be accomplished at the expense of potential low-income tenants. It would do nothing to alleviate the crushing rent burden of present tenants in the program.

Social Justice for All

HUD and Congress decided to help the owners and the tenants. The depth of the subsidy was increased. The 1974 legislation enacted both a deep subsidy program and a rental assistance fund to keep the Section 236 projects afloat. Under the former, 20 to 40 percent of the tenants could receive subsidies that would reduce their rents to 25 percent of their income. Under the latter, subsidies were paid to cover a portion of the increases in taxes and utilities.

In 1976, HUD implemented a program wherein Section 8 funds were earmarked for tenants in subsidized projects that had "loan management" problems. There was a hitch, the subsidy was hitched to the project. If the tenant moved out of the unit he could not take the subsidy with him. If the approach made questionable policy sense, it made good political and public relations sense.

As an appropriations staff investigation committee reported,

> The then Secretary [Carla Hills] of HUD initially refused this proposal as not being consistent with the intent of the Section 8 program. However, as FY [Fiscal Year] 1976 wore on, it became apparent the publicized goal . . . of 400,000 housing units was not going to be met. To avoid this embarrassment, HUD decided to implement a high priority program whereby $170 million of Section 8 funds were set aside for assistance to existing loan management multifamily projects. It was recognized by HUD officials this would permit the rapid commitment of about 100,000 housing unit reservations which would in effect take HUD "off the hook" in meeting its publicized 400,000 unit production goal.[3]

In 1978, HUD came back with a "better idea," a flexible subsidy which would be based upon what the project needed to keep it economically viable. This was almost too much for Representative Edward Boland, the Chairman of the House Appropriations Committee:

> With respect to the Section 236 projects, . . . we originally provided an interest subsidy. On top of that, we have piggybacked a rent supplement subsidy. It is also possible that we could have piggybacked on top of that project . . . additional Section 8 loan management subsidy, or some other form of operating subsidy.[4]

HUD's innovative approaches, money aside, made everyone feel good. Even the books were looking good. The tenant's rent burden was lightened. Foreclosures were forestalled. However, the solution was only a partial one for many of the non-profits, since the condition of their projects had deteriorated so badly that they needed a significant investment of capital to rehabilitate them.

A. Bruce Rozet suggested to the PUSH people, that the physical assets of the project could be transferred to a limited distribution entity. The former non-profit could be the nominal owner but the tax benefits of ownership would be sold to private investors. The funds from these sales would be used to rehabilitate the project and bring in experienced management. Bishop H. Hartford Brookings of the African Methodist Episcopal Church, one of the church leaders that were assembled as part of the PUSH study, recollected, "All of a sudden, Santa Claus had come."

In October of 1976, the HUD Assistant Secretary for Housing promulgated a memorandum facilitating the conversions of non-profits to limited distribution entities and the private investors were off and running.

The Ventures of Robin Hook

A. Bruce Rozet's life calling seems to be separating bucks from Daddy Warbucks and taking over ventures that were started by others. After a stint at the Stanford Research Institute, he put together, in 1964, a Beverly Hills conglomerate called Commonwealth United Corporation. Commonwealth's main asset was 800,000 shares of a company called Sunasco. Sunasco was worth less than nothing (it had a negative value of $25 million). With the help a friend, who tipped others to the rumor that Sunasco was going into the fashionable computer leasing field, the stock zoomed up in value and Commonwealth sold out at $10 a share, for an $8 million profit.

Given this success, Rozet decided to expand his takeover operations. In order to obtain the money, he went to Europe and more specifically to Investors Overseas Service (IOS) run by Bernard Cornfeld. The IOS in its times, through its Fund of Funds, raised billions of dollars around the world, keeping one step ahead of the authorities in various countries. IOS was not a kosher operation. As a major study of the operation concluded:

> It was an international swindle. IOS was the creation of Bernard Cornfeld and Edward M. Cowett. Together these two men built an organization so steeped in financial and intellectual dishonesty that it was absurd that it should have been entrusted with so much of other people's money, let alone be praised for the brilliance which they managed it.[5]

The core of the swindle, was the Fund of Funds (FOF), which was a mutual fund whose business consisted of investing in other mutual funds. Mutual funds make their profit by charging their customers a management fee. Out of this fee, they have to pay for investment analysts and the other cost of buying and selling securities. The FOF charged a management fee but the only "management" was channeling money into a mutual fund. Cornfeld and Cowett took the idea one step further, it created a set of mutual funds in which FOF was the only owner. "FOF was able to benefit from two sets of management fees; a second sales charge; now dressed up as brokerage commission, was appropriated by IOS for the onerous duty of transferring the customers' money from the Fund of Funds to the individual proprietary funds."[6]

The Fund of Funds was very good to Commonwealth and Mr. Rozet. It raised $30 million through a Eurobond issue in January of 1969. Unfortunately, Commonwealth became overextended in its attempt to take over the Rexall chain of drug stores. It needed another $30 million to close the deal. Rozet came ever so close. He had conditional commitments from two American financial institutions for $20 million and FOF was happy to provide him with an additional $10 million. Rozet was ready to pounce when he was struck down by a newspaper. The *Los Angeles Times* analyzed the profits of his company concluded that a third of its profits had come from a shady deal in the tropics.

> In December 1968 the real-estate division had bought a block of undeveloped land in Hawaii for $1,656,800 which it managed to resell in the same month for $5,450,000. From the gains . . . $2,963,000 was taken as profits by Commonwealth . . . .

> But information . . . [filed] with the SEC now revealed that the Hawaiian land . . . had been bought and sold on the same day, December 31, 1986, and the purchaser were . . . Commonwealth's own brokers. What was more, although nearly 3 million had been taken as profits, Kleiner and his friends [the brokers] had only paid $541,000 cash.[7]

The drug store deal unraveled. The banks refused to extend the $20 million. Rozet resigned. Stockholders and creditors (including the Fund of Funds) now owned a company which was $100 million in the hole. On the same day he resigned:

> [T]he SEC sued the company, charging that its filing in five takeover transactions were "false and misleading" Commonwealth United without admitting guilt consented to the court order. Kleiner Bell (the brokers] were forced out of the securities industry . . . for among other things selling Commonwealth United stock on inside information.[8]

Undaunted, Rozet turned his hand to real estate tax shelters. He could now not only take the rich for a ride but help the poor along the way. From 1971 to 1975, Rozet was chairman of the board and a 22 percent owner of Income Equities Corporation (IEC). IEC advised and consulted for various limited partnerships that specialized in the ownership of subsidized projects. It was a highly profitable business. IEC collected fees for locating, evaluating the investment potential of, and acquiring projects and then monitoring the activities and management of the projects.

In picking properties he wasn't much better than Cornfeld and Cowett. Quality was not a criterion. He concentrated on rehabilitation projects since they could be fully depreciated in five years. As an HUD area director from Los Angeles was quoted as saying, "It seems every time a problem comes up with Income Equities it was over a rehab job that was in trouble to begin with."[9] Rozet was involved in coast-to-coast disasters. Three of the eight buildings in the previously mentioned Diego-Beekman in the South Bronx were in his portfolio. By early 1975, HUD was foreclosing right and left. Rozet was not losing any sleep. In an interview at the time, Rozet conceded that even if the project were foreclosed his company had already earned its profit in its sales to the limited partners.

To assuage his investors, Rozet promised to bring in a fresh group of managers. The new management team was headed up by an old friend, Hugh Pike, whose main claim to fame was that he too was barred from the securities business by the SEC. Rozet continued on as a consultant - collecting fees for picking projects even after the management transfer. And in a giant shell game, RIA (Realty Investors Associates) managed the IEC projects and Rozet affiliates managed many of RIA's projects (in 1978 RIA had a portfolio of 24,000 units).

Ever restless, Rozet in 1975 continued to work his way through the forest of tax shelter financing. He came up with a new product—HIPPLE (Housing Partnership Investments Limited). When he spoke, E.F. Hutton listened. The latter's voice reached deep into pockets of investors. Sonneblick Goldman (a major real estate firm) was also part of his new team. He lined up projects sight unseen by far outbidding other investors. George DeFranceaux, chairman of the National Corporation of Housing partnerships, who sold two subsidized rehabilitation projects in Washington D.C.'s inner city, commented, "They paid me so much money for them I couldn't believe it. What's more they didn't send anyone to look at them first."[10]

When Rozet tried to register HIPPLE, the California Corporations Department refused to approve any offering in which anyone who had been connected with IEC was involved. No problem. Rozet stepped down as general partner and received $600,000 as a severance fee. Sonnenblick Goldman stepped in and hired a newly formed company (headed and staffed by IEC alumni) to help market HIPPLE.

The Federal sheriff, one step behind, then showed up. In October of 1977, the SEC pulled the plug on IEC. Rozet and another officer were accused of selling $60 million in limited partnerships illegally. IEC and twelve affiliates were barred from selling limited partnerships in housing and real estate. Rozet was charged with defrauding investors by extracting undisclosed fees and paying investors out of their original capital to create the illusion of profitability. Without admitting or denying guilt Rozet signed a consent decree that required that he sell his tax shelters through independent brokers instead of directly to the public. He was also barred from managing the affairs or the real estate of limited

partnerships. The consent decree, however, did not take Rozet's bow
away. He was left free to find properties for acquisition and offer
consulting services to limited partnerships.

A Glut of Housing Projects

The new business was the National Development Services Corporation (NDS) which planned, negotiated for, acquired, and converted
projects. It acted as a consultant to various limited partnerships formed
by "an independent and non-affiliated" National Investor Development
Services Corporation (headed by Stephen D. Moses[11]), a partnership that
acquired existing HUD-assisted housing projects. By March of 1981,
NDS and its Chairman Bruce Rozett could boast in a prospectus that it
had assisted in the transfer of over 150 housing project involving over
$400 million of real estate.

The operation grew so quickly because of the lack of selectivity.
Commissioned finders criss-crossed the nation looking for suitable real-
estate. Projects could be found in nearly every state of the union and
Puerto Rico.

Sellers were not limited to properties that were in need of substantial
rehabilitation. In fact, there were five main sources of projects: (1). There
were non-profits with ulterior motives. Non-profit and nobility are not
synonymous. One of Rozet's earliest finds was a group of projects in
New Mexico owned by the Carpenters Union that was under the thumb
of its President. The problem was not the condition of the projects but
rather the condition of the union's treasury. The President wanted a hefty
pension. Their only assets were the projects. Rozet provided the answer.
If the project were transferred to a limited distribution entity, the Carpenters
would receive sufficient funds from the syndication of the project to
investors to insure that the President would spend his retirement years in the
manner to which he had become accustomed. Not a penny went into the
project. (2). The elimination of aggravation was another factor. Project
ownership and management involves more than ribbon-cutting ceremo-
nies. It was quite difficult for many non-profits to evict a tenant who
couldn't pay rent (and in a number of cases they found it difficult to even
ask for rent) let alone to deal with the Federal bureaucracy in order to get
the needed additional subsidies to run the project. (3). The blessings from
the Bishop Brookings (for which he received paltry indulgences in the

form of a Rozet credit card that covered some of his first class travel expenses) brought in many projects. Brookings introduced Rozet to AME ministers who had over 10,000 units that were ripe for conversion.[12] (4). The community development corporations (such as the Woodlawn organization in Chicago) that came into existence during the poverty war, with OEO or Model City funding, to provide housing were also candidates. When their funding evaporated, their operation quickly disintegrated and they sometimes used the housing projects as a source of funds to stay alive. (5). Limited distribution partnerships that owned projects insured under the Section 221 (d)(3) below-market-interest rate program. The projects dated from the early and mid-sixties. Having lost their tax shelter, the original owners were waiting to be taken in from the cold. The tax crossover point had been reached. The rapid depreciation of the base in the early years of the project to produce losses meant that in later year profits for tax purposes would exceed cash flow.

The supply of money was no problem. Rozet had a network of lawyers and accountants and investment bankers with clients in high tax brackets, who were eager to enter into losing deals. Christmas time (coinciding with the end of the tax year) was an especially busy time for sales of limited partnership interests to investors who wished to do good by participating in the nation's efforts to house its poor citizens.

Price was rarely a factor since the interests carried a great money back assurance. The new investors were assured their money back almost as quickly as they put it in and a 3-to-1 return on their money.

For a typical project[13] in which the partner had to invest $42,500 over a five year period, the projections were for a 70 percent tax bracketeer as shown in table 3.1.

In addition, there were the less tangible benefits of a small amount of cash flow and the capital appreciation of the project.

Not all of the projects were doing that well. Many of the projects selected for NIDC were in trouble. Who was called in by HUD to give NIDC some help but a newly formed Rozet corporation Housing Resources Management Inc. As Bruce Rozet explained, "In 1982 HUD and the then owner of NIDC requested the assistance of our firm in reviewing the needs of some sixty six properties acquired by NIDC in the years between 1979 and 1981."[14] The result was a Master Workout Agreement between HUD and HRM regarding the 66 projects (including Tyler House) and the acquisition by HRM of the stock of NIDC.

TABLE 3.1

	Investment		Tax Loss		Net Benefit	
Year	Annual	Total	Annual	Total	Annual	Total
1	$8,500	$8,500	$22,418	$22,418	$ 7,193	$ 7,193
2	15,000	23,500	41,021	63,439	13,715	20,908
3	8,500	32,000	22,646	86,085	7,352	28,260
4	5,400	37,400	14,407	100,492	4,685	32,945
5	5,100	42,500	13,648	114,140	4,454	37,399
6	0	42,500	11,957	126,097	8,370	45,769
			• • •			
20	0	42,500	8,750	265,288	5,999	143,200

Modus Operandi

The transfers from non-profit to profit status did require HUD approval and HUD required that each limited partnership could only own one project. The Rozet deals had a two-tier ownership structure (reminiscent of Bernie Cornfeld's multi-tier mutual funds.) There would be an investor partnership that would invest its funds in a number of project partnerships. This satisfied HUD requirement of project accountability.

The investor partnership had a number of straight-out business advantages. The private-placement documents required to raise money from investors were lengthy and expensive to prepare. By packaging a number of projects within one placement there were economies of scale. The investor partnership format also provided flexibility. If one of the projects fell out, it could be replaced by another, or if the full amount of the offering could not be raised the number of projects in which the partnership would invest could be reduced.

The two-tier arrangement had other advantages. HUD would not see the whole deal. In any negotiation with HUD as to the amount of rehabilitation work that was needed, it would not be helpful if HUD saw how much money was available. Secondly, the deal was the state of the art and although Rozet couldn't patent it, he didn't want to publicize it. The investors valued their privacy. There was also the advantage that the upper-tier partnership could be on the accrual basis of accounting and the lower levels on a cash basis (the importance of this technicality will soon be explained).

The final sentence before the listing of the compensation and fees in the prospectus reads as follows: "The compensation and fees to the General Partners (none of which was determined as a result of arms length negotiations) . . . are described below." This admission is a result of legal prudence rather the desire for candor.

In the aforementioned offering, $1.488 million dollars were raised from the investors. Rozet walked away with at least $515,000. NDS received $200,000. Management Assistance Group, Inc. (MAGI)— whose president, Lois Hue, was Rozet's lady-in-waiting: Rozet was later to divorce his wife and marry Ms. Hue—provided asset management and received $120,000 over a 3 year period and an additional $195,000 in consulting and conversion fees.

Junk Notes

What made the deals sellable was the assurance that there would be sufficient losses to allow an investor to obtain a 300 percent return. At times, these losses had to be created out of thin air. Reminiscent of the Hawaiian land deal in which land suddenly appreciated when the buyer "paid" for the property with notes on which he bore no responsibility, the losses (which Rozet was selling) in the case of investor partnership came about through the artificial inflation of the price of subsidized projects.

The investor partnership, previously discussed, involved three Mississippi projects that were subsidized under the Section 221 (d)(3) program. The mortgages carried a 3 percent interest rate and had an unpaid balance of $3.9 million. The price (which included some repair and renovation work to be done in the future) to be paid by the seller John R. Johnson was $4.3 million. The price paid by investor partnerships was $5.7 million. Johnson was to remain on as a general partner of the project partnerships and receive a salary over the first three years of $240,000. Since the operations of the work was subcontracted to MAGI for $120,000 the balance of $120,000 could be viewed as a finders fee. In addition, the general partners were to receive a commitment fee of $80,000 for an agreement to loan funds to the partnership *if* necessary.

The contract for sale from the non-profit was initially held by Johnson and assigned to the Project Partnerships. The purchase price was paid with a $5.7 million mortgage note which was wrapped around the FHA insured $3.9 million first mortgage and the balance between the purchase price and first mortgage of $1.8. million. The note ran for thirty years and had an interest of 14 percent but there was no personal liability assumed by the project partnerships and the partners.

The project partnerships had to pay, from the rents, the FHA mortgages debt service (based on a 3 percent interest rate), real estate taxes, reserves for replacements and mortgage insurance premiums. There was not, however, sufficient funds to make payments on the mortgage note to Johnson. This fact was of little concern to FHA since the projects' books looked fine. All the payments required by the mortgage and regulatory agreements were being made. The fact that the additional payments could not be made since the cash flow was insufficient, did not threaten the project's financial health.

At the investor partnership level the books looked even finer. It was filing taxes on the accrual basis. Therefore, all of the unpaid interest payments on the loan were treated as expenses, thereby increasing the losses and the tax benefits to the partners.

The "wrap-around" scheme was walking on the borderline between tax avoidance and tax evasion. Deductions are limited to mortgage interest that did not exceed the fair market value of the projects. There seemed to be little justification for the jump in price given: (1)the short time period between the sales contract with the non-profit and Johnson and the subsequent assignment to the project partnerships; (2) the non--arms length nature of the negotiation; (3) there was no personal liability; and (4) the notes could only be sold at a substantial discount. The Internal Revenue Service had disallowed deductions in cases of non recourse debt involving such items as movie films, record masters, and print plates. In the disclosure in the prospectus after raising these and other questionable practices (such as whether the deduction for the payments to the general partner could be considered expenses), the defense is sanctimoniously made, "there are strong public policy arguments which would indicate that no claim of lack of value by the service should be upheld because such a claim would, in effect, *make it uneconomical for anyone to ever acquire an interest in government-assisted housing* [my emphasis]."[15] Put another way, unless fees equal to over 33 percent of the investment and profits equal to 300 percent are made by limited partners for doing absolutely nothing we can't assist the poorly housed. These statements were made even before the passage of the Economic Recovery Tax Act of 1981, which liberalized the tax laws.

The wraparound note also has a boa constrictor like feature on the investor partnership. It assures that any capital appreciation will be squeezed out to pay off the note which has been accruing interest at 14 percent per year and that any subsequent owner would be saddled with a very high debt structure. In many cases the projects will revert to the holders of the notes.

Rozet and many of the firms under Rozet's control hold such junk notes.[16] At best they are a source of mischief. The case of Charles Bazarian Jr. is illustrative:

[The] charges against Bazarian, an Oklahoma loan broker who is serving a two-year term for a 1987 bank fraud conviction, appear to represent a link between two of the year's biggest scandals—problems with HUD and the series of failed savings and loans.

According to charges filed in Los Angeles, Bazarian took part in complex schemes that involved an affiliate of Associate Financial Corp. [one of Rozets] . . . and two Orange County thrifts in an attempt to defraud federal savings and loan regulators. According to the information filed . . . Bazarian worked with Wilshire Investments Corp., the affiliate of Associated . . . to obtain upward of $9.5 million in loans from Consolidated [Savings].

Bazarian's collateral consisted of "fraudulent" promissory notes supplied by Wilshire . . . [that] Wilshire obtained . . " through investments in real estate, the value of which was "highly inflated."

Bazarian in turn used the notes to carry out fraudulent deals at savings and loans in California, Oklahoma and Texas . . . through much of the 1980s Bazarian dealt . . . Last year as Bazarian appealed his 1987 criminal conviction . . . Associated paid Bazarian $15,000 a month, Bazarian's wife testified in a bankruptcy proceeding.[17]

Making the Rules

Rozet did much more than maneuver amidst the murky water of housing regulations and tax rulings. As one reporter, noted, "They [Rozet and associates] not only know how to bend the rules, but also probably help to write them."[18]

Bruce Rozet was a beneficiary of Senator Cranston's constituent services. In the late 1970s, when the Senate Banking Committee was considering the suspension that HUD had reimposed on the conversion of subsidized housing projects from non-profit to for profit ownership, it was Cranston who led the push to reactivate the program.[19]

When Congress took on tax reform, in 1986, eliminating the tax-loss industry, the senator did his utmost to ensure that there would still be a money pump for low-income housing. Since the legislation provided for the distribution of the credits at the state level, Rozet's lobbyists were also busy with the distributors of the funds. When the tax legislation came forth from Congress, it fit his deals very well. He was first out of the starting gate. The Associated Financial Corporation was involved in twenty four low-income housing credit projects as of 31 December 1988.[20]

When Senator Cranston made his presidential bid, Rozet hosted a fundraiser in his modest $5 million home that has a remote controlled back yard waterfall and is considered the epitome of interior designer Waldo Fernandez's work. Rozet has claimed that he has raised as much as $1 million for the senator through the years.[21] When Cranston dropped out, he joined the Jesse Jackson bandwagon. He went to the Democratic convention as a Jackson delegate from California and served on the board of directors of the Rainbow Coalition.[22]

Cranston in the 1988 Congress, headed up the Senate Banking, Housing, and Urban Affairs Committee. He appointed Rozet to a commission headed by Senators Mitchell and Danforth, to fine tune the tax credits. Rozet had a host of ideas that were particularly attuned to his projects (he had close to an additional forty projects that he was ready to syndicate).

Although he was king of the hill, he did not fare as well at HUD. In spite of hiring Lynda Murphy, he couldn't even "buy" a Section 8 Moderate Rehabilitation Project subsidy at HUD. This was a minor irritant compared to his encounter with Jack Kemp.

The Deal Maker and the Reformer

In February 1989, two weeks into Kemp's tenure, Jesse Jackson, accompanied by Bruce Rozet, came for a get-acquainted visit. The initial encounter between Rozet and Kemp was cordial and Rozet was sure he had another friend in a high place. He assumed that the new secretary would want to use his expertise to straighten out the mess at HUD. How wrong he was!

Jack Kemp while touring his domain came across one of Rozet's projects, Tyler House, in the District of Columbia. Tyler House was part of the NIDC portfolio but Rozet's involvement goes way back to the 1970s. It was one of the examples of the good that converters could do in the paper prepared by Rozet's office and submitted by PUSH:

> This major project was three months delinquent, verged on assignment at the time it was converted. . . . Rapid action by a conversion sponsor and a significant injection of private capital combined with a workout agreement with FNMA has at least to date brought the project back to liquidity. The tenant situation, although unsettled is being addressed. the management problem has been stabilized. Some bills have been paid and repairs have been attended to. The new investor sponsors are dedicated to make this project work . . . . With additional effort and cooperation from the HUD office, this project can be saved and be made viable from both the physical and financial point of view as well as in terms of tenant concerns.[23]

Kemp when he arrived at the Tyler site, was horrified and outraged when he saw conditions at the project—described by his General Counsel, Frank Keating, as "Beirut after the bombing". Reports also began coming in from field offices requesting authority to foreclose on some other of Rozet's troubled projects—six in Oklahoma, Geneva Towers a 573-unit project in San Francisco, and Ujima Village near Watts in Los Angeles.

HUD charged Housing Resources Management (HRM) and the whole host of affiliate Rozet companies with irregularities in misusing funds in projects in Washington, D.C. and Tulsa, Oklahoma and temporarily suspended the firms and individuals from doing business with HUD. The decision was upheld by the HUD Board of Contract of Appeals and Rozet was suspended pending a complete investigation.

While Jack Kemp saw Rozet as a "malefactor of great wealth," Rozet saw himself as an innocent victim of a political vendetta by HUD. Nevertheless, as Bernie Cornfeld put the matter after his clash with the Securities and Exchange Commission, "They may be schmucks, but they're the Government." With HUD putting the brakes on Rozet funding requests and investors getting jittery, new syndications came to a grinding halt. The hardest blow fell on many of his associates, such as Steve Moses and Hugh Pike who never put money away for the rainy days. They moved from their tax shelters into the shelter of bankruptcy laws. At least one other associate is bankrupt as a result of the inability of Drexel Burnham Lambert, because of its bankruptcy, to make good on its commitment to provide funding for a series of syndications. Rozet, one assumes, was far smarter. Although he spent lavishly, he had some experience with bailing out of failing enterprises and with European finance. He surely knew the way to the banks of Switzerland.

"These Eggs Are for Speculating Not Eating"

The ultimate irony of the tale, is that Rozet was brought down for the same reason he was so beloved by HUD management staff. He would buy projects sight unseen. As Robert Kalish who helped coordinate many of the transfers for HUD was quoted as saying, "Most of the projects were in such bad shape that nobody would touch them. The judgement was made . . . that it was better to work out something with Mr. Rozet than to foreclose."[24]

Management of projects was not Mr. Rozet's forte. He was not a man for operational details. Management was not a profit center. When the highest bidder went out to the boxcar and complained that the eggs were rotten, the commodity broker's response was that "these eggs are for speculating not eating," Bruce Rozet passion in life was in making money not in housing poor people. He would have been just as happy doing leveraged buy-outs and selling junk bonds.

He would take just about any project. His goal was to get it syndicated and his money out. There was a parody of a prospectus by a departing Rozet marketing director, Vin Morreale, that illustrates the point:

AFC CHERNOBYL HOUSING PARTNERS LTD.
A UKRAINIAN LIMITED PARTNERSHIP

Marketing Strategy

With the anticipated changes in tax laws, it is increasingly difficult to offer investors the abusive tax benefits which we have generated in the past. Government subsidized housing fulfills an identifiable public need and can be useful in convincing investors that they are actually serving the community by hiding untold thousands in legitimate taxes from the government. But the subsidized projects are usually occupied by the unsavory tenants we wouldn't let wash our Ferraris . . .

In light of these limitations, the General Partners devised the strategy of taking damaged nuclear reactors and converting them to low-income housing units. The first success came when the Three Mile Island Nuclear Power Plant in Pennsylvania was converted to government-assisted housing and renamed "Priscilla Villa." This type of investment offers the following benefits:

• An accelerated depreciation schedule of less than 15 days as opposed to the standard 18 years.

- Eligible for generous HUD Flex-Subsidy loans and rehabilitation credits.

- Attractive financing terms: A standard $2 billion nuclear plant which has achieved partial melt-down can usually be acquired for under a dollar-fifty. It is then possible to convince a . . . certified appraiser to value the property at the original $2 billion, with accompanying documentation bearing all the integrity of cow chips.

How the Partnership Works

Seller kickbacks, mortgage finder fees, loan fees, and acquisition fees will each be absorbed by the Operating Partnership, which is formed solely to generate management . . ., oversight . . ., hindsight . . . fees, partnership acquisition fees, legal and organizational fees, marketing fees, accounting fees, consulting fees and General partner salaries. The Investor Partnership is then structured to give the investors the impression that they are getting something for their money. The Investor partnership is to generate management fees. . . . After which, we hire ourselves or Affiliate companies to generate consulting fees, due diligence fees, fees for processing TPAS [transfers of physical assets] and other less legitimate fees we will sooner or later figure out ways of justifying. We then deduct another 13% for Broker-Dealer commissions and reimbursements. However, despite our best efforts, a full 37% of each investor dollar escapes us and goes into the project.

Peasant Village

Located on 213 irradiated acres the 320-unit Peasant Village apartment complex benefits from an excellent location [and] unique amenities . . . . Among the many fine amenities are a newly installed skylight, swimming pool, incandescent trees, and flower beds more than 20 feet tall. . . Lights, heating, and cooking are supplied simply by contacting the glowing walls and appliances. Microwaves are provided but microwave ovens are not. . .

Due to the aggressive marketing strategies of KGB Property Management, the project offers a 100% occupancy rate. . . Yuri Lee Pismiov, the President of KGB . . . oversees more than 20,000 units in Afghanistan, Siberia and the Gulag Archipelago.

Individual rents range from 800 rubles for the one-bedroom units and 900 for the two-bedroom units to 32,000 rubles for any units with a bathroom. . . [t]he projects offers a Sector 8 HAPPY (Housing Assistance Payments Per Year) Contract which offers subsidy payments on 125% of the units. . . The Project is only 378 miles from Payof Plaza a major shopping and black market center. Numerous hospitals occupy the complex grounds and various churches of absolutely no denominations are nearby.

Actually few of the Rozet's projects are in scandalous shape and given the size of the operation some mismanagement was to be expected. If HUD were to have operated the projects it is unlikely the results would have been much better. Bruce Rozet is surely convinced that like, Al Capone going off to jail for tax evasion, he was gunned down by a cheap shot. The U.S. attorney general's probe of his financial operations, however, could lead to a shot at the heart and criminal charges.

Rozet may be down but he is certainly not out. At HUD's request he is selling off 35,000 units in his portfolio. His first attempt to sell the project was structured like the approach he used at the time he was forced out as a manager of the Income Equities Corporation in the 1970s. One of the principals was Arthur Penn, Rozet's longtime chief financial officer. Rozet was also dealing with only one group. A rival group was turned down since it rebuffed Rozet's suggestion that he be retained as a consultant.[25]

When that deal fell through, according to HUD sources because the group didn't want to jeopardize their reputation,[26] Rozet hooked up with a new partner, Vince Lane—the head of the Chicago Housing Authority and reported to be Secretary Kemp's favorite public housing director. The deal left HUD officials puzzled. They did not know that Lane had been a buddy of Rozet long before Kemp developed an interest in housing. Vince Lane had been the chief financial officer of Woodlawn Community Development Corporation, whose projects found their way into Rozet's portfolio, and in the previously discussed Mississippi deal, Mr. Lane was a general partner in charge of the project partnerships. HUD is left with another hard decision.

No Heart-No Sight

The government is also culpable for the whole affair. HUD refused to face the failure of programs that could work only by overestimating the income of tenants and underestimating expenses. When the days of reckoning came all of HUD's masons and all the heavy layers of financial and administrative patchwork were insufficient to shore up a program whose surface was undermined by structural defects.

HUD did not have the ability to value the projects and determine whether the amount of subsidy going into the project was in any way commensurate with the benefit of the tenants. During all the years, HUD never saw the fourth option of allowing the developers' fate to be determined by the market while protecting the tenants. Their fate should not have been tied to the project's. It should have gone the "free enterprise for the rich and social justice for the poor" route. Lacking the imagination, HUD turned to creative financiers. It was much better to let the

Treasury pick up the tab for the hundreds of millions in lost revenue arising from Rozet's elegant tax schemes.

The sides weren't fair. HUD's Inspector General couldn't decipher the trading and flipping of projects between Rozet's many corporations. As a top investigator said, "We thought it was part of a major scheme. They were slick. They were well-heeled. They were well protected. We could never prove [any fraud against HUD]."[27] On the other hand, agents from the IRS were being told that the questionable valuations and validity of the wrap around financing were absolutely necessary in order to help low income tenants and fully in accord with HUD's policies.

Rozet and HUD were a perfect match. Rozet's cupidity was matched by HUD's myopia. The man with no heart met the Government with no vision. The result was a government "robbed blind."

Notes

1. Remarks by Sharon Keilen, Executive Director, Advisory Services for Better Housing Inc., in *Hearings on Distressed HUD Subsidized Housing Projects, Senate Banking, Hsng., and Urb. Affairs Comm., 95th Cong., 1st sess.*, 28–29.
2. Quoted in *A Review - Conversion of non-Profit HUD multifamily projects to limited distribution entities* [No date or author is provided in the document. It was written in the late 1970s by somebody in the A. Bruce Rozet organization].
3. *House 1979 Appropriations Hearings*, 133–34.
4. Ibid., 167.
5. Charles Raw, Bruce Page, and Godfrey Hodgson, *Do You Sincerely want to be Rich*, 4.
6. Ibid., 86.
7. Quoted in ibid., 248.
8. Wartzman, Rick, "How a Big Financier of Housing Projects Ran Afoul of HUD," *Wall Street Journal*, 31 August 1990, AI, A4.
9. Stephen Quickel, "The Robin Hood Game," *Forbes*, 1 October 1976, 61–62.
10. Quoted in ibid.
11. He had headed up Boise-Cascade's hugely unsuccessful Urban Development Division. It had huge overruns in its attempt to rehabilitate Clifton-Terrace which remains a landmark failure of subsidized housing.
12. David Hilzenrath and Susan Schmidt, "Public Housing's Money Man," *The Washington Post*, 24 November 1989, 1,10.
13. *Confidential Private Offering Memorandum, $1,487,500, 35 Limited Partnership Interests, COLINA INVESTORS, LTD.*, 99. (20 March 1981).
14. *House Hearings on Loan Management Procedures for HUD Assisted Housing, 101st Cong., 2d sess.*, 104.
15. *Confidential Private Offering Colina*, 74.
16. There is some speculation that in the Mississippi projects, Rozet's NDS had a deal not disclosed in the prospectus to receive a substantial share of the note.

17. Dan Morain, "Bank Swindler Named in S&L, HUD Fraud," *Los Angeles Times*, 19 September 1989.
18. Byron Fielding, "Rozen Bobs and Weaves on Capitol Hill," *Housing Affairs Letter*, 2 March 1990, 2.
19. *Senate Banking and Urban Affairs Comm., Hearings on Housing Authorization Legislation, 96th Cong., 1st sess.*, 118.
20. Associated Financial Corporation and Affiliates, "Summary of Selected Operating Projects."
21. David Hilzenrath, "HUD Curbs Operator of Projects," *The Washington Post*, 2 February 1990, AI.
22. Ibid.
23. *Conversion of non-profit projects*, 54.
24. Quoted in Hilzenrath, "HUD Curbs Operator."
25. Fielding, Byron, "Rozen-Golar Deal Bears Watching," *Housing Affairs Letter*, 4 December 1990.
26. "Kemp Favorite Takes Questionable Partner," *Housing Affairs Letter*, October 25, 1991, 5.
27. Quoted in Dan Morain and Jill Stewart, "HUD: Entrepreneur Feels the Heat," *Los Angeles Times*, 25 November 1989.

4

Circles of Shame

The Tragedy of Sam Pierce

At his confirmation hearing Judge Pierce was introduced with gushing praise by Senator Daniel Patrick Moynihan of New York:

> May I just begin with the observation that if there were more men such as he in the country, Presidents would have an easier time filling their Cabinets. There are few men in our time who have served with such distinction as Judge Pierce has in such a broad range of response [sic] positions in public and private life.

> Judge Pierce . . . is a graduate of Cornell, NYU Law School and Yale University. Early in life, he became an assistant district attorney . . . and went on to become an assistant U.S. attorney for the southern district of New York. Thereafter, he went to Washington, where he served as an assistant to the Under Secretary of Labor in the administration of President Eisenhower. Thereafter, he went to the House of Representatives where he became . . . counsel to the Subcommittee on Antitrust of the . . . Committee on the Judiciary.

> He then turned to the practice of law. He became a Judge in the Court of Special Sessions . . . , then returned to Washington, where he became General Counsel to the Department of Treasury in 1970. . . .

> Judge Pierce was General Counsel . . . when I was a member of the White House staff . . . . I remember the awe that one associates with someone who comes to the Treasury who is not only a master of the legal issues but also cognizant of the fiscal and monetary consequences . . . . [T]this is an experience he acquired as a member of the board of a number of our most distinguished corporations.

> He is in every respect a singular man.[1]

71

After serving two terms as HUD secretary (more than twice as long as any prior secretary), praise continued to flow:

> Who should be remembered as Ronald Reagan's most effective Cabinet member? . . . By the only standard that ultimately matters—concrete achievements of Reaganite goals—the star of the cabinet has been its least visible, least charismatic member. Secretary of Housing and Urban Development Samuel Pierce has proved that an Eastern establishment Republican can be a successful Reagan revolutionary.[2]

Since that praise, in a Job-like change of fortune, former Secretary Pierce's life has been filled with scorn. He is now gauged by a new measure—the level of Washington scandals.

> In the mix of Washington scandals HUD ranks as historically less important than the Iran-contra and financially less costly than the S&L crisis. Yet in terms of breathtaking cynicism and hypocrisy it's hard to match. Over eight years ostensibly respectable people effectively became poverty pimps, getting rich and powerful by subverting programs intended to help the poor.[3]

The former secretary was thrice brought before the House of Representative's Employment and Housing Subcommittee of the Committee on Government Operations (Lantos Committee.) At his third appearance, he took the cover of the Fifth Amendment, becoming the third cabinet secretary (serving or former) to do so; the other two starred in the 1922 Teapot Dome scandal.

After investigating for fourteen months, the committee concluded that it had uncovered at HUD widespread fraud and abuse, influence peddling, blatant favoritism, monumental waste, and gross mismanagement. At the request of Attorney General Thornburgh (responding to a House Judiciary Committee request in November of 1989), the circuit court appointed former Federal 3rd Circuit Court of Appeals Judge Arlin Adams as Independent Counsel to look into these matters. After taking more testimony the Lantos Committee on 24 July 1990 requested Judge Adams that he widen his probe to include whether former Secretary Pierce violated federal bribery laws and perjured himself in testimony before the committee.

The Pierce Perspective

In 1974, after extinguishing the prior private subsidized housing programs, the Republican administration, with more than a little help from Congress, managed to create an even more expensive replacement

—the New Construction and Substantial Rehabilitation segment of the Section 8 Program. By 1980, even the Democrats had some inkling that they had a potential disaster on their hands. Representative Edward Boland (he of the Boland Amendment that was to bring such grief to the Reagan Administration in the Contra case), Chairman of the Appropriations Subcommittee in charge with funding HUD, introduced the bill covering appropriations for 1981 with the following discussion of the dollars:

> [S]ection 8 . . . is not unlike any other housing program in that it is the victim of the inflationary pressures felt throughout the housing industry. But I believe these numbers carry a special significance at a time when we are trying to get some control over what this government will be committed to spend in 5, 10, 20 years.
>
> Mr. Speaker, no other program commits the Government spending money down the road as dramatically as does the subsidized housing programs. So I would urge the new administration . . . to look hard at some of the options available to housing low-income and elderly . . . . The problem is how we can do that without committing a disproportionate share of our resources over the next 20, 30, or 40 years.[5]

The Reagan administration—budgetary conscious in social program areas—placed two main items at the top of secretary's agenda, shutting down the new construction and substantial rehabilitation portion of Section 8 and shifting assistance to existing housing. Secretary Pierce placed a third item on the agenda, obtaining fair housing legislation with meaningful penalties for violators.

Although the Great Communicator he wasn't and his relationship with the Chairman of the House Banking, Finance, and Urban Affairs Representative Henry Gonzalez were rancorous (he referred to Pierce as "Stepin Fetchit"), he achieved his main goals.

During his tenure, the policy pillars of fifty years of housing programs—of providing new housing for poor people—were pulled down. Housing assistance was being directed to existing housing. And late in his reign, fair housing legislation with strong enforcement provisions were enacted.

He set a high standard for ethical conduct. When the inspector general in 1982 reported that Charles Bazarian Jr. (who we met in the last chapter) was a bit too friendly with a number of high HUD officials, the secretary informed the general deputy assistant secretary for housing Philip Abrams:

> The investigation disclosed a degree of failure . . . to be sufficiently alert to the possibilities of creation of appearances of favoritism . . . .

I hasten to emphasize that . . . appearances only were involved. However, as you are well aware, appearances are of major importance to broad perceptions of integrity of public processes, particularly in those areas where public agencies conduct . . . business transactions with private interests. . . .

It is important for all Department activities . . . be carried out in an arm's-length, business-like manner without favoritism, or appearance of favoritism towards any-one.[6]

Ironically, the scandals did not come in any of the main line programs. The coinsurance program was perceived as a small off-budget program that provided a nice demonstration of privatization. The Section 8 Moderate Rehabilitation Program and the Urban Development Grant Program were being shunted off the main line and headed for extinction.

These micro programs were not to be micro-managed. Pierce was living in the Reagan era of majestic disinterest in management. Under the 1982 Federal Managers Financial Act, department heads were to report to Congress and the President whether they had reasonable assurance that their internal controls and accounting systems were in order. As reported by the *Washington Monthly*:

Pierce . . . wrote OMB in 1983 to say that he could not provide reasonable assurances. The fact that he was only one of three of 17 agency heads to do so might have put OMB with notice that all wasn't well at HUD. In 1984 and 1985, Pierce wrote again to say that reasonable assurances were beyond HUD's grasp. What's more, guess what problems he was having? Fraudulent escrow agents. Problems with the co-insurance program . . . . Congress yawned and did nothing. OMB went one step further and said "Hey shut up over there!" Jack McGrath, the HUD official who filed the reports, officials on the M-side of OMB pressured the agency to file a rosier report.[7]

OMB's mind-set is caught in an article in the *New York Times*:

The budget office cut the staff of its own management division by 42 persons . . . in its drive to set an example to other agencies. . . . James C. Miller budget director . . . says he never read any of the [management] reports. . . . "[T]he [Reagan] Administration was more focused on the philosophy of reducing Government than on financial details." he said, "That meant less attention was paid." Mr. Miller added, "Our perception was that waste came form Congress in the form of wasteful programs."[8]

Secretary Pierce by disposition and political philosophy fit in perfectly. Although he had sat on the boards of General Electric and the Prudential Insurance Company, he had never run any large organization, let alone a federal agency. He came to HUD with but the scantiest knowledge of HUD programs and never mastered the details:

At one meeting toward the end of his tenure, HUD staff members were talking about
the controversial Moderate Rehabilitation Program. "What is this Moderate Rehab
program anyway?" Pierce interjected.[9]

As a personal or political favor, he would occasionally dabble in the
selection process. He would bend over backwards to accommodate a
client of a politically powerful former secretary of HUD—a natural act
when all of the public positions on his impressive resume were political
appointments and he was hoping for one more to top off his career.
Although he had time on his hands, occasional soap operas, design of
campaign cravats ("Push for Bush"), travel to the Soviet Union (in his
five trips he spent more time there than the Secretary of State) and the
Far East, and thinking about the retirement of Thurgood Marshall and of
the black robes of the Supreme Court filled his day. They were certainly
to be preferred to watching programs, in which he had little interest when
they were alive, die. The details and the disposition of the bodies could
be delegated to his lieutenants.

Unfortunately, his lieutenants were young and restless. Instead of
mopping up, they were slopping around in the mud and having the days
of their lives. They were the bold and the beautiful children of the eighties
in which the lust for power was the guiding light.

Disappearance from the helm is not the way to prevent "appearances
of favoritism." A man who shied away from power was to find himself
in the midst of scandal dealing with the abuse of power and the appearance of deception. Integrity of public processes was replaced by partisan
favoritism and the fragile bond of trust between the electorate and
appointed officials was shattered.

Coinsurance: From Deregulation to Disaster

In the 1950s, coinsurance was tied to loss control. The risk-sharing
between private lenders and FHA was a way to assure that those who
issued loans that FHA insured would be prudent and careful in carrying
out their appraisal and underwriting responsibilities. The 10 percent
share of the risk borne by lenders in the Title I home-improvement loan
program cured their laxity.

In 1974, coinsurance was seen as a cure for the poor underwriting that
plagued HUD's inner-city home insurance program. An assistant secre-

tary tried to convince a skeptical Congressman, of the virtues of coinsurance:

MR. LUBAR: One of the main problems we have now is that in the central city area . . . [i]f you don't have 100 percent insured FHA loans there are no loans made, and since we insure 100 percent . . . standards aren't what they should really be.

MR. ST GERMAIN: In the event of a default . . . where you have a 10 percent coinsurance lender . . . [and] there is a loss of $5,000 . . . FHA's loss is $4,500 . . . . and the originator's loss is $500. [T]he HUD offices are going to watch over these insurers very carefully . . . . I think one of the big problems . . . is that you have not had sufficient competent staff to supervise these programs. What is going to turn all of this around?

MR. LUBAR: Well that is a good question. The concept is that HUD would go out of policing of every loan . . . . We would spot check and in effect be in the wholesale insurance business . . . The only checking is when there was a claim, much as . . . Title I.[10]

Legislation authorizing coinsurance was enacted in 1974 and became Section 244 of the National Housing Act. Congress in the same legislation also enacted a new paragraph (f) under Section 223 ("Miscellaneous Housing Provisions") that authorized the secretary to provide mortgage insurance for the purchase and or refinancing of existing buildings. During the 1970s there was some activity under the latter provision but no activity under the coinsurance provision.

In the eighties, Sheldon Lubar was gone. Fernand St Germain turned his attention to raising the federal insurance on deposits in savings and loan associations to $100,000 and then deregulating these institutions - now recognized as the initial steps that were to lead to the savings and loan debacle. HUD for its part in May 1983, began the Section 223 (f) coinsurance program. Mortgage insurance became a wholesale business. Private lenders had the power to commit the full faith and credit of the United States. The result was a debacle albeit on a smaller scale.

A Good Fit

Representative Tom Lantos, the chairman of the House Government Operations subcommittee investigating HUD commented, "When . . . a list is compiled of the most ill-advised ventures in the 1980s, on the top of the list of lemons, high above the introduction of the "New Coca-Cola" and the making of the film *Heaven's Gate,* will be HUD's coinsuring loans."[11]

For those at HUD in the early 1980s, without the benefit of 20/20 hindsight, coinsurance looked like a very good idea. A premise of the new administration's housing policy was that the construction of subsidized housing was a bad idea. Having decided to severely cutback new construction it was logical to reduce the HUD staff involved in mortgage processing—appraisers, underwriters, construction analysts, and inspectors.

A corollary of the premise was that HUD's role in multifamily housing was to insure the maintenance of the existing unsubsidized stock. The new administration found a ready-made vehicle in the Section 223 (f) program that permitted the refinancing and minor repair of existing buildings. Not having a staff to run even a small multifamily insurance program, HUD put its chips on coinsurance. It was good fit—real businessmen who didn't rely on the crumbs of subsidy, faster processing, fewer federal employees, and less red tape.

HUD felt protected. The coinsurer would be responsible for the first 5 percent of the loss. FHA would pay for 85 percent of the balance of the loss and the private lender would be responsible for the remainder. With this risk, the private lender was granted a great deal of power and responsibility. It was to perform all loan underwriting functions, monitor property management agents and handle the foreclosure and disposition of the projects.

After the acquired property was sold, the lender could apply to HUD for payment of HUD's share of the loss. The loss was the difference between the sales price and the unpaid mortgage plus costs of foreclosure, accrued interest, and maintenance of the property.

For its efforts HUD permitted the private lenders to collect from the borrowers up-front fees that could be included in the loan. These fees included an application fee of .3 percent, a financing fee of 2 percent, and a placement fee of 1.5 percent. The lender also received .35 percent from the HUD initial mortgage insurance premium. Thus, at the initiation of the loan, the fees totalled 4.15 percent. In addition, the private lender received a .10 premium from the annual renewal of mortgage insurance premium plus an annual loan servicing fee of .25 percent. If securities, backed by the coinsured loans, and guaranteed by the Government National Mortgage Association (Ginnie Mae), were issued the lender received another .07 percent.

While HUD focused on introducing the housing voucher, this off-budget unsubsidized program took off like a rocket. By the middle of 1988, 5 years after the program was inaugurated, participating lenders had coinsured 846 loans. The amount of the mortgages was $4.8 billion. By 1988, led by the highest flying firm in the business, DRG, the program went off course—106 loans, having an outstanding principal and accrued interest amount of $700 million, were in default. The largest coinsurer in the program, DRG, which had 272 coinsured mortgages, contributed seventy nine defaults and a half a billion dollar in losses. The program was in a free fall descent—sixty five of DRG defaults had occurred in 1988. By March of 1990 the dollar volume of defaults had reached $1.6 billion and HUD was rushing to shut the program down.

Donnie DeFault

Donald De Franceaux (Donnie De) was a nice guy, hard working, innovative, reasonable in his dealings, and he had a very rich father. His father had made millions dealing with FHA as a mortgage banker and after he made enough money he served as the president, chairman, and chief executive officer of the National Corporation of Housing Partnerships.[12]

In 1973, when Donnie De had passed his apprenticeship in the banking and real estate business, he formed a little company, called DRG. His father contributed some cash and cachet by agreeing to be named as chairman of the board. Donnie De was very ambitious. He wanted to make his father proud—or at least move out of his shadow.

The firm grew slowly in the 1970s. It was more successful in creating subsidiaries (DRG Financial, DRG Ventures, DRG Insurance and DRG Funding) than in making money. By the 1980s, with the real estate business drying up, Donnie De dabbled in various international ventures. He attempted to bring petrodollars to the United States by growing hydroponic lettuce and tomatoes for the Saudi Arabians. The money flowed the wrong way as he lost a few hundred thousand dollars. Then he found coinsurance.

Donnie De didn't need a great deal of money to obtain the government's insurance stamper. A license to play was $5,000 and $1.5 million in capital ($500,000 of which had to be liquid) and a small amount of experience (3 deals). In return you could insure billions of dollars of loans and receive all of the various and sundry fees.

Venture capital funds were able to stake DRG Funding to the $1.5 million and on 22 April 22 1983 it became the first company to obtain a license. It was a hunting license in a game preserve. With a staff of eager beaver employees, DRG closed twenty nine coinsured deals by the end of 1983. They were ninety-day wonders. Mortgages, that FHA would process in twelve months, were being processed in less than three months. DRG was operating on a national scale with loan officers who were right out of school. With diplomas in hand, they were processing and approving multi-million dollar deals. And then DRG found the Colonial House!

An article in *Regardie's* by Harry Jaffee tells the sordid tale:

In early 1984 . . . [t]he owner of Colonial House, a 1,818-unit apartment complex in Houston wanted to renovate and refinance to the tune of $47.2 million. DRG would stand to make more than $1 million in fees. . . .

Colonial House['s] . . . man out front was Michael Pollack, a California slickster who even in the halcyon days of the oil boom was known as the greatest renovation king west of the Mississippi. Pollack had long dyed-blond hair and sported thick gold chains around his neck, a shirt unbuttoned to his navel, and lizard skin cowboy boots. He was the Joe Willie Namath of real estate, driving around in a stretch limo and judging wet T-shirt contests between hustling real estate deals.

When HUD officials caught wind of the . . . deal, they called Fort Worth to notify Walter Sevier, the agency's number-two man in the region.

He flew to Houston to check it out . . . DRG had appraised the building for $60 million, Sevier believed it was worth no more than $13 million. "The oil market had already begun to soften," he said, "Oil prices were beginning to fall, housing prices were off, apartments were vacant. When you're underwriting in a declining market, you should be conservative. Instead they inflate the income stream and lowball the expenses. . . . The difference between $13 million and $60 million isn't marginal. Somebody is either incompetent or dishonest.

[Sevier indicated he wouldn't approve the deal unless directed by Washington]

Barksdale [the FHA Commissioner] checked with [the] General Counsel, who ruled that DRG could do the deal. . . . When the papers were signed on September 14, 1984, only 110 of the 1,818 units were rented. . . In early 1985, with renovations completed, Pollack ran a television spot that showed a bikini-clad woman erupting from Colonial House's swimming pool with a VCR on her head. The idea was that you got a pool, a VCR, and a woman inside. But by then Houston's economy had hit the skids. The morals of Colonial House's occupants had apparently taken a dive too; the apartment build became known as "Venereal House."[13]

A mere thirteen months after the $47.2 million mortgage loan was coinsured it was in default.

DRG was in trouble even before Colonial was sliding down the tubes. In November 1984, HUD moved to rein in DRG. HUD wanted a second look at the coinsured loans before approval. Since this would diminish the business by increasing the time to process loans, he hired a "lobbyist." This wasn't your everyday lobbyist. It was former HUD Secretary, Carla Hills, Esq., who had little trouble getting an appointment with Secretary Sam Pierce in April 1985.

To further soften up the Secretary, on 4 May 1985, a gala dinner was held in his honor to benefit the Georgetown Preparatory School. Large contributors to the Samuel Pierce Scholarship fund were invited to meet with the secretary in his office on April 25. First on the list of the contributors who accepted the invitation was DRG and its president Donnie De.

The meeting and dealing with Hills and the wining and dining didn't stop the secretary from writing a tough letter on 9 May 1985. Everything was tough, until the "therefore." The letter was a recitation of DRG's sins—failure to get HUD approval of its loan processors, inadequate review of borrower's financial statements, inflated income projections, underestimated expenses,and overvalued properties. *Therefore,* DRG was absolved. It did not have to submit loans to HUD before it insured mortgages.[14]

With the Colonial House default, DRG faced the danger of being thrown out of the program. Donnie De needed a real heavy hitter. He hired Lynda Murphy, an attorney who was a very good friend of Debbie Dean, Pierce's powerful executive assistant. The decision was to go to bed with Donnie De. Rather than pulling DRG's plug, HUD would paper over the problem. Dean, with a little coaching from Murphy, prepared and signed a workout of the Colonial House mortgage to forestall a claim on the mortgage.

Tom Lantos taking testimony from Lynda Murphy was puzzled by the process:

MR. LANTOS: You find it intriguing . . . do you not that the proposed work-out for Colonial House . . . an extremely complex transaction with enormous financial and legal

ramifications is signed by the Executive Assistant . . . and not the individual who
has program responsibility for this, Mr. Demery or the Secretary himself?

[As to why Mr. Demery didn't sign]

My hypothesis is it was very complex, very important, very serious decision and
he chose not to put his name on it. He bucked it upstairs. . . . Now having this . . .
document that only individuals with intimate knowledge of laws and regulations could
understand, why is this letter signed by Deborah Gore Dean, who clearly had none of
this knowledge, and not the Secretary? Does this puzzle you?
Ms. MURPHY: Yes, it does.[15]

The experience didn't chasten Donnie De. Emboldened by the knowledge that when a debt reaches a high enough sum it becomes the
creditor's problem and that he had low friends in high places, Donnie De
continued on his merry way. DRG closed more than sixty deals while the
Colonial House workout was being negotiated and another hundred deals
by 1988. The total dollar amount of the loans were well in excess of a
billion dollars.

What ultimately did DRG in was neither poor underwriting and
overmortgaging nor inspector general audits. DRG was an issuer of
Ginnie-Mae mortgage-backed securities. DRG was required to pass
through to the holders of these securities the sales proceeds of coinsured
projects that it had acquired and sold. It didn't. On 16 September 1988,
GNMA took control of the entire portfolio of coinsured loans, totaling
$1.1 billion. On 26 March 1989, HUD suspended DRG Funding. As of
October 1989, two-thirds of its 214 loans were in default—$709 million
out of approximately the $1.1 billion in mortgage loans it originated.

When HUD finally put DRG out of business, the U.S. marshals came
for DRG's files. When the FBI examined the files they found evidence
that Donnie De and his associates went beyond the bounds of poor
judgment. The pattern of overmortgaging suggested criminal reckless-
ness. Colonial House, originally valued at $60 million was ultimately
sold for $8.2 million. Forest Oaks was coinsured for $3.395 million on
1 October 1984. After default it was sold for $25,000. FHA had a negative
equity position. FHA's share of the loss was $3.4 million, since the claim
by DRG included a half a million dollars in accrued interest.[16]

There was also a pattern of self-dealing in which DRG Funding, the
mortgage company, facing enormous liabilities as a coinsurer, siphoned
off profits to its subsidiaries either as commissions for selling properties

or for advice. In addition DRG which grew by overappraising attempted to survive by underappraising. At a time when DRG was negotiating a $15 million loan and a $25 million line of credit from a Texas holding company, Southmark, the FBI alleged, it was selling buildings to companies controlled by Southmark at prices that were below their fair-market value.

Ironically, when GNMA took over DRG's portfolio of loans, it chose York Associate's Inc. to service the loans. The firm was headed by an alumnus of DRG. In July of 1990, the loans were back in GNMA's hands. It had to take control from York of $2 billion of mortgages (covering 80,000 rental units in twenty-eight states.) Although better than DRG, only one-sixth of its loans were in default, York was not solvent enough to provide GNMA with sufficient funds to enable it to pay the investors their monthly payments.

What Went Wrong?

Why did coinsurance quench the fires of scandal in the Title I home-improvement program and torch the Section 223 (f) multifamily program? Why was the default rate twenty five times higher in the coinsured program portion (12.5 percent) than in the fully insured portion (less than .5 percent) of the section 223 (f) program?

In Title I, coinsurance brought a modicum of risk and the glare of publicity that shamed bankers into not being part of a system that bilked some of their customers. The added risk was more than offset by the high return on their money under the program. The elimination of fraud could be accomplished by checking that the work had been done and that the homeowner was satisfied. And from FHA's perspective the loans were small, so that if a lender's default rate was out of line, FHA could step in before incurring a large loss.

The participants in the multifamily coinsurance business were not traditional moneylenders. They were in the business for the fees rather than the interest payments. Ninety-eight percent of the loans were pooled and sold to GNMA. Since the "profitability" of the lender increased with the size of the loan, overmortgaging was the way to go.

Borrowers' dreams came true. Lenders were competing for customers and the one with the most liberal appraisers and optimistic underwriters (no doubt many former HUD employees) made the loans. Borrowers by mortgaging out of existing buildings could make money without concern about occupancy of the building.

The coinsurers were in the same position as savings and loan institutions. GNMA's guarantee of the securities that were backed by coinsured loans was the equivalent of Federal deposit insurance. GNMA agreed to guarantee full payment (and FHA agreed to indemnify it against any loss from the coinsurers failure to pay its share).

Coinsurers were give access to a huge source of funds. Purchaser were willing to buy the government securities regardless of the quality of the loans, in the same manner as insured depositors in savings and loans could disregard the quality of the bank's portfolio. It was the "full faith and credit of the United States" upon which the reliance was being placed and it was the government that was left holding the bag.

The HUD Undersecretary, Alfred DelliBovi, in March 1990, testified that " the coinsurance scheme proved to be structurally flawed, administratively unfixable, and fundamentally unsound."[17] The vulnerability of the program and the awful temptation to inflate appraisals was recognized by FHA "old-timers" before the program started. Jon Will Pitts, a veteran FHA official and an old sailor, in reviewing the proposed Handbook for the program, in 1982, warned: "This is the most fraudulently prone system ever spawned by HUD" and pleaded:

> Before we launch this program we should perform the carefully planned vulnerability assessment. . . . We should search every nook and recess of the hold to be sure that all the sea cocks are closed before we launch this vessel down the waves or else she will swamp and settle in the mud before she clears the bar! Please give us a chance to make her seaworthy before we launch.[18]

The flaw was not in the concept of coinsurance. As of 31 May 1988, 114 lenders did not have any defaults. There is also the record of the single-family Direct Endorsement Program (in which approved private lenders could underwrite loans directly.) The program was enacted in 1983 as part of the broader effort to privatize processing that included the multifamily coinsurance program. It now accounts for 90 percent of FHA's single-family mortgage activity and the mortgages have consistently experienced claim rates that are below the claim rate of HUD-processed mortgages.[19]

Coinsurance does have some distinct advantages. It is (1) simple to administer; (2) permits speedy action; (3) relies on existing institutions; and (4) permits the government to operate on a wholesale rather than a retail basis. Coinsurance did all these things. Unfortunately, the institutions HUD was dealing with were not moneylenders concerned with interest spreads but rather fee-gatherers. When HUD gives someone its insurance stamper and allows a company whose total assets are $1.5 million to pledge the full faith and credit of the Federal government to a billion dollars worth of loans, it creates a terrific incentive to do terrible things. A modest profit on fees of 2 percent produces $20 million in a billion-dollar portfolio. Such an arrangement requires a good many monitors and people looking over the shoulder of the coinsurer. HUD cannot take on faith that the lender's judgment and honesty will not fall victim to greed.

HUD was a bit tardy when it came to providing sufficient monitors for the program. It was not until 1987, that a Coinsuring Monitoring Branch was made operational to monitor and evaluate the program on-site. However, as Inspector General Paul Adams noted, "Such an effort will be ineffective without an equally intensive HUD program enforcement effort consisting of the imposition of sanctions and other forceful administrative actions."[20]

The Lone Ranger or Program Ombudsman

The inspector general did not cover himself with glory in the coinsurance program. He had great difficulty in knowing what to do when he saw the program go awry. Thus, in the Executive Summary of his audit of the program after finding that HUD was in the hole for hundreds of millions of dollars and things were likely to get a whole lot worse, he expresses the following worries:

> HUD's failure to enforce program requirements in a more rigorous fashion is adversely affecting the *success* of the . . . program.

> HUD's approach has been to conduct . . . reviews of prospective . . . loans for those lenders not complying with the program, such as DRG. However, this tactic is costly to HUD in terms of staff resources and is also contrary to one of the primary objectives of the Coinsurance Program, which is to delegate loan processing for the purpose of achieving more timely processing of mortgage insurance. (my emphasis)[21]

The use of the word "success" is akin to watching the Hindenburg explode and talk about its successful trans Atlantic flight. Instead of suggesting that more staff resources are needed, the inspector general bemoans their use. When HUD is losing hundreds of millions, a few million for staff that could prevent some "fraud, waste, and abuse" would seem a prudent use of money.

In all fairness, the inspector general did suggest that HUD use its authority to suspend and terminate. Characteristically, he immediately backed off:

> [T]he suspension or termination of a lender such as DRG may place HUD in a difficult position since such actions could conceivably result in severe financial difficulties for the lender. *Without the income generated from the processing of new loans, it may not be possible for DRG to meet its continuing obligations to holders of GNMA-mortgage backed securities for the principal and interest payments on a its defaulted loans.* (my emphasis)[22]

The inspector describes, but doesn't recognize, a New Age "Ponzi Scheme." In olden times, new money was borrowed to pay old loans. Now, new money is lent to pay old loans.

He speaks no evil and is determined to make no waves. The Inspector General Act of 1978,[23] empowers investigations and audits. Nevertheless, he seems determined to defend the Department's handling of the program and in spite of all the hanky-panky at the secretarial level, his finger is always pointed downward, never upward.

In the case of coinsurance, the ideology of privatization and the low value given to public funds dominated the thinking of the upper echelons. The failure to terminate or even curtail DRG after the Colonial House fiasco cost the government hundreds of millions of dollars. The inspector general was more interested in not casting dirt on a program of the administration than in making sure that the public wasn't being plundered. He didn't have his priorities right. It is more important to make sure that the circus parade is going in the right direction than to make sure it leaves a clean trail.

Porkbarrel Programs

Section 8 inserted into the U.S. Housing Act of 1937 by the Housing and Community Development of 1974 contained an armada of programs under a single subsidy flag. It covered new, substantially rehabilitated and existing buildings. The framework was that the government subsidy would close the gap between the cost of housing ("the fair-market rent") and the amount a poor household could pay. HUD set different fair-market rents (FMR) for the various levels of construction and further

differentiated by locality, type of building (elevator, row, and single
family) and the size of the apartment.

In 1979, HUD added a new ship to the fleet—the moderate rehabilitation program to cover as the name indicated more modest repair and
modernization in the $5,000 range.[24]

HUD "fair-shared" the funding. Money was allocated according to the
relative needs of the state "as reflected in data as to population, poverty,
housing overcrowding, housing vacancies, amount of substandard housing and other objective conditions specified by regulation".[25]

The program was operated on an "invitation only" basis. The field offices
invited applications for the program from PHAs from appropriate areas. If
there wasn't enough money to fund all the PHAs, projects would be selected
on the basis of (1) demonstrated capacity of the PHA or the contractor; (2)
the financial resources to get the work done; (3) the PHA's experience with
the Section 8 program; (4) the potential for the rehab and leasing being done
speedily; and (5) the overall feasibility of the proposed program."[26]

The PHAs that received funding were to advertise the availability of
funds and select owners to participate in the program through a competitive process. The local PHA guaranteed Section 8 rent subsidies for
fifteen years, so that tenants of the development could pay the rent. Since
the program dealt with small-scale rehabilitation, the understanding of
the designers of the program was that the maximum rent level would not
exceed 120 percent of the HUD determined fair market rental of existing
housing in the locality.[27]

As programs go, the moderate rehabilitation program was small
potatoes (with the great bulk of the 130,000 units covered by the program
preceding 1985). Nevertheless, as the result of the activities of a number
of wretches it resulted in the raunchiest episode in HUD's history.

Bad Times

The second half of the eighties was a bad time for the developers who
had relied on the subsidized housing market. The Reagan Administration
had dropped the guillotine on the new construction and substantial
rehabilitation portion of the Section 8 program. A program that was
providing subsidy contracts for hundreds of thousands of units in the late
seventies and early eighties was stopped in its tracks.

At the same time, the roof was ripped off the "tax shelter" of the real estate industry. The generous provisions of the Economic Recovery Tax Act of 1981, was replaced by the "Tax Reform Act of 1986." The Fed giveth and the Fed taketh. However, much more was taken than given. The depreciation period was doubled to thirty years; losses could not be used to offset non-real-estate income; the maximum tax rate was dropped to 28 percent (reducing the value of paper losses by 40 percent); and the special treatment of capital gains was eliminated.

All of this was replaced by a low-income housing tax credit.[28] There was a ten year tax credit available to property owners for each unit set aside for low income renters for at least fifteen years of low-income use. When initially implemented there was a 9 percent annual credit for ten years for new construction or substantial rehabilitation. A separate 4 percent credit covered the cost of acquisition of an existing building that was to be used for low-income housing. An example may be helpful. A new $50,000 unit (of which $5,000 represents land) has a annual tax credit for ten years of $4,050 (9 percent x $45,000).[29]

The tax credit program is unique in that there is a cap and the credits are allocated by the states. In the 1980s, the state limit was $1.25 for each resident. For example, a state with 4 million residents would have $5 million worth of credit authority per year ($50 million for a ten-year period) to allocate among projects.

From Pseudo-Precision to Discretion

The Reagan Administration had decided that the Moderate Rehabilitation Program was also an expendable housing program. At the same time, the program had become so small, that Congress in the Appropriations Act for Fiscal Year 1984 (which began in October of 1983) allowed HUD to waive the "fair share" allocation method.

In a conversation with the general counsel, John Knapp, the secretary "heard" a legal opinion that when Congress waived the fair share requirements, the project selection process became inapplicable. Mr. Knapp during testimony indicated that he did not recall the conversation and then by letter denied making it. In a dictum in his letter, he did make it clear that if he would have been asked, he most likely would have held that there was "good cause" for suspending the regulation.

Mr. Knapp received a good deal of criticism from Congressman Bruce Morrison who complained that "the scandal is that there were no standards"[30] The congressman did not understand the political culture of the office of general counsel. The latter has only one client—the secretary. His guide in interpreting the law is to allow the secretary as much discretion in the policymaking area as possible and to interpret away legal impediments. He is a neutral in the world of policy. He is willing to give the secretary sufficient rope to swing with. If the secretary displays the wisdom and discernment to swing to the rhythm of the heavenly spheres he will watch with glee. If the secretary hangs himself he will watch with dismay and have to explain his interpretations to an unfriendly Congressional committee. While we're in the heaven's, the Reagan's administration could not have gone forward with its "Star Wars" program but for the broad interpretation of the 1972 Anti-Ballistic Missile Treaty by Abraham Sofaer, the State Department's legal adviser.[31]

The fair share requirement was inserted in the legislation when Section 8, with the shining promise of hundreds of thousands of units, was enacted. In the middle of the eighties, when the sun set on most of the programs, Congress recognized that it made little sense to fair share a handful of units. The program was so small and the number of eligible recipients so large—over 3,000 PHAs—that no good cause was served by cutting the pie into miniscule slivers.

The absence of the fair share requirement seemed to result in a geographical misallocation to those at the short end of the allocation. To others, it was a redress of a previous distortion. As Philip Abrams, former HUD official and now developer, explained it:

MR. ABRAMS. I never really focused . . . when I was at HUD on how skewed the formula . . . is against the newer parts of the country . . . The only statistical substitute [for substandard housing] . . . is "housing built before 1940" which means any area . . . [in the West] gets very much skewed to its disadvantage.
The amount of funds distributed in 1986 . . . went disproportionately away from the areas that had benefitted [previously] . . . You are talking about a disproportionate share of millions versus an offsetting disproportionate thousands."[32]

The mystery to Congress was how HUD got away from any objective criteria in allocating funds once the process moved to Washington. The project selection criteria in the regulations were themselves quite judgmental and discretionary. The Field office were instructed to "invite" applications only from PHAs in areas where the program was "appropriate"—a near-total grant of discretion. And, if there was to be so much discretion, it made more sense to leave the decision to the judge in Washington rather than to the cop on the beat in some distant field office.

The regulations even if they had been fully enforced would not have changed the outcome. The selection criteria were only applicable if a field office invited PHAs to apply for more units than were available. They were written on the assumption that the rehabilitation was being done by small inexperienced contractors. The criteria related to competence—the ability of the proposal to be come to fruition. In practice, the regulations were rarely applied in the field offices. PHAs would only be invited if they showed interest, had a particular property in mind *and* there was enough money. When the substantial rehabilitation and new segment of the program were running, field offices viewed moderate rehab allocations as consolation prizes for PHAs that weren't awarded the more lucrative projects and wanted to get involved in small scale rehabilitation (the regulations had to require *$1,000* dollars worth of work be done.) Nowhere, in six volumes of hearings by the House investigating committee is mention made that the developers selected to do moderate rehab work couldn't get the job done.

Regulations and strict statutory formulas provide little safeguard against political interference. This can be illustrated by two incidents with regard to the Section 8 programs. The *Boston Herald* in June of 1979 reported that 70 percent of the money raised by the Carter campaign, as of April 15 of that year, came from Section 8 developers. All the contributing developers subsequently won approval for their new projects.[34] To shore up the senatorial candidacy of Millicent Fenwick, President Reagan intervened and was able to announce at a photo opportunity the following sound bite, "The Department of Housing and Urban Development has advised me that they've agreed to approve Section 8 funding for 125 units of elderly housing at Park Place in Ewing, New Jersey. And if you don't elect her senator, we'll take it away."[35]

The Urban Development Action Grant Program (UDAG), another program that was embroiled in scandal, had a strict numerical formula and was believed to be immune from political influence and manipulation at the federal level.[36] In fact, it was anything but tamperproof:

It was . . . who was pushing each project rather than the merits . . . which determined the funding level. The manipulation began early in the process. . . First, he [DuBois Gilliam, a Deputy Assistant Secretary for Community Planning and Development who at the time of his testimony was serving an 18 months prison sentence for bribery and conspiracy to defraud to the government in using his position to steer funds to a project in Biloxi, Mississippi] would direct Halcyon consultants to HUD on the UDAG program, to work on the application. Next Gilliam would alert Stanley Newman, Director of the UDAG office, to any UDAGs which had to be funded, so that Newman could maximize the points on the application. If it appeared that the UDAG would not be placed high enough on the list to guarantee funding, Gilliam would advise the developer and the city to obtain congressional support to lobby for the program.[37]

The Anatomy of a Deal

The drop in funding for the Section 8 moderate rehab program was quite dramatic. In 1979, 34,000 units were funded. Moderate rehab was a small sideshow to the hundreds of thousands of units being allocated under the Section 8 program. In the late 1980s, with the new construction program gone, it was a far smaller show. However, it took center stage since it was the only show. A grand total of 318 funding allocations were made between 1984 and 1988. Except for 1986 in which slightly over 100 projects were funded, the average number of allocations hovered around 50.

As the program got smaller, the projects and the amount of rehabilitation got larger. The average size of project, for which funds were allocated between 1984 to 1988, was over 100 units. In a group of projects that were audited, the average rehabilitation cost exceeded $26,000 per unit.[38] In fact, the program went way beyond the fixing up of apartment buildings. Hospitals, schools, factories were converted into apartment buildings. In Worcester, Massachusetts, a historic mill was converted into the Crystal Park Apartments at a per unit cost of over $80,000. The Regulations were followed to a tee. Section 882.504(c)(4) required that in selecting proposals, the one and only preference, went to projects that had the greatest dollar amount of rehabilitation per unit.

The moderate rehab projects were profitable to developers. Large amounts of money were being made and once again the cry of "windfall" was heard in the land. One of the prime examples was Sierra Pointe Apartments, a project in which Philip Abrams was involved. The project was a 160 unit multifamily rental development, built in 1963 in Clark County which is on the outskirts of Las Vegas, Nevada.

The rehabilitation was financed by a nonsubsidized FHA loan processed by the Benton Mortgage Company (a coinsurer that found a profitable and *safe* niche in the mod rehab program). In December 1986, the loan was initially endorsed for insurance and a Section 8 assistance contract was executed with the housing authority. The amount of the loan was $7.4 million and the cash proceeds from the sale of tax credits was $2.34 million.

When the rehabilitation was done, the average rent was $599. After the allowance for utilities, the average tenant paid $11.85. The average annual subsidy was $7,054—$1,264 more than the average family income of the residents.

The General Accounting Office prepared a report that zeroed in on Sierra Pointe and concluded that the developer had on a small investment of $54 reaped huge profits and to make matters worse there were units in the $400 range that did not need rehabilitation in the area so that more people could have been helped for the same amount of subsidy.

Abrams, although admitting the tax credits produced windfall profits (Congressional action on tax bills being totally unpredictable), challenged the GAO's hindsight analysis of the initial risks and its lack of foresight of future risks:

> [I]n December 1986, we had approximately $230,000 expended that was contingent on FHA initial endorsement and contingent on the housing authority executing a contract . . . . In June 1988, . . . we had $405,000 in cash invested in addition to the mortgage proceeds. After the final endorsement . . . we had $507,000 invested . . . since then we've put another $180,000 . . . [W]e have a 1 percent guarantee to GNMA . . . [W]e have an operating deficit guarantee and a guarantee that these credits will remain in existence for 15 years, because although the tax writeoffs are taken over 10 years, the credit obligation is over 15 years. The project had a negative cash flow in 1988 . . . [T]he cash flow for 1989 may be as high as $17,000; however, that goes to the people who bought the credits, because . . . they also bought the cash flow and . . . a portion of the of the residual value of the project at the end of 15 years. So, I would take issue with the saying that there was no risk.[40]

The Clark County Housing Authority also disagreed with the GAO. It had 2,400 people on its waiting lists and there was little likelihood of getting very many certificates or vouchers for existing units. Mod/rehab was the only game in town. Even if the authority had received the funds for existing units the GAO analysis would have been wrong. The Section 8 program was shifting from certificates to vouchers. Under the latter format HUD sets the Fair Market Rent—in Sierre Pointe the payment standard of $599 was the same as the FMR. The subsidy the tenant would receive would be the difference between the standard and 30 percent of his income. If the $400 unit were obtained, he would pocket the money and no additional households would be helped.

Mr. Abrams was not crying poverty. For the talented developer there was money to be made. There was the availability of tax credits which could be sold to eager investors. There were also the high levels of the payment standard in many areas. The FMR reflects the upper half of the rents in the locality—being set at the rent at the 45th percentile of recent movers (who pay a higher rent than longer term residents in the locality). As such they were high to begin with. These seemingly scientifically derived numbers are based on old, shaky, and skimpy data. For a place like Clark County, Nevada, the FMRS were set almost $200 above the rent for which standard units were available. It meant that developers could rehabilitate projects up to the stage of nearly new (thereby qualifying for large tax credits) and still have rents that met the HUD standards. The most important job of the developer was often pinpointing the areas where there was a mismatch between HUD FMRs and the real world.

One of the ironies of the Sierra Pointe project is that Mr. Abrams, when he was at HUD, fought for doing away with the entire FMR system. On the other side of the fray was the entire establishment of the office of policy development and research, which saw the housing voucher based on an FMR as the fruit of the $200 million Housing Allowance Experiment. The decision was left to Philip Winn the assistant secretary for housing in whose bailiwick the program resided. Abrams lost. Winn decided to go with a system that was "tested" rather than trying a new system. Sierre Pointe could be considered as Abrams' silver lining. For Winn, who was a partner in Sierre Pointe, there were no clouds.

The Lucky Few

The secretary decided to select the lucky developers by using a panel that consisted of his executive assistant, assistant secretary for housing and the undersecretary to chose the PHAs to be funded. He testified that he never got into the decision making progress and no complaints were brought to his attention to necessitate any involvement.[41]

The awards were made on a subjective basis. Subjectivity can be the handmaiden of experience and wisdom. The key dimension is whether the judge's decision was disinterested rather than the "objectivity" or "subjectivity" of the process.[42] On this criterion, the panel failed miserably. As Deborah Gore Dean, the debutante daughter of a political family, informed the *Wall Street Journal*, "It was set up and designed to be a political program. I would have to say that we ran it in a political manner."

The term "political" encompasses being responsive to requests by congressmen to fund a project as a constituent service. And there was a great deal of funding in the UDAG and Section 8 Moderate Rehab that was political. The secretary and the staff received many calls—from Senators McCain, DeConcini, D'Amato, Hawkins, Specter, Heinz, Thurmond, Denton, Lott, Cochran, Moore, Wilson, Grassley, Dole and a host of other senators and congressmen. And there were cases for which a call wasn't necessary. The fact that the Springfield-Holyoke area, received at least nine funding allocations and was represented by Edward Boland the chairman of the subcommittee that dealt with HUD's appropriations and held the power of the purse strings, cannot be chalked up to coincidence.

Government agencies are postgraduate schools. Many of the top tax specialists have put their time in working for the Internal Revenue Service and there is no better training available for litigators than the Justice Department and the Office of the Solicitor General. Likewise, there is no better preparation for work in the field of subsidized housing than HUD. We are dealing with a combination of technical expertise and knowledge of the agency ranging from having the latest phone book and the ability to walk the corridors without getting lost to a substantive knowledge of the programs.

In obtaining scarce allocations, we are also dealing with a continuum that runs from friendship, to contacts, to networks and political influence. The water hole is fenced in, but the fence has many gates and the people in charge have their eyes on leaving and still having access to the scarce resource. As Joe Strauss, a dear friend of Debbie Dean (she even sent him a teddy bear when he was sick),[43] put it, "I perceived during my last year or so at HUD that there was a niche in the private sector for an individual who had an understanding of HUD programs."[44]

Among the door revolvers, the team with the best batting average when it came to allocations was the "Winn Group"—J. Michael Queenan, Phil Abrams, Phil Winn, and Lance Wilson—who came together on specific limited partnerships. All the members brought housing expertise to the table. They also had much more than talent. As Congressman Shays commented to Mr. Queenan:

> [Y]our partners are an illustrious group . . . Philip Winn who was the former FHA
> Commissioner in charge of giving out mod rehab . . . hires . . . Philip Abrams, who
> ultimately becomes FHA Commissioner . . . the Undersecretary, the number two
> person at HUD. So you teamed up with two of these individuals . . . And then you
> teamed up with Lance Wilson who was the Chief of Staff. He was at the very center
> of HUD and, in the judgement of many had more control than the Secretary . . . [45]

Others, however, needed consultants. And many of the latter had as many credentials in housing as the emperor had clothes. The personification of the political consultant was the former secretary of the interior, James G. Watt whose "only known experience in the field of housing was making Bambi homeless."[46] In his previous incarnation, he warned against the dangers of being "lured by the crumbs of subsidies, entitlements, and giveaways—lured deep into the forest of government regulation." In his dealings with HUD, he avoided the dangers. He didn't deal in crumbs—he received over $300,000 for his services and he never got very close to the forest. He was never in danger of eating from the tree of knowledge.

MR. SCHUMER: What you testified is that before you met with Secretary Pierce, I think
  you named four people, you called each of them to let them know that you were
  meeting with Secretary Pierce.
MR. WATT: And told them afterward I had done it. That is right.
MR. SCHUMER: I would submit it is pretty clear on the record, Mr.Chairman, that for
  one-half hour meeting, and eight phone calls, each of which were described as
  perfunctory, Mr. Watt got $169,000. . . .
MR. SCHUMER: Have you ever visited all three of these projects you worked on . . .?
MR. WATT: I have not visited them. I have seen the pictures.

A headline and the first paragraph of a story in the *Wall Street Journal* characterized what was going on: "Favored Friends—Housing Subsidy Plan for the Poor Helped Contributors to the GOP . . . A federal program to provide subsidized housing for the poor may be better remembered as a pot of gold for fat cat Republican contributors, well-connected developers and Washington consultants."[48] The cast of influence peddlers included: Fred Bush (no relation) who had been Vice-President Bush's deputy chief of staff; George Murphy, the former California senator and Hollywood hoofer; Edward Brooke, the former senator from Massachusetts; Gerald Carmen, a former head of the General Services Administration; Richard Shelby, Reagan White House personnel officer, William "Bill" Taylor, "Member for Florida" (who would do his business with HUD using the letterhead of the Republican National Committee); Paul

Manafort, head of a leading lobbying firm and a campaign adviser to President Bush (who bestowed on Seabrook, New Jersey a $43 million rehabilitation of dilapidated housing that the community didn't want); and John Mitchell, the former and late attorney general. He was family, the stepfather of Debbie Dean.

Little Additional Waste

The selection process in the House Committee's words had all the "competitiveness of professional wrestling." Nevertheless, the mismanagement of the selection system did not involve much more waste than was intrinsic in the programs.

Were the funds well spent? If the question relates to the quality of the projects that were rehabilitated, the answer would be a qualified yes. The House committee could only find one horror story, the Seabrook Apartments: "row upon row of cinder block barracks that appeared to rise from the middle of a cornfield which could be entered from a narrow, unpaved, and unlighted dirt road."[49] In general, the money was about as well spent as in any HUD production program.

Could the government have gotten more for its money? No doubt if the program were truly moderate and the rehab was in the $5,000 range more units could have been upgraded. But that was not the way the regulations were written. You didn't get a preference for moderation. In addition, if the government had just relied on the existing units, less would have been done. If the tenants would have rented the cheaper units in Clark County and a host of other areas, there would have been no savings and no more poor people housed. Under the housing voucher the full subsidy would be provided regardless of the actual rent. Since most of the rehabilitated units were priced at or near the FMR for existing units HUD actually got more for its money—an assisted tenant and a rehabilitated unit. A prudent result from a perverse program.

Could the UDAG money been spent more wisely? Could the grants have induced greater private investment or more jobs? The following colloquy by the author of the program Senator William Proxmire and its administrator demonstrates how hard it can be to reach a rational result:

SENATOR PROXMIRE: Another UDAG that was approved for $1,255,000 to partially fund a podiatric clinic . . . [in] Cleveland. [T]his project . . . will only create 10 new jobs. That means the taxpayer puts up $122,500 for every new job. . . .

MR. STOKVIS: The reason that this happened is because . . . . the UDAG selection formula
 . . . gives 70 points . . . for the impaction and distress of the community. As a result
 . . . the two most distressed communities . . . Buffalo N.Y. and Hoboken, N.J.[50]
 would in all probability always get a UDAG . . . .

SENATOR PROXMIRE: Are you telling me the law mandates you have to go ahead under
 those circumstances.

MR. STOKVIS: . . . . The law sets up the selection process.

SENATOR PROXMIRE: . . . . [W]hen you see $122,000 for a job . . . this is ridiculous isn't
 it? [Give the author a Golden Fleece Award] Could you conceivably get down to
 a point where you have one job, $1 million a job and say "Well, go ahead, it is a
 very distressed area.

MR. STOKVIS: [W]e are not asking for money for the UDAG program.

SENATOR PROXMIRE. Well that is good.[Laughter][51]

Did the fat cats and favored few milk the moderate rehab program at
the expense of the poor? The fees that the consultant's received came out
of the developer's pocket and were not recognized as a cost of the project,
which in any event were limited by the FMRs.[52]

Why were the developers so eager to pay? The projects were profitable. The greatest rewards, however, were not attributable to HUD.
Rather, they came from the states. It was far from a discriminating
operation. As the GAO noted, "[T]ax credits were awarded up to a
maximum amount allowed by regulation on a first-come, first-served
basis rather than the needs or merits of individual projects."[53]

At best, the cost of the tax credit was far greater than the benefit. The
GAO estimated in the syndication, 55 percent of the value was lost. A
significant portion of the loss is because the investor will place a lower
value on the ten-year credit than the government.[54] In addition (actually
subtraction) Sheldon Baskin, explained the high handling charges this
simple subsidy required:

> The credit . . . can be used by any investor, but only in relatively small amounts. . . .
> The result is that most [credits]. . . were sold . . . to small investors through publicly
> syndicated funds. These funds require . . . brokers, who have to get 8 percent off the
> top—in fact it's not much compensation for selling a very complicated $5,000 or
> $10,000 investment. But the securities liability laws being what they are, the broker-
> age firms has to show the deal to lawyers, and the lawyers will require the firm to do
> its due diligence—appraisals, feasibility studies, and have their own accountants run
> projections and do tax analysis in addition to the ones done by the . . . syndicator . . .
> [who] has to pay *its* lawyers, financial analysts and marketing people to make a profit.
> Furthermore, the profit has to cover deals the syndicator bids on and negotiates but
> which are never consummated.[55]

Circles of Shame

The Centers of the Universe

There may not have been much waste but oh was there an abundance of misuse of power, arrogance, greed, hypocrisy and a little bit of fraud. At the center of HUD's concentric circles of shame was the binary star, the team of Secretary Sam Pierce and Debbie Dean. When it came to dealing with power,. Sam was the yin and Debbie was the yang.

He shied away from power. He identified himself with the halfback he was in college, rather than the coach. "When I played football at Cornell and the coach sent in a running play, I didn't call a passing play. My coach is sending in the plays and I'm just running them the way he sent them in."[56]

He was also a product of his times. As noted by the *U.S. News And World Report*:

Living with racial prejudice, . . . [left him with] a firm conviction that for a black man to get ahead he had to play by the white man's rules. "Sam was exactly what the Republicans wanted to put in the cabinet," says Gloria Toote a longtime friend from New York politics. "He's not brash; he knows his place."[57]

In the big game against the "Social Pork Barrels," the Coach David Stockman, was making the big calls in the housing area and Pierce turned out to be an excellent ball carrier. When victory was assured, there were no more calls from the bench. He was now the coach, but his voice which was never very loud, nearly disappeared.

As far as his involvement in the selection of moderate rehab projects, the House Committee concluded that he was damned if he did and damned if he didn't. "At best Secretary Pierce was less than honest and misled the subcommittee about his involvement in abuses and favoritism in HUD funding decisions, At worst, Secretary Pierce knowingly lied and committed perjury during his testimony on May 25, 1989."[58]

Without getting into the question of perjury, even had he not misled the committee, he certainly failed to fulfill his duty to keep himself informed of the organization's activities and he was woefully lax in exercising control over subordinates. Unlike a member of the board of directors who occasionally visits but keeps his hands off the operations, the head of the organization is a full-time, hands-on job.

As a former judge, he knew he was holding his position as a trustee of the people. As Justice Benjamin Cardozo wrote:

> Many forms of conduct permissible in a workaday world for those acting at arm's length are forbidden to those bound by fiduciary ties. A trustee is held to something stricter than the moral of the market place. Not honesty alone, but punctilio of an honor most sensitive, is then the standard of behavior.[59]

He was not even alert to enforce the standard he set for others, that "All department activities be carried out at in an arm's length, business-like manner without favoritism or appearance of favoritism."

His major sin of commission came in the cases in which Lance Wilson, his first executive assistant was involved. Like a doting father, he had a great deal of difficulty saying no to Lance. Gilliam testified about a meeting with the secretary dealing with a project in Belle Glade,Florida with a low UDAG rating:

> I said this is Lance's project . . . He indicated to me . . . I don't like Leonard Briscoe [the principal]. He said Leonard Briscoe was a crook and greedy. He said, you tell Lance, this is it; no more. And the Secretary agreed at that point to make the cut-off Belle Glade, Florida.[60]

He attempted to protect Lance Wilson from a civil servant in the UDAG office, David Sowell, who was unduly diligent in checking about the bonafide nature of a commitment letter issued by Lance's new employer, PaineWebber. After the ever-loyal office director, Stanley Newman, informed Gilliam, the latter took the matter to the secretary. Unable to send Sowell off to the field, he was given a new desk in front of Mr. Gilliam's office, where the latter could keep an eye on him.[61]

If Secretary Pierce is to be condemned for his activities at HUD, it should be because of his misplaced loyalty and tragically because of his "get along-go along attitude." The attitude that took him so far turned out to be his Achilles' heel at HUD. The most damning and expensive example was his handling of the DRG coinsurance affair and the deference he showed former Secretary Carla Hills in the Colonial House coinsurance case.

In November of 1984, after the Colonial House closing and some other examples of poor processing, the then assistant secretary for housing, Maurice Barksdale, decided that DRG should lose its privilege to close deals without a HUD review before closing. His successor, Shirley Wiseman, who was later to head up the National Association of Home

Builders, agreed and rejected Carla Hills' request the review requirement be lifted.

Attorney Hills then met with the Secretary. Although she argued the merits of the case, the Secretary's letter lifting the requirement indicates that the decision could not have been made on the "merits":

> You have been advised that the majority of these cases were unacceptable as processed. We have not, in fact, found the improvement in processing policy which we hoped to find.

> You continue to use, in violation of regulations and handbook requirements, non-HUD approved personnel to process cases.

> Your approach to the financial and credit analysis requirement indicates that you place little importance on this part of the underwriting process, when, in fact, it is one of the more important aspects. The ability of the principals to meet the initial cash requirements as well as to meet contingencies . . . is an important concern in determining whether to insure a loan. . . .

> The rental analyses usually consist of . . . analyses that support an opinion . . . rather than a comparative analyses showing the adjustment process used to arrive at an estimate.

> Expense analyses are sketchy and poorly documented. Fee appraisers frequently estimate current project expenses after a repair/renovation program that are significantly *below* the past operating history of the property. Often management fees are tailored to the project instead of being based upon typical experiences found for competitive projects. Too often management fees are established on an identity-of-interest basis.[62]

To conclude the letter, that DRG had been rehabilitated and that DRG was ready to be released, to continue its pillaging, is akin to the release of Willie Horton. It was a shameful and costly dereliction of duty.

Debbie Dean, his executive assistant, reveled in power. Coming from a well-connected family. There is the sense that her pablum was laced with power. As her boss, Sam, said, "She liked power. She liked the idea that 'I can call the shots, I can get this for you if I want, I can stomp on you, I can kill you.' That's the kind of thing she liked."[63]

Debbie Dean went from barmaid to receptionist in the private sector. At HUD, she went from heading up the correspondence unit, to executive assistant to the secretary, and a nomination to be assistant secretary for community development. She missed the latter job by the narrowest of margins. Twelve of the twenty members of the Democratic-controlled Senate Banking, Housing and Urban Affairs Committee supported her nomination but the chairman, William Proxmire refused to call for a vote. Opposition was based in part on charges that she had required subordinates to perform personal services for her during office hours such as cleaning and painting her apartment.[64]

In her appearance before the Senate panel considering her nomination, on 6 August 1987, she also lied. When asked about the mod rehab process, she made the following statement:

> [T]he field office receives applications from public housing authorities. They are rated and ranked, sent to the regional administrator, who forwards them to the Assistant Secretary for Housing. . . . [T]hey bring it to a panel. . . . That panel goes solely on the information provided by the Assistant Secretary for Housing. He gives us the information and the three of us make recommendations to the Secretary, who is the person who approves the units.

> I have never given or approved or pushed or coerced anyone to help any developer. Those funds go directly to the public housing authorities.[65]

As the secretary retreated from power and remained in his office or up in the air, Debbie Dean filled the vacuum. She did not need a seeing-eye dog to spot an important Republican or an old associate from a hundred paces.

She was the de facto boss of HUD. She operated the secretary's autopen and was his representative on the Secretary's Committee on Waste, Fraud and Mismanagement. She was also the key link between the White House and HUD on personnel issues.[66] She was the "panel" in the case of moderate rehab. Individuals such as Silvio DeBartolomeis, Shirley Wiseman, and Janet Hale who served as acting assistant secretaries for housing and John Knapp, who was acting undersecretary were unaware of the panel's existence. The process of obtaining scarce moderate rehab funding "could be aptly described as 'making the Dean's list.'"[67] She was having such a good time that she was trying to revive the program, her Administration was trying to kill. She was lobbying Congress, for more funding:

> "Debbie Dean was always pushing for more mod-rehab money, she came up and lobbied me personally," said Thomas L. van der Voort, who until last year was the top aide on the Senate Appropriations subcommittee that oversees HUD's budget.

> He recalled one 1987 visit to his Capitol Hill office in particular. "All I remember is her coming and making a pitch for mod re-rehab. She said, 'There are a lot of people out there doing marvelous work with this program and we have a lot of applications.'"[68]

The exact disposition of decision making between Dean and Pierce may never be known. She took the Fifth and he, before taking the Fifth, managed to speak with a forked tongue—not a bad bureaucratic technique except if one is under oath. Thus, he claimed he never asked that a proposal be funded[69] and vigorously objected to the suggestion that Debbie spoke for him.[70]

Debbie Dean also played her part in the DRG fiasco. When Colonial House came tumbling down, it was she who orchestrated the papering over of the problem. She was having the time of her life. And if Henry Kissinger is right that power is the ultimate aphrodisiac, it didn't hurt her social life.

The Masters of the Universe

Clustering around the center were a number of people who had been at HUD and who remained in very close orbit. Lance Wilson was, by far, the nearest to the center. The secretary brought Lance down to Washington to serve as his executive assistant from March 1981 to June 1984. And if Secretary Pierce would have had any real power in the administration, he would have been the assistant secretary for housing.

Lance was a member of the next generation. One may even view him as the son of Sam. He had all the confidence that Sam lacked. He was smart, slick, and suave. Within two years after leaving HUD, he had joined PaineWebber as first vice president in its Municipal Securities Group. He was, in Tom Wolfe's term, a "master of the universe."

His universe was HUD. If Sam had to play by the white man's rules, Lance played by nobody's rules. In April of 1984, a UDAG was approved for a project in Fort Worth, Texas. The developer was Leonard Briscoe. HUD career staff in Texas had unanimously recommended that it be disapproved. Lance Wilson, on the other hand, applied a great deal of pressure on the UDAG staff in Washington. Shortly after leaving HUD, Lance called Leonard and suggested they form a corporation. Leonard did not recall the purpose for which the corporation was formed. The corporation in fact had no income in 1984, 1985, 1986, and 1987. Lance, however, received checks from the corporation for $23,500 in 1986.[71]

In spite of being barred from lobbying HUD for one year, shortly after leaving HUD, Wilson was putting together another UDAG deal with Leonard Briscoe and meeting with Debbie Dean. Debbie was quite accommodating; she even wrote a letter to a mortgage company to inform them that Mr. Briscoe "has shown he has the ability to plan, develop, and operate successful projects." The secretary was of even greater help. Briscoe was named minority contractor of the year by the secretary two years running and Debbie, at his request, had called 20 to 25 banks to line up financing.[72]

Once Lance Wilson made it to PaineWebber funding ceased to be a problem. When Mr. Briscoe needed a firm financial commitment to move his UDAG application, Lance would produce it on PaineWebber letterhead. "Paine Webber is pleased to issue its firm commitment (subject to the award of the Urban Development Action Grant) to underwrite taxable bonds in the amount of $79,360,000.[73] The fact that he did not have the authority to make the commitment and was committing fraud did not seem to trouble Mr. Wilson.

Lance was an equal opportunity violator of rules. Just as he failed to follow HUD's conflict of interest rules, he failed to follow PaineWebber's Code of Conduct. The latter required written permission to be engaged in any other business; be employed or compensated by any other person; serve as an officer or partner of another organization; invest in limited or general partnerships, other than those offered by PaineWebber.

He failed to disclose his interest in six Winn partnerships. He failed to disclose his consulting work for Alexander Naclerio. Naclerio was having trouble getting FHA to insure his project. because, as he told Wilson, Hunter Cushing [the deputy assistant secretary for multifamily housing] was out to hurt him—to quote Naclerio's version of Hunter's remarks, "Why should I do anything for that f'ing guinea from New York."[74] Naclerio took his problem to Wilson. Lance speared Hunter and the project was approved. For his consulting work, he received $10,000. He picked up at least another $65,000 for consulting work for lobbying Assistant Secretary Tom Demery.

Lynda Murphy was a very good friend of Debbie Dean. Although she left HUD, she remained a presence for a long time. When asked if he knew Murphy, former assistant secretary, Maurice Barksdale, indicated that he met her when he first came to HUD and Ms. Murphy was working there. She had officially left five months before he arrived. Not being on the payroll did not end her access to internal HUD documents.

She was intimately involved with the DRG coinsurance case. She was given draft HUD letters before they were issued and she helped draft a letter for Dean's signature. She also was fairly successful in obtaining moderate rehab financing for her clients. Lynda, a loyal friend, was ever so helpful to Debbie who, after failing to be confirmed as an assistant secretary in September 1987, left HUD and formed her own company. Murphy's firm awarded the company a consulting contract paying $2,500 for seven months.

HUD's Flotsam and Jetsam

As administrations age, the holders of key policy positions get younger. At the beginning of Secretary Pierce's reign, most of the key political appointments were seasoned middle agers with a modicum of substance. As they finished their tour of duty, they were replaced by ambitious younger folks special assistants, whose main claim to fame was that they were masters of ceremony at the HUD Christmas talent show. They had also developed the peculiar Washington mind-set of cynicism and naivete. Being "overwhelmed" by the imperfections of the government and the sense that nobody seems to be watching or care, they fell rather easily into the swing of things.

The one who went the fastest, at least to jail, was the star witness of the hearing, DuBois Gilliam, who headed up the UDAG operation. Gilliam had no illusions about his inability to resist temptation or his qualifications.

Mr. Gilliam. Shortly after you walked in . . . [it was] downright power and greed. . .

I never should have been hired at HUD. I should never have been hired by the Federal government . . . I got in there because I was political. . . I was placed over at HUD. Samuel Pierce got loaded up on him a group of Young Turks who were very political on a must-hire list, and we had no housing skills whatsoever.[75]

Although he never received vicuna, he was wined, dined, and clothed and given a good deal of pocket money for exercising his housing skills. He eventually had built up enough confidence to apply for the assistant secretary's job during one of its vacancies. Lance was kind enough to make available to Gilliam and the Mrs. limousine service, hotel service and tickets to *Cats* on a jaunt to New York. Mr. Gilliam claimed he received $100,000 while at HUD and $17,000 monthly retainer after he left—a substantial portion from Sam Pierce's "minority crook of the year" Leonard Briscoe. He also received a bit from Michael Karem.

Mr. Karem, a former deputy assistant secretary for multifamily housing had come to HUD hot off the campaign trail. He was executive director of the Kentucky Reagan for President Committee.

By 1981, he was under investigation for charges of "receiving financial compensation for steering HUD properties to favored developers."[76] After he resigned, the secretary wrote to him that although the inspector general failed to uncover evidence of criminal misconduct, there was a in his office a "degree of failure to be sufficiently alert to the possibility of creation of appearances of favoritism of a kind that the office's operation are particularly susceptible to."[77] His exit didn't affect his access—he received over $12 million in UDAG grants.

Silvio DeBartolomeis, before coming to Washington had been a "gofer" for Philip Winn, who had been the chairman of the Republican party in Colorado. When he was brought to Washington as a special assistant to deputy assistant secretary Philip Abrams, he had great difficulty convincing the personnel office that he had the qualifications to receive the pay of a low-ranking manager. Within a few short years, he was the general deputy assistant secretary for housing and the acting federal housing commissioner. When he left the government, he joined the Winn Group, in his words, to "learn more about the management of multifamily residential real estate." Better late than never!

There were others. As a former inspector general commented, "HUD was a turkey farm. Some of the political appointees are still having trouble finding the men's room." R. Hunter Cushing arrived at HUD with the knowledge that Catholics and Puerto Ricans breed like cockroaches. His condescension was matched by his ability to fawn before power. As a reward for these skills, he was appointed to the position of deputy assistant secretary housing for multifamily housing in charge of the key housing subsidy programs.

It is unlikely that either Hunter or Silvio took any money. Hunter was rich and Silvio was amazed to have made it so big in government. He also had some political savvy. Mr. DeBartolomeis, sensing that at a future time he would have to explain the HUD funding process to a Congressional committee at first brought a witness to see that Debbie was ordering him to sign a moderate rehab funding order. He then took to being out of town much of the time so that a deputy such as Hunter Cushing would sign in his stead. He would see evil, hear evil, but not sign evil. Alas, he finally succumbed. Why get on the wrong side of

Debbie when he was still hoping to be nominated for the position of assistant secretary for housing?

Thomas Demery, who got the job that Silvio wanted, came to Washington to do good works. He had a favorite charity, Food for Africa, that raised money for the poor children of Mozambique. Contributions went up substantially after his arrival in Washington. It became a favorite charity to developers and consultants who had a hunch that Mozambique was on the route to a moderate-rehab project. The inspector general led a huge safari across the land without finding the path. The main result was a 700-page report entitled "Thomas T. Demery, Former Assistant Secretary, Section 8 Moderate Rehabilitation Program," which triggered the House investigation. The irony is that 75 percent of the projects audited preceded Demery's tenure.

Actually Mr. Demery's power was quite limited. When Demery tried his hand at selecting a project, his deputy Hunter told him he would not sign off on the project unless Deborah Dean told him to do so.[79] When he took the matter up with the secretary, he was told that the program was not his but the secretary's and he would speak through Dean.[80] The only thing he asked of Demery regarding the moderate rehab projects was that he be kept informed of the developer or the person behind each project. If Demery is to be believed, the secretary's lawyer is going to have a difficult job in convincing a jury that his client didn't lie to the Congressional committee.

The Order of the Garter

A majority of the developers of subsidized housing were Democrats in their hearts and pocketbooks. Faced with a Republican administration doling out the funds on a political basis meant they had to find a Republican lawyer or lobbyist. As Paul Manafort explained:

> Black, Manafort & Kelly is a lobbying . . . firm, founded in 1980. It is a bipartisan firm. . . . It is not unusual to have an entree be made so that your case can be heard, but ultimately in the process, the merits of the case, in my judgement, are the bases on which decisions get made.[81]

He said it with a straight face. With his $326,000, he received for obtaining funding for the Seabrook apartments he should have also been given the Order of the Garter. As Representative Barney Franks noted, "I don't think you, frankly, had any idea what the merits were. . . . [T]his reminds me of Viscount Melbourne's announcement of why he'd like the Order of the Garter—because there was no damned nonsense about merit connected with the award of it."[82]

A Rogue Elephant

The scandal at HUD was not that the allocations had been done on a political basis. Had all the allocations been made to congressmen to "buy" their vote on Contra aid (or the Kuwait war resolution) or to obtain a Republican majority or support for fair housing legislation it would at worst have been called hardball politics. It should be remembered that in spite of a lengthy review procedure in the Model City Program the announcements of the selected cities (all of the cities that applied) were made at the White House.

The revolving door aspects, although carried a bit too far by some of the former employees, was part of a larger problem of the complexity of programs. It cannot be expected that experts that are brought in from the private sector would as a result of government service be barred from pursuing their specialty after they return to the private sector. Conversely, it would be unfair to bar for lengthy periods government employees—at the executive and legislative levels—from making use of their expertise after they leave government. Although these lubricants of the government machinery, from an outside of the beltway viewpoint only have dirty hands to show for their labors, they are a necessary part of the process of achieving public purposes.

The heart of the HUD scandal was the adoption of a process that resembled a tribal potlatch. Through the granting of gifts in the form of allocation of units, affection, power, and aggrandizement was bestowed upon the givers. The recipients of these gifts were glad to pledge their fealty and to make sure that before any public purpose would be achieved their pockets would be lined and their mansions adorned.

The shame of HUD was that it had become a law unto itself. The fact that those in power at HUD didn't like the law didn't give them the authority to shift its focus from the welfare of the poorly housed to lavishly housing the poorly prepared—the Manaforts and Wattses of the world. They turned HUD into a rogue elephant.

Notes

1. *Senate Banking, Housing and Urban Affairs Comm. Hearings on the Nomination of Samuel R. Pierce, Jr.*, 1-2 (13 January 1981).
2. Lawrence Uzzell, "The Unsung hero of the Reagan Revolution: Secretary of Housing and Urban Development Samuel R. Pierce," *National Review*, 9 December 1988.
3. "The HUD Ripoff," *Newsweek*, 7 August 1989, 16.
4. Letter to the Independent Counsel in Subcommittee on Employment and Housing of the Committee on Government Operations, *Hearings on Abuses, Favoritism, and Mismanagement of HUD Programs*, 101st Cong., 1st sess., 1989 (Lantos Hearings) part 6, 1.
5. 126 *Cong. Rec.*, Part 24:31,520. (1980).
6. Quoted in House Subcommittee on Housing and Community Development, *Hearings on Loan Management Procedures For HUD Assisted Housing*, 100th Cong., 2d sess., 1391-92.
7. Jason DeParle, "What the Smartest Man in Washington Doesn't Understand. And Why it Will Hurt You," *Washington Monthly*, November 1989, 36.
8. Gerth, Jeff, "Regulators say 80s Budget Cuts May Cost U.S. Millions in 1990s," *New York Times*, 19 December 1989.
9. "The HUD Ripoff", 17.
10. Subcommittee of the Committee on Government Operations, *Review of FHA –Update of FHA Mortgage Insurance Fund Deficits*, 93rd Cong., 2d sess., (1974), Part 2, 171-73.
11. *Lantos Hearings*, part 3, 99.
12. A federally chartered private corporation (but with three of the fifteen directors appointed by the president) to act as a catalyst in mobilizing private housing investment, for low-and-moderate income housing through the incentive of existing tax advantage. It is presently one of the largest owners of apartments in the country.
13. "The Rise and Fall of A Real Estate Dynasty–R.I.P. DRG", *Regardie's*, March 1990, 50, 57.
14. Letter is in Senate HUD/Mod Rehab Investigation Subcommittee of the Committee on Banking, Housing, and Urban Affairs, *Hearings on the Abuse and Mismanagement at HUD*, 101st Cong. 2d sess., 1990, (*Senate Investigation*) Vol. I, 366-75.
15. *Lantos Hearings*, part 3, 444.
16. Inspector General, "Audit of Section 223 (f) Coinsurance Program, 9 December 1988.
17. *Senate Investigation*, Vol. I, 539.
18. *Lantos Hearings*, part 6, 410, 412.
19. IFC, "*Final Report*—The Characteristics of HUD-Processed and Direct Endorsement Mortgages." i. (prepared for HUD 18 December 1989).
20. Inspector General, "Audit of Section 223 (f)," 12.
21. Ibid, ii,iii.
22. Ibid, 14.
23. P.L. 95-452., 92 *Stat.*, 1101.
24. Testimony of Secretary Patricia Harris, *Senate Hearings on HUD's 1980 Appropriations*, 96th Cong., 1st sess., 1979.
25. Section 213 (d) of the Housing and Community Development Act of 1974.

26. 24 *Code of Federal Regulation*, Sec. 882.501.
27. In exceptional cases this amount could be exceeded by 20 percent.
28. The difference between a tax deduction and a tax credit can be seen in the following example. Assume $10,000 in income and a tax rate of 10 percent. A tax deduction of $900 would result in a tax bill of $910 [(10,000 - 900) x 10%]. A tax credit of $900 would result in a tax bill of $100 [($10,000 x 10%) - $900.]
29. As in all matters relating to the tax code, its a bit more complicated. The percentages are defined as 70 percent of the present value of the property amortized over ten years. Thus, if the Treasury borrowing rate were 8 percent, the present value cost over 10 years of the annual $4,050 payment is $27,176. The present value benefit to an investor who is seeking a 12 percent yield is $22,833.
30. *Lantos Hearings*, Part 1, 330.
31. Gordon Michael, "Within the Arms Debate a 2d Debate," *The New York Times*, 9 February 1988, 3.
32. *Lantos Hearings*, part 2, 240-41. The geographic distortion in the East, where Puerto Rico with one fifth the population of New York received twice as much mod rehab funding resulted from the influence and desires of the Republican Senator from New York.
33. *Lantos Hearings*.
34. *Lantos Hearings*, part 2, 738.
35. Quoted in Kuntz, Phil, "At Least Once in the Reagan Era HUD Favors Came From the Very Top," *Congressional Quarterly*, 30 September 1989.
36. There was near total discretion at the local level. As a study of the program at the local level advised, "[T]he potential for scandal is so great that city officials should set up countermeasures in advance, such as requiring more uniform negotiating procedures, arranging for independent analyses of developer agreements, tightening the restrictions on former officials who want to do business with the city." Bernard Frieden and Lynne Sagalyn, *Downtown Inc. How America Rebuilds Cities*, 226.
37. Committee on Government Operation, *Twenty Fourth Report, Abuse and Mismanagement At HUD*, 45-46.
38. Office of the Inspector General, "Audit of the Section 8 Moderate Rehabilitation Program," appendix 1 (26 April 1989).
39. General Accounting Office, "Use of Subsidies," 27 February 1990.
40. *Senate Investigation*, part 1, 166.
41. *Lantos Hearings*, Part 1, 192.
42. I would like to thank Professor Michael Teitz for pointing out the distinction.
43. *Lantos Hearings*, Part 6, 393.
44. *Lantos Hearings*, Part 2, 161.
45. *Lantos Hearings*, Part 4, 590.
46. *Lantos Hearings*, Part 1, 2.
47. *Lantos Hearings*, Part 1, 396-40.
48. Cited in ibid., 195.
49. *24th Report*, 18.
50. The wizards who devised the formula had a different concept of distress than the thousands of yuppies who have ferried to Hoboken.
51. HUD-Independent Agencies Approp. for FY 1988, *Hearings before a Subcom. of the Senate Comm. on Approp.*, part 2, 967, 969-70 (1988).
52. See legal opinion by Betty Park, Acting Assistant General Counsel Assisted Housing Division, "Consultant Agreement Section 8 Mod" in *Lantos Hearings*, part 1, 96.

53. "Rental Housing Inefficiencies From Combining Moderate Rehabilitation and Tax Credit Subsidies," 5 (June 1990).
54. See 27.
55. *Senate Investigation*, part 1, 223-24.
56. Quoted in the "Undoing of Silent Sam Pierce," *U.S. News and World Report*, 18 September 1989, 29.
57. Ibid., 29, 32.
58. *24th Report*, 4.
59. *Meinhard v. Salmon*, 249 N.Y. 458, 464; 164 N.E. 545, 546. (1928)
60. *Lantos Hearings*, part 5, 75.
61. Ibid., 99-100.
62. *24th Report*, 40-41.
63. "Ex-Housing Secretary Says Aides Were At Fault in Disputed Program," *New York Times*, 26 May 1989.
64. Senate Banking Committee, *Nomination of Deborah Gore Dean*, 32. (6 August 1987)
65. Cited in *Lantos Hearings*, part 3, 724.
66. *Senate Hearings*, part II, 122.
67. *24th report*, 87.
68. Kunz, Philip, "Killing 'Mod-Rehab' With Kindness," *Congressional Quarterly*, 22 July 1989.
69. *Lantos Hearings*, part 1, 221.
70. Ibid., 221.
71. *24th Report*, 101-2.
72. Ibid.
73. Ibid.
74. *Lantos Hearings*, part 4, 152, 174.
75. *Lantos Hearings*, part 5, 116.
76. Alan Berlow (Nation Public Radio Reporter) quoted in *National Journal*, 31 October 1981, 1, 960.
77. Quoted in Fitzgerald, Sara, and Sandra Sugawara, "Executive Notes," *The Washington Post*, 10 May 1982, A 15.
78. Quoted in "The HUD Ripoff," 19.
79. *Lantos Hearings*, part 5, 335.
80. Ibid., 336-37.
81. Ibid., 105.
82. Ibid., 107.

PART II

THE MANAGERS AND THE OVERSEERS

5

The Circle of Neglect

What is remarkable about the last forty years of HUD scandals and fiascoes is how so many were overlooked or out of the line of sight of the overseers. The media, Congress, General Accounting Office, Office of Management and Budget, and Office of the Inspector General fiddled while HUD was lighting up the town.

The Media

Time magazine couldn't understand why Washington's corp of investigative reporters were napping during the capers of the Pierce Administration:

> Big bucks. Heaps of Hypocrisy. Influence peddling by prominent Republicans. The unfolding scandal at the Department of Housing and Urban Development is the kind of story that guarantees front-page play. It is also the kind of story that could guarantee brilliant future careers, perhaps even Pulitzer prizes . . . . So reporters have pounced on Washington's latest example of sleaze. There is just one hitch: it's yesterday's news. All that murky bureaucratic back scratching and buck passing happened during the heyday of the Reagan Administration Where was the ever vigilant press corp back then.

The short answer: sleeping.[1]

The sleep of the media rivals Rip Van Winkle's. The name of HUD and issues of housing policy conjure up a potion that causes drowsiness. Covering HUD is not the fast track to fame and fortune. It is the "Gulag

of Washington."[2] Jack Anderson, the syndicated columnist, who has
made a career of uncovering the sleazy details of Washington noted, "We
don't have enough eyes to look at HUD. the very name HUD says
dullness, dullness, dullness."[3]

The general media has been nearly totally oblivious to housing issues
and programs. In part this is due to the generalized education of reporters
and the premise, which they share with lawyers, that given a few days
almost any subject can be mastered. It makes them the victims of the
readily visible and interviews with high officials. Of course, after a few
years on the job, a reporter would gain sufficient expertise to safely
navigate through the alphabet sea of programs. However, unless he plans
to go into the trade newsletter business, the career path will take him to
a more glamorous assignment such as the obituary desk.

Success is not a story and even Pulitzer Prize winning stories may only
make matters worse. As a former director of the former Bureau of Budget
put it:

> The public servant learns that successes rarely rate a headline but government
> blunders are front page news. This recognition encourages the development of
> procedures designed less to achieve success than to avoid blunders. Let it be
> discovered that the Army is buying widgets . . . while the Navy is disposing of widgets
> at a lower price; the reporter will win a Pulitzer prize and the Army and Navy will
> establish procedures for liaison, review, and clearance that will prevent a recurrence
> . . . . It may cost a hundreds time more to prevent the . . . occasional widget episodes,
> but no one will complain.[4]

The focus on scandals and simple stories is a good part of the
explanation of why coverage is so poor. Bad news sells papers and what
better bad new is there than low behavior by high officials. Unfortunately,
the causes of most of the incidents discussed were a bit more complex.
They were buried in the structure and the fine print of the programs. In
the Section 608 program, the small changes in the program limitations
from "reasonable replacement cost" to "necessary current costs" or the
change from room limits to apartment limits went by unnoticed. A
journalist bearing reports of the future effect of the underwriting and
processing changes wrought by Congressional technical amendments on
the subsidized rental programs would not have been received with kudos
by the editor and the publisher. The big news in the early 1970s was the
battle between HUD and the Department of Transportation as to which
agency would have the largest flagpole.

It takes some human interest and the klieg lights of a congressional investigation to awaken interest in HUD. The poorly applied siding flying in the wind in the Title I scams and the pictures of the tavern in Paterson will get HUD off the back pages. "Robbin HUD" (Marilyn Louise Harrell) the talkative and charitable blond embezzler who gave a fifth of her take to charity has gotten far more copy than "Robin Hook" (A. Bruce Rozet), the West Coast schemer who controlled tens of thousands of subsidized apartments and who with his band managed to siphon off more than half the money that was raised to rehabilitate the housing of the poor.

The demolition of a single project, Pruitt-Igoe, made headlines and the evening news throughout the nation (and is still the lead in on most public housing stories). Has any reporter ever raised the possibility in print or over the airwaves that a far more insidious problem in public housing relate to the rent calculations? As Gorbachev now knows only too well, management of a system in which price has no relation to quality is a recipe for financial disaster that can bring the whole system tumbling down.

If it ain't photogenic and simple, its on the real estate pages. *Sixty Minutes* could do a story about the Section 235 when it had footage of toilets coming through the ceiling. The issue of homelessness is a perfect story, especially if the people are neat and clean. Robert Hayes, Director of the National Coalition for the Homeless, told the *New York Times* that when he is contacted by television news programs or congressional committees, "they always want white, middle-class families to interview." With the realization that the problem is interwoven with drug addiction, alcoholism, mental health, illiteracy, and domestic violence the story has receded from media and public attention.

The Lantos hearings with stories of political influence by a cast of famous characters made the headlines and the nightly news. The hearings of the Senate investigating subcommittee that explored ways of strengthening HUD management and Congressional oversight were treated by news editors as the essence of dullness—even C-Span didn't cover the hearings.

Congress

Congress has done a much better job of hindsight than oversight. The Section 608 and Title I investigatory hearings came only after President

Eisenhower, relying on reports by the Internal Revenue Service and the Federal Bureau of Investigation impounded the files of the Federal Housing Administration. In fact in the case of the Section 608 program, the hearings occurred four years after the program had ended.

In the following decades, except for the report by the staff of the House Appropriations Committee that uncovered the rip-offs in the Section 235 program, there was no meaningful oversight by Congress. They were more often more interested in fighting rear guard actions defending failed programs.[5]

They never did understand the structural flaws of the interest subsidy programs. The efforts by Democratic and Republican administrations to overlook and paper over the massive defaults so that current budgets wouldn't look bad were aided and abetted by Congress. Rozet became a hero in Congress for all his good works in this endeavor to keep the budget looking slim while he fattened up on fees for flipping projects. Congress was so enamored of the new Section 8 projects that they killed a regulation that HUD was proposing to limit the budget overruns. And they came ever so close to approving the nomination of Deborah Dean for the post of assistant secretary for community planning and development, not realizing that this represented a step down in power and authority.

A student of the Congress informed the Senate investigating committee that oversight is not in a congressman's job description:

> There is a wealth of political science studies to explain why an ordinary person of good intentions would probably behave just as today's legislators do. Heavily over-worked elected politicians are not likely to pay more than episodic attention to signals of executive mismanagement. Their political interests favor mainly those investigations that will make a noticeable splash. Their need to advocate constituent's interest often lead to interventions in agency decision making that can lead to mismanagement. On the top of all this is the inherent tiresomeness of the oversight work.[6]

The House Government Operations report on the "Abuses and Mismanagement at HUD" issued on 1 November 1990, suggested that:

> HUD funding decisions should be based on merit and competition. There is a need to take politics and discretion out of housing programs. This applies equally to the executive and legislative branch. Just as it was wrong for HUD to dole out housing units . . . just as it was not right for President Reagan in 1982 to give units to New Jersey to influence a Senate race, so too Congress should not earmark funds for housing projects in appropriations bills, Last year's Supplemental Appropriations bill for HUD earmarked nearly $30 million for 40 housing grants.[7]

The suggestion fell on deaf ears. Within weeks after the report, Congress in the 1991 appropriations bill earmarked $73 million for specified projects. In 1992, moving into an election year, the set-aside was doubled to $150 million.

The General Accounting Office

Where was the General Accounting Office (GAO), Congress's watchdog, while the head of the agency was asleep? GAO had 40 auditors settled in offices in the HUD building. What did these auditors see or hear? Nothing.

In their first evaluation of HUD's efforts to improve its program management and internal controls, HUD got better than average marks. John Heileman in an article entitled "Congress's WatchDog: Mostly It Still goes for the Capillaries," marked the markers:

> "The Department of Housing and Urban Development has played a major role in upgrading the nation's housing and providing community development aid to cities and counties." It was downhill from there, 212 pages of pap. Dig down through it long enough (as embarrassed GAO officials recently have) and you'll find a few remarks that are vaguely on the mark. "HUD's top management changes frequently. . . . As a result, institutional memory at a high level does not exist to understand the causes of HUD's longstanding management problems . . . ." Revisionist stories in the press have seized on lines like this to cobble together an argument that GAO was ringing the bell while HUD was burning down. More to the point were lines like these: "HUD has made significant strides towards resolving many of its management problems. HUD has increased its efforts to prevent fraud, waste, and mismanagement and is improving its financial management activities." Now if these words were superfluous bromides, they didn't belong in the report. And if they were candid assessments of the evaluators then they didn't belong in the report.[8]

They had an instinct for the irrelevant and the green eyeshades shielded the forest from the underbrush. They found evidence of mismanagement in projects here and there but they did not see the bigger picture. They did at least two reviews of the moderate rehabilitation program without finding much amiss.

In 1988, the GAO was asked by members of the staff of the Senate Housing and Urban Affairs Committee to look into allegations made by HUD employees, that cronyism was rampant in the agency. They looked, but did not see.[9]

The jury is out on whether the GAO has the qualities one seeks for in a good watchdog. Everyone agrees that it is not a Grand Champion. What is left open is how far from the mark the GAO is. The views differ from the extreme that its no damn good to a more middle ground that it is a good dog with a tendency to be lulled into inaction. John Payne takes the former view: the GAO is "more a decrepit hound than a watchdog, it has to be led by the nose to the expiring fox."[10] John Ols, who took over GAO's HUD oversight function after the Pierce period, tends toward the view that the problem lies in an occasional lack of alertness:

> I guess we got a little too complacent, HUD was not a big priority in the administration and Congress didn't care enough to give it decent oversight. Nobody cared about HUD—and we just went the same way as everyone else. You get very settled. You start to see the agency like the agency sees itself.[11]

The Office of Management and Budget

The title "Office of Management and Budget" was a misnomer during the 1980s. It was the "Office of Budget." Trying to set an example of cutting staff, the management side of OMB which had a staff of 224 in 1970 was reduced to forty seven by 1988. The belief was that only Congress and Democratic administrations could screw up.

OMB, however, has promised to mend its ways and it has begun to add staff (fifty members in the management area.) And there is a promise that the future will be different. William Diefenderfer, OMB's deputy director, informed Congress in April of 1990 that:

> OMB is reorienting itself to ensure earlier detection of major management problems. Oversight will be aggressively pursued by both Budget and Management examiners. I believe OMB working with agency management and inspector generals can build the necessary safeguards to reduce waste, fraud, and abuse, and provide effective stewardship to the public's business.[12]

H. Hugh Heclo, a professor at George Mason University, who has studied OMB for a score of years, is skeptical about OMB's latest promise:

> This is a splendid theory. Its main problem is that it has never worked in practice. OMB has become more a part of the government management problem than a resource for its solution. . . . Taken as a whole, the record does *not* show that OMB can be counted on to play the ongoing critical role that leads to management improvement. On the contrary, the management function within OMB has never been institutionalized to provide a sustained capacity for overseeing administration in the rest of the executive branch. Organizational turmoil has prevailed on the management side of OMB. Management improvement initiatives have been launched with great

fanfare, only to turn into paper exercises that are soon abandoned. Budget staff and management staff have been separated, merged, reseparated and remerged. . . . [T]his sorry history . . . should give anyone pause about what is to be expected from any new round of management reform.[13]

The statement that OMB is part of the problem is literally as well as figuratively true when it comes to the situation at HUD during the 1980s. The "M" of its name could stand for "messenger" of politically driven project selection decisions. In 1987, a $10 million UDAG was awarded to build a shopping center in Albuquerque, New Mexico. DuBois Gilliam describes the process:

[T]wo days before we are going to sit down and make a determination on what projects we were going to fund I received a call from [OMB] . . . to inform me that OMB was funding the Albuquerque project. . . .

I subsequently found out . . . that representatives from Albuquerque had visited with UDAG staff and had learned . . . there were problems. They . . . went and saw . . . Senator Domenici. [H]e . . . spoke with . . . former Senator Baker who was the Chief of Staff to the President and indicated that they needed the project funded. He informed them that the project would be funded and that is what triggered the phone call. . . .

I went upstairs. I saw Debbie Dean. . . . She in turn called Carol Crawford and they got to arguing. Deborah says, OMB cannot make announcements on UDAGs. We haven't even done due diligence on this project yet . . . Mrs. Crawford's response was *"We're OMB, we can do what we want to do."* (My emphasis)[14]

The Office of the Inspector General

The work of the inspector general won plaudits as far away as the other side of the Atlantic Ocean. In London, the headline in *The Economist* proclaimed "Hooray for Auditors."[15] Paul Adams was credited with blowing the whistle at HUD so loudly that it could be heard on Capitol Hill. Congress, at the insistence of the new secretary, with great alacrity, in 1990, passed reform legislation that rewarded the inspector general by increasing his power and staff.

The inspector deserved neither the adulation nor the reward. Based on the performance during the Pierce years, the inspector general seemed more interested in protecting HUD's good name than the public's property. This junkyard dog was a sheep in wolf's clothing. The audit reports arrived so late that they were swept into the next Administration, were written in a style that was more a bureaucratic jargon than a means of communication, were poorly targeted and timid—tough on those below but oh so soft on those above.

The audit of the Section 223 (f) coinsurance program was issued on 9 December 1988, when the secretary was a political lame duck. In the case of the Section 8 moderate rehabilitation audit, the inspector general spent so much time directing his troops after the wrong horse (the charitable activities of Thomas Demery) that he didn't get around to interviewing the secretary until the latter had one foot out of the door. The audit report was ultimately issued after Secretary Kemp had settled into office. The timing raised some eyebrows:

CHAIRMAN GONZALEZ: [W]hen did you begin your investigation?
MR. ADAMS: February 1988.
CHAIRMAN GONZALEZ: Why would you have waited . . . until January 19 of this year [1989] to interview the HUD Secretary, Mr. Pierce, who was going out of office the next day . . . ? Was it that you didn't learn until, say, 2 days before of the possible involvement of Secretary Pierce?
MR. ADAMS: No sir. It was just a matter of scheduling.[16]

The reports of the inspector general were remarkably circumspect, never suggesting the possibility that there was a disaster brewing. In reporting on the coinsurance program that was gushing red ink, the auditors were worried that the failure to enforce the program requirements would adversely affect the *success* of the program, that adding monitoring staff would taint the program's purity of purpose, and suggested that DRG should stay in business in order to earn fees so that it could make its GNMA payments. In the moderate rehab audit, as late as April 1989, the Inspector General could not declare, "The program is being run on the basis of favoritism and political influence." Instead, we get the phrase about the "widespread perception that exists . . . that the MRP is headquarters-driven favoring certain PHAs, owners, developers, etc."

The writing style of the inspector general was described by the House Investigating Committee as a "combination of pablumese and account-ese."[17] The writing problem reflects a generic personality flaw and a flaw in the law. On the first point:

When most government auditors discover a problem they couch it in terms that are least likely to arouse the bureaucracy's enmity. Rather than scream "the building is on fire," they will remark, alongside some comment about the excessive number of staples purchased last year, that "signs of combustion were evident in several hallways"—and be certain to add that corrective anti-combustion action is being taken by the agency. "No one is going to say, "The building is on fire". You'll get in trouble for that, "is how one former budget examiner describes the average inspector general report. "Everyone is covering their ass."[18]

The "Inspector General Act of 1978" makes the inspector a Presidential appointee and his semi-annual reports are transmitted to the appropriate committees in Congress. Although he is under the general supervision of the "head of the establishment" (the secretary) the latter cannot "prevent or prohibit the Inspector General from initiating, carrying out, or completing any audit or investigation, or from issuing any subpena during the course of an investigation." Nevertheless, in an important way he is beholden to the secretary—monetarily. In 1982, Paul Adams, then the deputy inspector general was nominated by the secretary and received a meritorious executive award which carried with it a $10,000 bonus. In 1986, Paul Adams was nominated as HUD's "Executive of the Year."[19] It is poor manners to bark at the hand that feeds and strokes.

The audit report in the moderate rehab case was the product of 15.5 staff years of auditing and 2.5 years of investigating. It contained over 700 pages. Quantity did not translate into thoroughness. There were gaping holes in the report. It did not meet the scandal head on. Rather it focused on Assistant Secretary Demery who came in on the tail end.

This lack of focus was a matter of notice for a number of representatives who participated in the House Hearings. In the following cross examination, it becomes quite evident that the inspector general bears no resemblance to Sherlock Holmes:

MR. MORRISON: Why is it that you focused and concluded that the problem starts and ends with Mr. Demery when the abuse—and I would like to say that the Worcester grant is a classic targeted abuse of giving away units to a developer. . . . Who targeted these units? . . . It couldn't have been Mr. Demery because he wasn't there. . . . What is not in these documents is who at HUD was making these promises. That is the question that you guys do not answer. You are investigating developers. That is the U.S. attorney's job. Your job is to investigate HUD officials, and you don't come to the bottom line at that. Who at HUD promised the units to the State Street Development Corporation?

MR. ADAMS: The information we have is that the information was communicated by former Senator Brooke.

MR. MORRISON: Who at HUD - he doesn't work there either? Who at HUD told Ed Brooke? . . . Did you ask Ed Brooke?

MR. ADAMS: Yes.

MR. MORRISON: What was his answer?

MR. NERI [a member of Mr. Adams' staff]: [H]e said that he had not lobbied for units to be awarded there.

MR. MORRISON: So you just said that Senator Brooke did it. Senator Brooke said he didn't do it. Who did it?

MR. ADAMS: We don't know, sir?

MR. MORRISON: But no criminality, nobody lied to you? I don't know how you have an agency that carries out investigations that when you get conflicting stories just walks away from it, which is apparently what you did. I mean you just collected paper.[20]

The inspector general's posse, "the gang that couldn't shoot straight," was in such hot pursuit of Tom Demery that they galloped right past Debbie Dean. Tom Demery when he finally stopped to talk to his congressmen complained that the only explanation for the inspector general's activities was a personal vendetta and that the investigation centering on Food for Africa was a coverup of the real story. His explanation has an element of credence. As Representative Christopher Shays, after perusing the inspector's report, mused at the Lantos hearings:

> I feel it was so incomplete, I feel it wasn't even in conformity to any general accounting principles. I even feel when Mr. Demery made the comment that it was in so many ways vicious and it singled out his activities. He even used the word "coverup."

> I have been haunted by that because I feel in some ways there was a coverup. Whether it was intended, whether it was significant remains to be determined. But I sincerely believe the key people were not looked at by your office.[21]

The final remarks from the halls of Congress on the work of the Inspector General go to Representative Bruce Morrison:

> I can't figure it out, whether this is an intentional coverup of the wrongdoing of certain individuals, whether your participation is totally incompetent, or there is something else going on here that doesn't fall into either category. . . .

> It is amazing the *Wall Street Journal* and the *New York Times* and the *Los Angeles Times* and the *Washington Post* can find out more in a few weeks about these individuals than you can find out in months of investigations with hundreds of investigators. Doesn't that make you a little uneasy about the quality of job done by your shop.[22]

The circle of neglect is closed.

Notes

1. Riley, Michael, "Where was the Media on HUD," *Time*, 24 July 1989, 84.
2. Ibid.
3. Ibid.
4. Kermit Gordon quoted in Herbert Kaufman, *Red Tape Its Origins, Uses and Abuses*, 14.
5. See "Suspension of Subsidized Housing Programs," *Hearings before the House Subcommittee on Housing*, 93rd Cong. 1st sess. (1973) and the report by the Congressional Research Service of the Library of Congress, "Analysis of the Section 235 and 236 Programs," (1973). The latter was prepared for the Senate Subcommittee on Housing and Urban Affairs and written by Henry Schecter, a former HUD official, who while at HUD prepared estimates of the cost of the programs that, at least in the cases of Section 236, were, to say the least, a trifle optimistic.
6. Heclo, H. Hugh, "Statement," *Senate Investigation*, vol. II, 170.
7. *24th Report*, 8.
8. John Heileman, "Congress's Watchdog: Mostly It Still Goes for the Capillaries," *Washington Monthly*, November 1989, 42.
9. "Whatever Became of Oversight," *National Journal*, 22 July 1989, 1, 886.
10. Payne, James, "The Congressional Brainwashing Machine," *The Public Interest*, Summer 1990, 7.
11. Heileman, "Congress's Watchdog," 48.
12. *Senate Investigation*, vol. II, 138.
13. Ibid., 17172.
14. *24th Report*, 15354.
15. 1 July 1989, 19.
16. "HUD Investigations," *Hearings before the House Subcommittee on Housing and Community Development*, 100th Cong., 1st sess., 25.
17. *24th Report*, 8.
18. DeParle, Jason, "What the Smartest Man in Washington Doesn't Understand. And Why it Will Hurt You," *The Washington Monthly*, November 1989, 18.
19. *Lantos Hearings*, part 6, 459.
20. *Gonzalez Hearings*, 5153.
21. *Lantos Hearings*, part 1, 493.
22. Ibid., 518, 523.

6

Good Management of Bad Programs

Its been a long time since anyone associated the name of HUD with good management. The dialogue between Marilyn Louise Harrell ("Robbin HUD")—a contract closing agent who failed to transmit to HUD $5 million—and Representative Tom Lantos indicates how far from ideal some of HUD's operations were:

MR. LANTOS: United Airlines has a whole lot of agents a ticket counters selling tickets. Most people buy their tickets with credit cards, but there are some who walk up to the United ticket counter with cash, and they buy a ticket to New York or wherever, and at the end of the shift the agent . . . must have, as any cashier does, hundreds of dollars, large quantities of money which she then has to account for. . . . Something must have given you the idea, correctly, that at HUD the controls are so inadequate that you can get away with that. . . . Clearly, had you worked for United Airlines, at the end of the day you wouldn't have put the cash in your pocket and the next day and the next day until it reached a pile of dollars, $5 million, because before the first day was over, United Airlines would have said, there are tickets you sold where is the money?

MS. HARRELL: Well . . . the very lowest people on the employment spectrum were . . . inputting the computer work that was actually the account process. . .

MR. LANTOS: "And you felt there were no controls of any kind that could have made this scheme obvious to the higher-ups at HUD?"

MS. HARRELL: Not really.[1]

There is much work to be done in the boiler-room and backroom operations of HUD. There is a need to fix the faucets and the pipes so that money doesn't drip away and when the pipes are leaking it is quickly discovered. It is work for the auditors and accountants of the inspector general and the Federal Housing Administration.

Management and Scandals

The management needs in the policy and program areas of HUD were recently summed up by Morton Schussheim, a senior housing specialist at the Congressional Research Service of the Library of Congress:

> To get an administrative unit to implement a policy or program three conditions must obtain. First, the agency must identify with the goals of the policy. Second, there must be clear communication of what the top officials really want. Third, a penalty and reward system must be available to back up the official policy. Outside the administrative apparatus the intended beneficiaries of a program must be convinced that real benefits will be forthcoming and the community at large has to be persuaded that the policy or program is worth the cost.[2]

These rules are necessary conditions for an efficient organization. However, when we apply these rules to the previous cases, they are not sufficient to affect the outcomes. In the Section 608 case, FHA identified with the policy of increasing production of rental housing. The bureaucracy got the message. Program managers were rewarded for increasing the volume of business. The term "beneficiaries" is ambiguous. It can refer to the developers, the renters, or all of those seeking rental housing who were indirect beneficiaries of the program. The former and the latter had little reason to complain about the program. The renters, although some were unhappy because of the level of the rents, had only a short-term commitment to the building. They had the option of moving to another apartment or to become homeowners.

The problem came from the community at large, represented by their congressmen, who were "outraged" not by the cost of the program (the era of subsidized private production had not yet arrived) but by the enormous profits of the developers. At a time when the average salary of a baseball player was $15,000 and the entire payroll of the New York Yankees was $450,000, some developers were making millions.[3]

In the Title I home improvement case, the agency believed, that as long as the premiums kept rolling in and the claims were low, the responsibility for managing the program could be delegated to the private sector and local law enforcement. It was an early instance of deregulation and it was profitable. The fly in the ointment was that some of the intended beneficiaries were bitten by fly-by-nighters. And the problem of these victims would not disappear. Every time they would approach their house and see the aluminum siding their veins would bulge with aggravation.

In the case of the inner-city homeownership debacle, management was too enthusiastic. The top leadership of FHA and the staff were like repentant sinners seeking atonement for their deeds in prior decades—only 2 percent of the new FHA-insured homes were open to blacks between 1946 and 1959. FHA rushed into areas in which even angels fear to tread. They were dragged out. Few of the subsidy recipients were hurt badly in a monetary sense. They were beneficiaries only because they were in a bad monetary state. The hurt was to the heart in the shattering of dreams and expectations. Even in the absence of the thieves that flocked to the program it was doomed to failure. The subsidy was sufficient to buy the house but not to properly maintain it.

In the case of the Section 236 program, we again have a case of enthusiasm outrunning intelligence. To encourage production, the agency forgot about management. The entire agency was geared toward development and the production of new rental housing soared. The situation that one of the many commercial developers in the 1980s finds itself in the 1990s is analogous to the fate of HUD's production division.

Crow employees . . . took pride in the company's unusual culture, with its egalitarian management, low base salaries intended to motivate creative development.

New top Crow officials say the compensation structure worked too well. . . . It encouraged only one kind of activity. That was development. You had to keep on development. . . . It forced new partners to make some incorrect decisions.[5]

HUD also had second thoughts, when it realized that in the program it and Congress had concocted, the price of production successes were management disasters. The deck chairs were perfectly aligned. The dining tables were set with fine china and lace tablecloths. The beds with their goose down pillows were made. Leona Helmsley would have been proud. Alas, the Titanic was sailing into an iceberg.

The job of cleaning up the problems fell into the hands of the management staff. The term "management" was a euphemism. It was a job for an undertaker charged with disposing the remains. HUD and the Congress saw the specter of very large appropriations to restock the FHA insurance funds if the projects were to be foreclosed and buried. They looked for a savior.

HUD and Congress were perfect candidates to be taken for a ride. They wanted dearly to believe that someone would come and take the projects off their hands. When the Robin Hooks showed up on their doorstep bearing promises of cash and a willingness to fix up projects, (if HUD would only give them small pittances to help the poor) it would have taken an ungrateful soul to monitor the delivery of funds and assure they would be used to rehabilitate the project or what the ultimate cost would be to the Treasury in lost taxes on sheltered income.

In the coinsurance program, HUD deregulated and took a fiscal shellacking. As in the savings and loan industry, it was on the right track but it didn't go far enough. As Alfred Kahn, the father of government deregulation, wrote,

> [I]t was deregulation . . . removing of ceilings on the interest rates that the S&Ls were permitted to pay, and then necessarily relaxing the kinds of lending and investment activities in which they might engage led to a lot of irresponsible lending and investing. But that would have come to an end, but for our retention of federal deposit insurance-the distorting effect of which was enormously increased when the government increased the original deposit from $10,000 to $100,000 and failed to prevent depositors from multiplying their effective protection by holding or participating in a number of insured accounts, at a number of institutions. Federal insurance protected depositors from the discipline of the market and in so doing made it possible for S&Ls to continue to attract deposits no matter how imprudent their lending and investment activities—when they were effectively insolvent.

> Deregulation does not and should not mean total laissez-faire . . . [It] doesn't mean you fire your police force. You don't fire your bank examiners . . . or call off the antitrust enforcement agencies. In many ways, deregulation makes these responsibilities of government more important, not less.[6]

The Section 8 moderate rehabilitation program is the one case in which the Schussheim strictures seem to apply. The secretary opposed the programs (although not necessary the goals) of his agency. The civil service was shut out of the program. The reward system was askew. And, much that occurred was outside the administrative process. The only caveat is that the manipulation of the moderate rehabilitation program, however, had been going on for decades.

From a Policy Scandal to a Political Scandal

Until 1965, the sole approach of the federal government toward meeting the housing needs of low-income families had been to provide a subsidy to a public or private entity to enable the latter to produce and maintain a unit that a poor family could afford. The Housing and Urban Development Act of 1965 contained a new program that followed a completely different path. It moved the PHA from the role of landlord to tenant. Under the program—dubbed "Section 23" since it was tagged on as the 23rd section of the United States Housing Act of 1937 (the enabling legislation for public housing)—the public housing agency (PHA) was granted the power to lease units in privately owned buildings. The units would then be subleased to low-income tenants. The PHA would pay the owner the market rent and the occupants would pay the PHA what they could afford. The Federal government would provide the difference between what the PHA paid and what it received (plus a small amount to cover handling charges.)

The program had a number of apparent advantages over the traditional approach. With production lagging in subsidized housing, this approach offered the possibility of providing the poor with decent housing almost instantaneously. The housing would not be stigmatized as housing for the poor. The units would be scattered and the program would not result in the segregation of poor families. The subsidy also would be significantly lower since a used unit would generally cost less than a new unit. The final and perhaps most important thing was the political palatability of a used housing program. The prior programs that had emphasized new housing had been criticized as providing "penthouses for the poor." The criticism would not apply to a used housing program. It was therefore, no coincidence, that although the Housing and Urban Development Act of 1965 contained two new programs, one stirred waves of controversy (the rent supplement program which was geared to new construction), while the other scarcely caused a ripple (the Section 23 leased-housing program.)

Nevertheless, HUD was unenthusiastic. The program had started life on the wrong side of the aisle. Sponsored be Rep. William Widnall, it was the Republican alternative to rent supplements. Although Section 23 was enacted it was seen as a throwback to the housing allowance idea that was first put forward in the late 1930s. The Democrats, who defined (and continue to define) the housing problem as a shortage of decent housing, could not see much use for a program limited to older units. It was a sop to gain Republican votes for the important construction oriented program.

In spite of its dubious pedigree, Section 23 gained a foothold. In many localities, owners would moderately rehabilitate their units, in order to obtain a lease with a PHA. And, then the program was turned on its head. A shrewd lawyer, Joseph Burstein read the term "existing" so literally as to deprive it of any meaning—the lease could not take effect until the building was completed. This was not a waiver or disregard of a regulation but rather the negation of legislation.

HUD was quick to adopt this means to get around the clear meaning of the statute. By the end of 1972, about half of the leased units under management were either new or substantially rehabilitated. The radical remodeling of the program can be seen in the breakdown of the units that were in the planning stage in the June 1971-June 1972 period: 16 percent were to be in older buildings, 10 percent were to be in substantially rehabilitated buildings and 74 percent were to be in new buildings.

As a program that produced new units, the best that could be said about it was that it was no uglier than its step sister, public housing:

MR. BOLAND: Most long term leases (10-20 years) are barely financially feasible. . . . If escalation clauses cannot be fully funded, and this seems to be the case in many of the areas of the country, LHA's will face disas-terous financial consequences. . .

MR.GULLEDGE [HUD's assistant secretary for housing]: Yes, but no more disastrous than all the other units they have under management.

The mountainous HUD housing study after the moratorium produced only a molehill of evidence about the new construction segment. *The Housing in the Seventies* report concluded that it cost $1.03 to produce $1.00 worth of housing under the leasing program compared to $1.40 in the conventional subsidized housing programs. Unfortunately, those statistics only covered the used housing portion of the program. The evaluation team didn't have the time to look at the portion that relied on new housing. Nevertheless, Section 23, as a low-income construction program, was viewed kindly by the new rulers of the land. And so in the fall of 1973, the leasing program was spruced up, given a new title—up 15 notches from Section 23 to Section 8—and nominated to be the sole heir to the low income throne.

What emerged from Congress was a program that stressed new construction. The Democratic administration, at the end of the 1970s, however, tried to bring a portion of the program back to moderate rehabilitation, the original Republican concept. And then in the 1980s, contrary to the Republican administration's goals of relying on used housing, the combination of high fair market rents and tax credits turned the moderate rehabilitation program into a "close to new" program. Nearly the same physical result on a smaller scale occurred in the early 1970s. The only difference is the former policy scandal was ignored and the latter, because of the blatant political favoritism, turned into political scandal that made headlines.

The Other Guy

The importance of management can be gauged by looking at HUD's oldest subsidy program—the problem-laden public housing program. There is near universal agreement that the core of the public housing problem is poor management. There is total agreement as to who is at fault—the other guy.

Management failure is a villain made in heaven. Saddled with a mess, a new administrator can pass the buck back to the former administrators. Republicans, at least prior to the 1980s, can blame the Democrats who know how to legislate and tax but next to nothing about how to manage and operate. Democrats, at least prior to Jack Kemp, can blame the uncaring attitudes of the Republicans and their lack of commitment to the poor. Congress is quick to grab onto the issue of poor management, since it absolves faulty legislation. In a true exercise of federalism everybody at the federal level is ready to shift the blame downward to public housing agencies. When all else fails there are the victims—the tenants. All bemoan the good old days when subsidized housing served the deserving poor rather than a significant proportion of the underclass.

Management makes a difference but, in public housing, it is often marginal. The best management in the world would not solve its problems. The faults are so embedded in the system that if Solomon were to administer the program at the federal level and he would be able to appoint housing directors of equal wisdom at the local level things would not be much better.

From the beginning, the relationship between the federal government and the independent local PHA have been muddled and the rewards for good management undermined:

> The 1936 bill had provided [that] . . . "The Authority [U.S.] shall embody the provisions of such grant in a contract guaranteeing . . . fixed and uniform annual contributions over a fixed period."

[T]he 1937 bill introduced a quite new and, in the context, a remarkable provision as follows:

"Such annual contributions as are contracted for shall be strictly limited to the amounts . . . necessary to assure the low rent character of the housing project . . . "

Here was in the words of Gilbert and Sullivan, a most ingenious paradox. The first two sentences declared unambiguously that the grants be made . . . in "fixed and uniform amounts." The third said equally explicitly that the same annual contribution were to be neither fixed nor uniform . . . but were to vary as necessary to limit them "strictly" to the amounts deemed necessary by the Authority.

[T]he local housing agencies were put on notice from the beginning that prudence and efficiency in management would result, not in a somewhat more comfortable and stable financial position but in a reduction of the Federal subsidy.[8]

The right mix between federal control and local independence continues to evade HUD in a framework in which nearly all the money is federal. For example, a major initiative of the 1980s was the Public Housing Decontrol Initiative. In order to concentrate a lean federal workforce on PHAs loaded with troubles, monitoring activities were relaxed for PHAs meeting certain performance standards.

And then came Passaic. The executive director, Paul Margugio, collected salaries for four jobs—full-time executive director, full-time modernization director, part-time contracting officer, and part-time purchasing agent. Paul had no shame. He also charged compensatory time for overtime hours and was given a $7,500 expense account. Being a good husband and provider, his wife, Louise was paid more than $95,000 for working one day a week. The family income was approximately $350,000. The money came out of the modernization account.[9]

If the legislation spoke with a forked tongue so did its sponsor (Senator Robert Wagner) when it came to defining who the program was to serve:

MR. WALSH: I insist its benefits reach the lowest income group and that those of the lowest income get the tenements provided for in this measure.

MR. WAGNER: I do not want to interrupt the Senator in his presentation. As has been so often stated he and I are together in this proposition . . . that none but the lowest income group will secure occupancy of these homes. . . .

There are some people whom we cannot reach I mean those who have no means to pay the rent minus the subsidy, This after all is a renting proposition.

MR. PEPPER: Yes and yet the language . . . will limit the availability of these quarters just to those people. That is not what the Senator had in mind.

MR. WAGNER: I doubt whether it would be so interpreted.

MR. PEPPER: The senator means then, if I may inquire further, the lowest income group that is able to pay the rental that will be required by the authorities that administer the act.[10]

The legislation was interpreted according to Mr. Pepper's understanding until 1949 and the housing authorities prospered. In 1949, Congress worried that public housing competed with private housing, insisted that the Walsh view be adopted. The families to be served were to be those of the lowest income. But where was the money to come from?

Senator Joe McCarthy, an opponent of public housing, but with a demagogue's need to portray himself as a champion of the masses, made the following suggestion:

> [I]f we are to accomplish the purpose desired we must add an amendment to the bill so as to provide, in cases where the incomes are so low that in selecting those who most need the housing, we get down below what is called economic rent . . . we must advance a step further in granting a subsidy and make the subsidy cover not merely the cost of amortization . . . but where it is found necessary . . . make the subsidy sufficient to cover a part of the cost of administration.[11]

The amendment placed proponents of the legislation in a predicament. Were they or were they not interested in helping the very poor? If they chose the amendment, it would take more money to serve the same number of households. They would then be open to sharp attacks from Mr. McCarthy's Republican colleagues on the high cost and limited coverage of the program. If they accepted the amendment and didn't ask for money, the inequity to all those who were eligible and would not receive assistance would be intensified. If they rejected the amendment, which they ultimately did, how would they serve the very poor. The proponents mumbled about good management and threw the problem into the future:

> No one could estimate what would be required. . . . An open-ended authorization would therefore appear to be necessary.

> To authorize annual contributions without any limitation would be a most un-businesslike procedure. Public housing should be run on a business-like basis, and the Congress should fix a definite limit to the commitments which it is authorizing.

> If future experience should prove that larger contributions are necessary in order to meet the urgent needs, the facts can be presented to Congress for such action as appear suitable.[12]

The subsequent years were lean years for public housing. The very poor did arrive in public housing and the subsidies were inadequate in many projects. Money was needed to pay the operating as well as the debt service costs. A prudent management solution was found. Instead of requiring the return of excess subsidy from projects in which the full debt service was more than what was "strictly needed" at a time when the debt service subsidy was insufficient in other projects, the PHAs would consolidate their contracts and the successful projects would subsidize the unsuccessful ones.

The consolidation of contracts effectively eliminated the ability to oversee the financial operations of local public housing authorities. It put HUD in a position of doling out money with blindfolds. HUD does not know and has no way of finding out the amount of subsidy that is allocated to any tenant or any unit, let alone to a particular tenant in a particular unit. It merely postponed the day of reckoning.

By the late 1960s both the PHAs and their tenants were hurting. Public housing had originally had a requirement that 20 percent of income should be paid as rent. This uniform ratio made sense in the early years when all the projects were new and few of the tenants were very poor households. Time, prosperity, and a new tenant selection policy made the system an anachorism. The original tenants incomes and families were growing. Public housing could only offer a deteriorating physical and social environment, small units (because of the original cost limits were based on a unit rather than a room basis) and higher rents.

Site selection difficulties and the inability to provide better maintenance (since the PHAs needed every penny to cover the cost of maintaining the older and elderly building in which rents did not fully cover the operating expenses) left lower rents as the only alternative to retain moderate income tenants. PHAs were given the freedom to change from fixed ratios to fixed rents. These "ceiling rents" were, however, no match to the attractiveness of the private market.

At the same time, the fixed rents caused problems for the lower-income tenants who remained in public housing. They were now bearing heavy burdens (high ratios) for low quality units. It should come as no surprise that many of the urban rioters came from public housing projects. Senator Brooke, a member of the Riot Commission, after visiting a number of projects introduced legislation that would have limited the rents to 25 percent of income and provide $75 million in relief to PHAs.

In 1969, although the Senate passed the 25 percent limit and authorized the $75 million, the House bill had the 25 percent limit and a
provision that clarified HUD's authority to pay 2 percent over the debt
service as an annual subsidy. HUD foreseeing financial troubles, wanted
to put Congress on notice that it might have to give stopgap relief to
fifteen cities that were running at a deficit. The Conference Committee
did not authorize any specific figure but indicated that HUD should use
its authority only to cover operating deficits and to make up the difference
between operating expenses and 25 percent of income in the cases where
rent was being reduced. The Conference Committee, forging into a new
sea of red ink, sought to shift blame and found its scapegoat. It was
"management."

> The committee is deeply concerned over cases of lax management in many public
> housing projects which have led to high operating costs, deterioration of property and
> an intolerable environment for the families living there . . . Much of the blame for
> these conditions lie with project and local government officials. Too frequently
> individual projects have filled up with problem families to the exclusion of others
> with resulting vacancies which have caused local deficits.

HUD, to the chagrin of Senator Brooke and to the pain of PHAs,
interpreted its authority quite stringently. The new money was limited to
PHAs that were in trouble as of 4 December 1969 (the day the legislative
change was enacted into law) and only if they demonstrated that satisfactory standards of management and tenant responsibility would be
achieved. HUD also redefined income to reduce exclusions and deductions thereby reducing the fiscal drain. HUD was so successful that it
only obligated $7 million.

HUD's victory in its first battle of the bulge turned out to be pyrrhic.
Senator Brooke was back with a second amendment. Congress enacted
the Housing and Urban Development Act of 1970 which re-redefined
income and authorized an additional $75 million. HUD continued in its
fiscally prudent ways and by early 1971, sixty one authorities, that owned
400,000 units, were insolvent.

By the middle of 1971, Congress began to realize how costly the
bailout was becoming. The Senate Appropriations Committee chided
HUD for its lack of administrative control. The effect of the desire for
greater control was to speed the outlay of federal funds. Instead of
looking at budgets after the money was spent while the PHAs dangled
in the wind, HUD improved its management and moved to forward

funding. The combination of retroactive and forward funding in the fall of 1971 resulted in a HUD budget request to OMB that hit three figures (in the millions) and the following letter from Caspar Weinberger, then head of OMB, to Secretary Romney in November 1971, "While the need may well exist for operating subsidies at the level requested [$215 million], I am concerned that we lack a clear understanding of the long term federal role and objective in subsidizing the operation of public housing."

Congress was not rushing forward in its funding. In the spring of 1972, although it criticized HUD both for a laxity of funding and auditing, it never got around to appropriating the $170 million HUD had requested. By the end of June, HUD had run out of money and PHAs were forced to make deeper cuts in maintenance. It was not until the fall that Congress appropriated $150 million.

The moratorium came and went. In the spring of 1974, HUD came asking for $430 million to meet the projected deficits. Nevertheless, even the projectors guessed that the amount might be over $100 million too low, as a HUD official explained, "We've got to get a handle on where we're going with operating costs."

The seventies and eighties were marked by an intensified emphasis on sound management. The campaign was on two fronts—reducing the need for revenue by increasing the income of PHAs and imposing some limit as to two open-ended authorizations—operating subsidies and capital improvements.

In 1974, Congress, tried to turn the clock back to the good old days. It ordered HUD to instruct the housing authorities to establish tenant selection criteria that assured a "broad range of income" in each project. Morality, mathematics, and good local management got in the way. In 1979, the General Accounting Office found that the attempt was a failure since "no simple solution exists to motivate housing agencies to house a broad range of low-income families instead of the poorest households. . . . Formidable problems of a moral and administrative nature exist."[13]

The policy was predicated on the assumption that the poor are mathematical idiots. Two families arrive at the doorstep of a PHA. The only difference between the families is that one has an income of $16,000 and the other has an income of $4,000. Let us assume the PHA has two vacancies. The first is a brand new apartment located in a pleasant middle-class neighborhood. The second apartment is close to a half-a-century old in shabby condition and located in a neighborhood in which even dope pushers fear to tread. The very bad project has more than its fair share of the very poor so it is offered to the family with the higher income. Under the rules, in the seventies, the rent of each of the units was 25 percent of income. The "role-model" family is asked to pay $333 a month. Is there any likelihood that the family will chose the unit? If the PHA wants to snare this tenant it will have to offer more attractive bait —the new unit. The $4,000 family is then offered the old unit for $75 a month. Its an offer the family cannot refuse if it wishes to have a roof over its head. The correlation between tenants with very low income and the very bad condition of the project may be more a result of pathological rent policies than of the pathologies of the poor.

The tenant placement policy is good local management. The higher income tenant's contribution will exceed the operating costs thereby giving the PHA more breathing room. The fact that it is perverse Federal policy—if one includes the cost of the debt service subsidy, the higher income tenant gets the larger subsidy—is not the local manager's concern. He didn't create the system.

Evenhandedly, the system often works against the local PHA. Congress had mandated 25 percent as a *maximum* rent to income ratio in public housing, it used the same 25 percent to set a *minimum rent* in the Section 236 program. And, in the Section 8 program it was the standard. In the 1980s it was decided to serve primarily very low-income households. In order to squeeze a little more income out of the poor the rent standard in all the programs was set at 30 percent of income.

This has two results. Public housing loses its most successful tenants since the private market alternatives for them are better. They are usually replaced by lower-income households so that the total take of the PHA and federal government is reduced. Second, it continues the internecine warfare among housing subsidy programs. When a new project is located in the vicinity of an older subsidized project, there is an exodus from the old to the new. As the following letter from a PHA official indicates the same phenomenon can occur with older units in the Section 8 program in which the fair market rent is always above the median rent in the locality:

> Your Section 8 program is drawing people out of our local housing projects. You are creating an occupancy problem because your Section 8 Existing units are better than our public housing projects. Unless you are willing to subsidize us with greater

operating subsidies, because our occupancy factor has gone so far down, our local housing projects won't be able to make a go of it.[14]

To add insult to injury, HUD then admonishes local authorities for their high vacancy rates, without realizing that in some cases the fault is at the Federal level.

Congress, in 1974, finally faced the issue of operating subsidies and asked HUD to develop a formula. This was a very difficult task. There is no way of knowing whether high costs are a result of controllable factors such as a high level of services, poor cost controls, waste and fraud, or uncontrollable factors such as inflation. In the real world there is countervailing pressure against high costs because they must be reflected in a tenant's rent. In public housing there are no market signals—the government pays the deficit.

HUD developed the Performance Funding System (PFS). The standard was incestuous—other public housing projects. The reference point was a "well-managed authority" in the previous year (an atypical one since HUD was still playing budget games with the PHAs.) The measurement was subjective—the satisfaction of HUD Field staff PHA personnel and tenants with the PHA. The assumption was that a well-managed authority would be more efficient and have a lower costs (adjusting for such uncontrollable factors as the age and the height of the buildings). It was true in 1974.

But, it was not true in 1978. There were no significant cost differences among authorities. In fact as HUD reported, "Many of the high and low performers in 1973 shifted to the opposite group in 1978 to a degree that suggested unreliable measurement of performance or large shifts in performance or both." The performance element fell out. Only the name remained for what today is a funding allocation system. PFS had turned into a $2.5 billion pumpkin. Congress, like the young prince in Cinderella, has continued to search for the silver slipper. Section 524 of the Cranston-Gonzalez National Affordable Housing Act, asks the secretary to study the funding system and to compare and contrast the public housing and Section 8 funding system. As in the Cinderella story the Prince's first stop is with the ugly sisters.

A final item on the efficacy of good management is the relationship between maintenance and capital improvements in public housing. It makes very good sense for a PHA manager to let some of the buildings deteriorate so that he can qualify for modernization funding. And here again the lack of a pricing system bedevils federal managers. The private entrepreneur has limits and guides as to the level of capital investment. The cost must bear some reasonable relationship to the expected rents or the value of building. In the case of public housing, the building has a negative equity (rents don't cover operating costs) and the improvements don't result in increased rents. If its free, tenants want only the very best and PHAs have a strong desire to do a swell job and spend the largest amount possible. Priceless housing is a costly commodity.

Table 6.1
What Has Modernization Purchased

Funding FY 1981–88 (Millions)		Modernization Per Unit*	Vacancy Rate	
			1985	Current
Boston **	$168.2	$11,769	18%	10%
Providence	46.5	7,741	12	29
New Haven	33.8	9,248	13	21
Bridgeport	40.5	15,667	3	24
Camden	59.6	13,169	17	18
Newark	111.4	9,371	38	39
Washington	95.8	8,614	15	22
Philadelphia	157.0	7,034	9	14
New Orleans	66.5	4,400	2	11
Tampa	25.4	2,600	3	12
Detroit	56.7	5,897	32	41
Cleveland	79.7	7,155	23	21
Chicago	135.0	3,595	12	16
Virgin Islands	109.2	24,100	15	17

Source: Modernization Approval Data System (MADS) FY 1988 Reports

* The per-unit represents all units under management. The numbers, therefore, understate the dollars spent on the units that were modernized.

** The case of Boston is due to its exceptional status of having been run during most of the 1980s by a judicial receiver.

One would think that if large amounts of money were spent on rehabilitating and modernizing buildings at a PHA, that the buildings would become more attractive to tenants and that the vacancy rate would drop. As Table 6.1 indicates such is not always the case.

The PHAs listed in the Table are admittedly HUD's most troublesome authorities. Given the amount of money and attention HUD has lavished on these authorities it does point out the futility of HUD's monitoring activities given the undefined division of functions between the local housing agencies and the Federal government all the way back from square one.

HUD and Congress have thrown in the towel and come up with another formula, this one to allocate modernization money. This one is also only theoretically related to actual needs (only New York City had a sufficient number of inspected projects to give precise needs estimates.)16 The new Comprehensive Modernization Funding Formula will hopefully work as well as the Performance Funding Formula.

Even good management in this framework will often lead to counterproductive results. Managers focused on their projects don't see the city around them. At the same time PHAs are modernizing obsolete projects, private landlords are boarding up buildings or are allowing the city to take them rather than continue to pay the real estate taxes. The money being spent to lavishly modernize public housing units can be better spent outside its walls. The $20,000 and up (the maximum is in the $60,000 range) going to public housing modernization can fix many a roof and many a boiler in private rental housing and the resulting rent increases will be far smaller and the subsidies needed to place tenants in these dwelling far smaller than in public housing. The end result of a successful public housing modernization is likely to be a longer waiting list.

Given the jerry-built framework of current housing programs one can be thankful that HUD does not have a history of excellent management. A good deal more damage could have been the result.

Notes

1. *Lantos Hearings*, part 1, 568.
2. "The Missions and Management of HUD," *CRS Report for Congress*, 10. (5 July 1990.)
3. The players in the starting lineup of the New York Yankees in 1988 had an average salary of $694,000. Halberstam, David, *Summer of '49*, 16.

4. Arnold Hirsch, "The Causes of Racial Segregation: A Historical Perspective," in U.S. Civil Rights Commission, *Issues of Housing Discrimination*, 70. (November 1985)

5. Christi Harlan, "Giant Trammel Crow Finds Texas Slump Only Round One," *Wall Street Journal*, September 26, 1990, 1,10.

6. "The Deregulation Experience - A Roundtable Discussion with Alfred Kahn," *Harris Conversations for the 90s* 2, 67.

7. *Hearings on HUD-Space-Science-Veteran Appropriations Act for 1973, Part 3 before a Subcomm. of the H.R. Approp. Comm.*, 92nd Cong., 2nd sess., 1364.

8. Milton Semer, Julian Zimmerman, Ashley Foard and John Frantz, "A Review of Federal Subsidized Housing Programs," in *Housing in the Seventies Working Papers*, vol. 1, 96.

9. See "Abuses in the Administration of the Passaic NJ Housing Authority," *Hearings before the Employment and Housing Subcomm. of the House Comm. on Government Operations*, 101st Cong., 2nd sess., 1990.

10. Quoted in "A Review of Federally Subsidized Programs," 101, 1013.

11. 95 *Cong. Rec.*, Part 4:4808, (1949).

12. Ibid., 4809.

13. GAO, *Serving a Broader Range of families in Public Housing Could Reduce Operating Subsudies*, 3.

14. *Senate Appropriations Committee Hearings 94th Cong. 2nd sess., HUD Appropriations, Fiscal Year, 1977*, 187.

15. HUD, *Alternative Operating Subsidy Systems for the Public Housing Program*, 13.

16. "Comp Mod Funding Formula Proposed," *Housing Affairs Letter*, 3 May 1991, 7.

7

No Better People and No Greater Honesty

The Cost of On-the-Job-Training

The notion is abroad in the land that HUD is peopled with incompetents and corruptibles. If we could only get some new and better people many of the problems would disappear.

In truth, HUD has been headed up by a group of very distinguished and able Americans: Robert Weaver, Robert Wood, George Romney, James Lynn, Carla Hills, Patricia Roberts Harris, Moon Landrieu, Samuel Pierce, and Jack Kemp. All came with impressive resumes; two of the group were presidential candidates before taking the job. Robert Weaver and Robert Wood went on to become distinguished professors at major universities, James Lynn went on to head up OMB and to be listed by Fortune, as one of the top fifty executives in America; Carla Hills became the U.S. Trade representative and Pat Harris had been a law school dean and went on to become secretary of health and human services.

Although they were distinguished, few were well versed in housing. This is a systemic flaw. As Henry Kissinger, wrote before he entered government service,

[O]nly in the rarest cases is there a relationship between high position and great substantive knowledge. Most of our elective officials had to spend so much of their energy getting elected that they can give little political attention to the substance of what they are going to do when they get elected.

[T]he typical political leader of the contemporary managerial society is a man with a strong will, a high capacity to get himself elected, but no very great conception of what he is going to do when he gets into office. This is true of many of the cabinet officials.[1]

The knowledge problem is compounded by the fact that the typical secretary is unlikely to have the time to think about the policies of his agency. As a career executive commented:

[A]s quickly as political executives come into office, they have to resist pressures that would make them prisoners of their agency. They have to meet so many demands, make so many contacts, and attend so many meetings all at once they have little time for such matters as defining objectives. There is an inexorable Gresham's Law of public administration: Day-to-day problems tend to drive out long-range planning.[2]

The Good Old Days Were Terrible

There is a tendency to look back nostalgically to the pre-Pierce era in the 1970s as a golden age of administration at HUD. Thus, when Carla Hills appeared before the House Hearings investigating the Pierce scandals, Representative Lantos greeted her with the comment, "I am looking eagerly to our witness today to find out . . . what is missing in today's structure that, obviously, was in place in prior administrations that made it function . . . in the taxpayer's interests and the government interest."[3] Actually, it was a decade of on-the job-training with the nation paying the tuition in terms of wastefully poor housing programs. A study for the House Appropriations Committee in 1977 (a year after Ms. Hills left office) opened with the following paragraph:

Over the last several years a number of problems have arisen in connection with Federal housing programs suggesting that the programs are poorly designed, run in a lax manner, incapable of being properly administered by the Government or all of these factors combined.[4]

The decade started out well. George Romney had done his training in the sixties in bringing to life the high production interest subsidy programs that turned into management disasters in the early seventies. He was, however, a unique individual. He could admit that he made a mistake. The admission that he had been "brainwashed" about Vietnam cost him his frontrunner position and ended his race for the Republican presidential nomination against Richard Nixon in 1968.

In the fall of 1971, he realized that he had been brainwashed about housing programs. The programs which he had initially enthusiastically endorsed he concluded were lemons. He told the National Association of Realtors at a convention in Honolulu:

In 1969 and 1970 we rapidly accelerated our brand new subsidized housing programs. . . .On the surface, this seemed a highly successful effort. We built more subsidized housing in 3-1/2 years than in the previous 31 years of Federal housing programs. But, unfortunately, the 235 and 236 programs were untested. . . .We have discovered through bitter experience that there is a world of difference in operating . . . in the older central cities as to operating them in the suburbs. And importantly, we should assess the fiscal effect. . . . The maximum run-out cost is approaching one hundred billion dollars. . . . We need alternative methods. . . . We must ask what are getting for our money with our current programs. While Section 235 and 236 programs appear to be working in many parts of the country, these programs are not subject to the usual competitive market disciplines. The public housing area is also in crisis.

He was on the verge of a new policy, when he was removed by Nixon in 1972. After a landslide victory, the latter had little use for anyone but the most trustworthy.

James Lynn had the golden opportunity of writing on a clean slate and he chalked up the most costly and inequitable program in the history of HUD— the Section 8 New Construction Program. In retrospect he wasted tens of billions of dollars. He was trying to learn and change the system at the same time. As Robert Bell, who studied the moratorium period concluded,

The team charged with developing alternative policies needed either a structured adversary process designed to explore the arguments for and against all plausible courses of action or explicit guidance from policy level officials about which policies to study. Without either, the team lacked focus. Reflecting on the organization of the study, one HUD executive remarked, "It soon became apparent that the thing had started off on the wrong track. The hurry in trying to get it off the ground made it misdirected. . . . The first thing you should do in a study of this kind is write an options paper for the president. That will lead you to the right questions to ask. The process was started in the reverse direction—the option paper was supposed to be the end point. If HUD had begun this way, it might have made better use of its staff and produced a more policy relevant report."[5]

Hills and Harris can be faulted for getting "Lynn's folly" up and running. They had to pledge allegiance to the HUD programs in order to pass muster with the Congressional committees considering their nomination. By intelligence and diligence they succeeded in winning the confidence of Congress by implementing poorly crafted programs.

Sam Pierce, in contrast to his more energetic predecessors, can almost be considered a success in the area of housing policy. He was the hands-off administrator, par excellence. In some ways it was not a bad approach since

during his tenure the major housing policy change since the 1930s occurred—
the ending of new construction programs. Unfortunately, he didn't realize or
didn't care how subject to abuse his portfolio of discretion-prone smaller
programs were.

The Crook Factor

In all of the cases examined, there were the garden variety crooks and
chiselers. In the Section 608 program the criminal figures were on the inside.
At the top of the totem pole was the assistant commissioner for multifamily
housing, Clyde C. Powell. Before coming to FHA, he was a minor league
crook. During his tenure he became major league. Although his salary was
less than $10,000, his bonuses, in the form of payoffs from developers, ran
into the hundreds of thousands of dollars.

In the Title I home-improvement case the criminals were on the outside.
the suede shoe boys and the tin men were bilking consumers across the length
and breadth of the country. It takes only a small percentage of rotten apples,
when over a million homes a year are involved, to ruin the entire vat and
cause a stench that reaches from California to the banks of the Potomac.

In the Section 235 subsidized homeownership program for poor people,
there was the instigation of panic selling and the over-appraisal of shoddy
merchandise. In the Newark office, the chief appraiser and 10 other appraisers
were indicted for taking bribes.

There were few criminal scandals in the Section 236 program, although
in some areas, such as New York, a corrupt selection process was an open
secret. The Lantos committee probed why the Yonkers Housing Authority
was required to award a construction contract to the highest bidding contractor (JOBCO) before HUD would approve the contract. A former employee
informed the committee that this had been going on for decades.

> In those days, HUD would turn down a project proposed by a worthy sponsor on a
> good site if the proposed general contractor was found . . . to be unacceptable by the
> "The Office." Alternately, and here that meant either Monticciolo [the Regional
> Administrator during the 1980s] or Naclerio—HUD would arrange a "marriage"
> between a sponsor of Joe's or Al's choosing. That's how the game was played even
> then . . .

> Similarly, Monticciolo's connection goes way back—probably to the 1960's. Cer-
> tainly, every senior person on the technical staff, and many junior people as well,
> knew that JOBCO was Joe's favorite developer.[6]

On a smaller scale, FHA officials or closing attorney's rec room have been known to be paneled by developers eager to get to the head of the line for commitments or for early closings.

In the 1980s, there was DuBois Gilliams, who headed up the Urban Development Action Grant program (UDAG) who testified before the Lantos Hearings while on leave from Lampoc Prison. There was also the much publicized activity of Robbin HUD—the good-hearted closing agent who was so busy doing good and quoting the Bible that she failed to send to HUD $5 million in proceeds. She had many poorer and equally infamous cohorts.

HUD is by no means unique. For the dishonestly disposed holders of discretion or information opportunities abound. John Ruskin wrote about the "splendid mendacity of mankind." Bribery has been known to occur in the letting of government contracts and in the sale of its land and resources. Gifts have been given to inspectors and law enforcement officials who saw no evils and to tax collectors who did not question questionable deductions. As Herbert Kaufman has noted the opportunities to force gifts also abound, "Permits can be delayed, licenses held up, deliberations protracted, proceedings prolonged unless rewards are offered. Inspectors can charge violations by the score if their requests for payoffs are rejected."[7]

This is not to say that the government need be at the mercy of the crooked. From October 1984 to March 1989, 1,864 alleged perpetrators (to use police-speak) were indicted and there were 1,626 convictions of folks for their HUD related activities. However, just as the cost of defense, albeit necessary, doesn't buy a better country, the necessary cost spent for surveillance, do not buy better programs.

> We have attempted to suppress such practices. Many of them, such as bribery, have been declared crimes, but criminal penalties deter only if there is a good chance that the forbidden act will be detected. Corrupt bargains, however, are difficult to detect. We have therefore gone beyond deterrence; we have tried, by elaborate procedural safeguards, to make the commission of these acts almost impossible. These tactics are executed through torrents of laws and regulations and cumbersome procedures; it is sometimes said the prevention costs more than ailment. But our attitude toward public property is typified by the comments of a famous economist [Arthur Okun] ordinarily inclined to reject costs that exceed benefits in dollar terms: "The . . . [OMB] *should* spend $20 to prevent the theft of $1 of public funds." Not only are public property and public discretion held to have a special moral status; they occupy a special political position because abusing them eats away at the foundations of representative government.[8]

The Character of Staffing

The problems of HUD go beyond the question of criminality. During the 1980s, at the upper levels of the department appointees came and went with the seasons. Lower-level appointees were characterized by their loyalty (from campaign baggage-handler to deputy assistant secretary and beyond) rather than by their knowledge. Reductions in force followed up by sloppy reorganization cut muscle as well as fat out of the ranks of the civil service.

During the 1980s, the position of assistant secretary for housing was held by ten different people (including acting assistant secretaries) during the eight years of the Pierce Administration. The average length of stay in the position was less than 8.4 months. Between January 1986 and May 1987, the under secretary's position was vacant. During this period the three-person troika that Secretary Pierce had set up to decide on funding the moderate rehab program had only one person with continuity, Deborah Dean.[9]

At the civil service level, many believe (especially former employees) that there was a "brain drain" during the 1980s that contributed to scandals.[10] Many left or were forced out because their jobs were vestigial when HUD moved out of the business of insuring new subsidized construction. Unfortunately, HUD failed to realize that to monitor a coinsurance program more than a skeleton force of underwriters and appraisers were necessary.

The conventional viewpoint, that the bureaucracy hamstrings new administrations is more a testament to the inexperience of the new administrators than to the nature of the bureaucracy. The case studies give many examples of a civil service that gets the job done. When given a clear message, 608 projects are developed, homes are insured in the inner city in the Section 235 program, hundreds of thousands of insured subsidized units are produced under the Section 236 program, and in the Section 8 new construction and substantial rehabilitation programs hundreds of thousands of units are built.

Often there is fidelity to a fault. Loyalty at the expense of memory. Fearing the accusation of "nay-saying" or "skepticism," civil servants will stay silent and let the institution rush headlong into the abyss. Others will often be all too eager to curry favor with the new team. This goes beyond the question of policy. The silence of the technical staff in the face of abuses (the above mentioned letter about contractor selection in New York was written by an anonymous former HUD employee), the doctoring of UDAG applications, and the flight by the same senior career executive to his political superior to inform on a possible "whistleblowing" subordinate (who was too zealous in checking on whether Lance Wilson had the authority to make $79 million commitments for PaineWebber)[11] are examples of acts that are explainable but not excusable. Careers need to be furthered (few whistleblowers win distinguished service awards and matters that require investigation often do not make the inspector's agenda), and children must be fed, housed, and educated. The ultimate rationale is that of the good soldier, "if I don't do it someone else will." However, as Dennis Thompson, in *Political Ethics and Public Office*, has written, "When these lower-level officials come to recognize how certain bureaucratic routines cause them to perform in morally questionable ways, they acquire, as do other officials who work within defective structures, a specific responsibility to call attention to the defects, even if they cannot correct them."[12] Unfortunately, the civil service system does not test for character.

As to competence, John Rhinelander, an undersecretary in the Ford Administration, saw the difficulty of getting able people as a relatively new problem:

> For 12 years there has been bipartisan—President Carter and President Reagan—dumping on the Federal Civil Service. It was really quite the order of the day. It made the service unpopular.
>
> The pay situation, we're all familiar with that problem. I tell the young lawyers in my law firm that when I first got out of law school and clerked at the Supreme Court, I was paid exactly the same amount as a starting lawyer on Wall Street. They found it totally amazing. . .[13]

His knowledge of the law is not counter-balanced by his knowledge of history. The problem of salary is endemic. Things are not that much different from the situation in the mid-1950s, when a Brookings Institution report concluded:

> Government executives are employed at salary levels well below those in private industry in roughly comparable positions. In all likelihood government will never be able to reward its executives with salaries as high as those available in industry, and perhaps it never should. Nevertheless, existing wide discrepancies in executive salaries deter promising men and women from pursuing careers in government, make it more difficult to keep able executives . . ., and obstruct the interchange of executive personnel between private life and public service. Salary differentials would, however, be less significant if prestige of government employment was greater. Not only must government executives anticipate financial sacrifices, but he must also expect low prestige and considerable abuse and harassment from Congress and the public, who will occasionally question his integrity, the sincerity of his convictions, and his suitability for public employment.[14]

Discretion and Control

When all is said and done, the problem at HUD has little to do with criminality, staffing, or competence. For every dollar stolen or misappropriated as a result of fraud and abuse, thousands have been wasted as a result of poor programs and policy. We are spending far to much time on procedure and precious little on substance.

The continuous cries of windfall profits have been misguided. The problem has been the locus of the profits rather than the existence of profits. The profits in programs ranging from the Section 608 to Section 8 have not resulted from marketplace activities. They were not rewards for wise investments or for the delivery of an excellent product. Instead they have in the main been garnered even before the product has been market tested. The ability to mortgage out in Section 608, the syndication of tax losses in Section 236 and the sale of tax credits in the Section 8 made the housing aspect an aside. The prize came not from producing a winning project but rather from winning the project. The reward came from receiving the commitment not the commitment to housing (as the case of Robin Hook illustrates) and the skill that was required was HUD and Washington savvy.

When competition was removed from the market, it was placed in the halls of HUD. The story behind the headlines is that HUD when it acts in the housing area is involved in a negative-sum game. Every community qualifies and receives block grants. In the case of housing, there are very many more losers than winners. Even when the programs are running at full throttle such as the Section 608 program in the late forties, the interest subsidy programs in the sixties and early seventies and the Section 8 new construction program in the late seventies, there are many more applicants than recipients. When the brakes are applied, as during the Pierce administration, the discretion factor rises exponentially.

Since the winners have a leg up on the market and are likely to win big, when abuses occur the natural reaction is to put into place checks and balances throughout the process. There is a strong temptation to get rid of wrongdoing by making sure that there are no winners. In this type of atmosphere no one can get into trouble for being slow in approving a project. Discretion becomes caution and timidity. As a developer sadly recounted recent history,

> In December of 1989, HUD allowed tax credit funding to expire for projects throughout the country seeking HUD subsidies—more than 50 projects by some counts—rather than make a decision to fund those projects and be second-guessed

by Congress and the media as to whether the subsidy allowed excessive developer profits. A lot of families will suffer from that decision, but since they aren't well organized and most of them don't even know who they are, HUD seems to be vindicated in its assessment it would be more at risk in approving these projects than in letting them die. Ironically, Congressional hearings designed to expose abuses in HUD programs meant for poor people have resulted in termination of almost all HUD multi-family programs for low, moderate and middle income tenants instead of reform of those programs.[15]

Even when the secretary is a champion of capitalism, no one is to get rich doing the Sovereign's work or if anyone is to get rich as a result of Federal largesse let it be a poor person and serve as an example of an American success story. The incentives of the programs are tinkered with to assure that a private developer (or a Public Housing Agency) doesn't get a penny more than he deserves. As Sheldon Baskin a developer and scholar told the Senate Investigating Committee,

As a young man studying economics, it always seemed to me that socialism made a lot of sense, especially as a way of avoiding the grinding poverty for some that so often seems to be endemic in capitalism. What bothered me was the many *socialists* who seemed to be much more concerned that some people might be too rich than that other people were too poor. Similarly on the subsidized housing issue, there are too many who are so concerned about windfalls that they would rather see more people ill-housed and homeless than take a chance that someone will get "too rich" housing the poor, whatever their definition of "too rich." The irony is that this category now encompasses both a substantial number of so-called housing or tenant advocates *and* conservative, business oriented top level administrators at HUD.[16]

Ironically, if there is anything a federal agency is not particularly adept at, it is fine finger work. The rosiest result of the effort to fine tune and coordinate subsidies is longer regulatory delays, more rolls of red tape, many levels of review and a shrinking away from decision making. In the interim the subsidy partners at the state or local level are likely to leave or recalculate their subsidies so that they also are only paying their fair share. Michael Stegman, mixing mathematics and liquor, drew an even bleaker picture at a housing conference sponsored by Fannie Mae: "Not every agency and financing source that participates in a project can be, in Reggie Jackson's words, "'the straw that stirs the drink.' Like an equation that has too many unknowns to have a unique solution, a creatively financed tax credit project that requires virtually all financing components to be locked in before any will be committed cannot be underwritten."[17]

In an attempt to forbid speech with evil-doers, the agency ceases to speak. As a housing newsletter reports:

Officials reconsider proposed rule for implementing a controversial 1989 HUD Reform Act provision after a *Housing Affairs* story reveals gag effect on HUD staff.

Section 103 says that HUD employees "shall not knowingly" disclose information concerning the selection process for financial assistance and multifamily mortgages.

Publication of final rule is delayed until it can be clarified and revised to avoid further "information paralysis" sources tell us. . . .

HUD's Ethics Office, which will oversee responsibilities for Section 103, won't comment on the delay.18

To put the problem in more general terms, David Packard, a former deputy secretary of defense who chaired the President's Blue Ribbon Commission on Defense remarked to a GAO sponsored round table on "Ethics and the Defense Industry":

I don't think you can make the Department look good by making the industry look bad. . . . When you try to deal with procurement problems through ever-increasing inspections and the imposition of penalties, you can do serious damage. We found that purchasing people and contractors had already become much more cautious. Contracts that should have been negotiated in a few months were taking a year or more. This added to costs, simply because time is money. But much more important, the delay in placing contracts reduced our technological lead over the Soviets, which had already been shrinking in recent years.[19]

Acting with Discretion

Perhaps it is time for HUD to act with discretion and realize that what needs reform is the framework of Federal housing assistance. Scores of inspectors and reams of regulations will not give HUD better control of the 3,000 housing agencies and the thousands of private developers within its realm. If quality subsidy delivery vehicles are going to be our number one product, the process will have to begin at the design stage rather than at the inspection station.

Whenever a subsidy program provides someone with a large benefit and the process involves a great deal of discretion, temptation rears its ugly (or beautiful) head. When a program is structured so that only a small percentage of either the developers or the consumers are selected, we are asking for trouble. When we bestow upon private entities the credit card of the federal government we should expect that they will go on a spending spree and they will have the bags and HUD will have the bills. If HUD entices, it will surely be seduced.

A large part of the red tape that ensnares programs represents attempts to secure movable objects from the sticky fingered among the general populace. Often the government only acts to rectify past mistakes—to fight the last war. In response to the "mortgaging out" expose of the fifties, the paper wall of cost certification was built. It turned out to be a Maginot Line against developers who used the latest tax vehicles to outflank it.

It is time to realize that our road is a rut. The real housing scandal is that after 50 years so few of America's poor are being assisted. And even of those assisted, a substantial number are treated to shabby housing or still paying a crushing percentage of their income. A recent Congressionally mandated GAO study found that close to a third of Section 8 subsidy recipients were paying more that 40 percent of their adjusted income for housing (the top (or bottom) twenty unlucky households in the sample were averaging 74 percent of their income.[20]

In order to improve on our past record we must proceed by a different path. I would suggest that it is time for HUD is to leave the project selection process and let the marketplace chose which subsidized developer will succeed and which will fail. The success of public housing authorities should depend on how well they satisfy their consumers rather than how well they submit their requests for assistance. Since this sounds like the ravings of a libertarian, (or even worse, an economist) let me spend the last chapter in explanation.

Notes

1. "Bureaucracy and Policymaking: The Effect of Insiders and Outsiders on the Political Process," in Kissinger and Brodie, *Bureaucracy, Politics and Strategy*, 14.
2. Marver Bernstein, *The Job of the Federal Executive*, 13.
3. *Lantos Hearings*, part 3, 101.
4. Francis Parente, "Housing Management Problem Survey," *HUD-Independent Appropriations for 1978 Hearings*, part 8, 57.
5. *The Culture of Policy Deliberation*, 176.
6. *Lantos Hearings*, part 6 (appendix), 386.
7. Herbert Kaufman, *Red Tape*, 523.
8. Ibid.
9. HUD/Mod Rehab Investigating Subcommittee of the Senate Comm. on Banking, Housing and Urban Affairs, *Final Report and Recommendations*, 182 n. 61.
10. Ibid., 17071.
11. *Lantos Hearings*, part 5, 82.
12. Dennis Thompson, *Political Ethics and Public Office*, 644.
13. *Senate Investigating Comm.*, vol. 1, 42.
14. Bernstein, *Federal Executive*, 208.
15. Sheldon Baskin, *Senate Investigation*, vol. I, 227.

16. Ibid.
17. "The Excessive Cost of Creative Financing," *Housing Policy Debates*, vol. 2, Issue 2, 265. (1991).
18. *Housing Affairs Letter*, 3 May 1991, 4.
19. *The GAO Journal*, Spring 1988, 5, 7.
20. GAO, "Assisted Housing - Utility Allowances Often Fall Short of Actual Utility Expenses" vol. 1, 4. (March 1991)

PART III

HUD IN THE MARKETPLACE

8

HUD in the Marketplace

When there is a housing shortage and there are poor people who cannot afford decent housing, it seems obvious that we should build more housing for the poor. Hitting two birds with one stone is a simple and powerful idea. It is a maxim that every child learns and few adults forget. It is reinforced in the case of housing by two elements—goodness and greed—that have resulted in a powerful lobby supporting the need to build housing that poor people can afford.

Alas, attempting to hit two birds with one shot violates the elementary rules of gunnery. It is a sure way to miss both targets. In the case of subsidized housing, the errant missile has often gone astray and ruptured the fabric of communities and neighborhoods. The results have been neither philanthropic nor all that profitable. Making a poor family "housing rich" by providing it with new housing goes far beyond any concept of philanthropy. And for all the billions spent and all the windfalls, HUD may have placed some developers on top of the foothills of wealth, but, nowhere near the mountaintop where the *Forbes* list of 400 reside (Lance Wilson ranked 560th in compensation among PaineWebber employees.)[1]

The approach is expensive and unfair both to rich and poor alike. The situation is analogous to a meal ticket program in which for 10 percent of the recipients, the meal ticket is honored at the best restaurants (living in the newest apartments). For twenty percent, the ticket is honored at fast food establishments (the remaining subsidized units). For the balance, it is honored at soup kitchens and at the Thanksgiving and Christmas dinners at the Salvation Army.

It is not only unfair to the poor. HUD was asked to respond to the following letter in the early 1970s:

> As a member of the usually silent majority. . . I believe that I should bring to your attention some things . . . that should be corrected. . . . I am a young man of 25, employed as a personnel supervisor of a growing concern where my wife is also employed. Between us we earn approximately $11,000 and live within our means in a modest three-room apartment in a 40 year old building. A new [subsidized] housing area is now open for tenants who earn less than $3,000 per annum . . . These apartments are as large or larger than ours and in beautiful condition and the rent is actually less than what I am paying. Is it possible that this situation can be justified.

Taxing Paul to help Peter to obtain decent housing may rest on sweet virtue. Taxing Paul to help Peter to obtain better housing than Paul is a bitter pill.

In the context of corruption, programs that aim at supplying new housing for poor people are fraught with danger. The inverse relationship between the size of the subsidy and the size of the program means there will be many more applicants than winners. The selection of the few projects that will be well insulated from the discipline of the market involves a great deal of discretion. The dragon of temptation will be out of his lair.

Two Herds of Horses, Two Stacks of Carrots

Begin at the beginning. There is housing production and there is housing assistance. The focus of housing production is the creation of a new dwelling unit; its prime justification and purpose is the community's need for an additional *supply* of dwellings. The focus of housing assistance is the need by some citizens for a subsidy if they are to be able to afford decent housing; its prime justification is the community's sense of obligation to satisfy the *demand* of those citizens for suitable accommodations.

Unfortunately, we have made a fundamental error. We have combined the production and assistance function. The main thrust American housing policy has been to assist poor people by supplying them with new housing. In the 1980s, the Reagan Administration concluded that America had a sufficient supply of housing and, therefore, did not need a production program. It need only focus on the assistance side.

The error, however, remains deeply embedded in our housing policy. The catchword, at present, is "affordable housing." The latest law enacted is the Cranston-Gonzalez National Affordable Housing Act which has as one of its objectives "to increase the supply of decent housing that is affordable to low-income and moderate-income people." If the poor cannot afford food, we earmark assistance and give them food stamps. We don't create farms that only grow "affordable food" or build "affordable food" supermarkets where only the poor can shop. If the poor have a transportation problem we don't subsidize General Motors to build "affordable Buicks."

The premise that a housing supply program can only be justified if it is for the poor is a political one. Any production program aimed at the middle class will be met by the "horse and the swallow" analogy. We will be feeding the middle-income horse and the swallows, representing the poor, will feed on the drippings of the horse that filters through his system. This unattractive picture makes a difficult political sell.

The analogy is fortunately a false one. The true analogy is to two herds of horses and two stacks of carrots. The well-fed horses, the middle class, will be fed sparingly. They will receive only a small part of one of the stacks. The remainder will be reserved for the "lean horses." The housing that will be turned over to the poor as a result of the middle class being enticed into new housing will not pass through and out of the market since the poor will be receiving sufficient assistance to afford these older but good units.

Is there a housing shortage so that we need to fund a supply program? If one examines the national housing statistics there is ample evidence that the supply is ample. In the second quarter of 1990, the rental vacancy rate was 7 percent. It was even higher in the low-rent sector of the market—9.6 percent in the $200 to $249 range and 9.0 percent in the $259 to $299 range.[2]

There are, nevertheless, a number of good reasons to enact a supply program.

1. As a result of years of bombardment by testimony from interest groups and full page advertisements in the *Washington Post* and the *New York Times* by the Federal National Mortgage Association about the need for "affordable housing" there is a consensus in Congress (that was never moved by Reagan's beliefs) that there is a housing shortage.

2. What is true nationally may not be true in every locality. Housing markets are local in nature. There is no national market for housing. A vacancy in Dallas does not help a person looking for an apartment in San Francisco. There may be areas where the supply is very tight.

3. A large housing assistance program for the poor is dependent on a loose market. At present close to 40 percent of those who receive rent vouchers are unable to finding units that meet HUD standards.

4. In a tight market, a large injection of housing vouchers may have an inflationary effect and thereby increase program costs. The renters with incomes near and above the median income—who will not be eligible for a subsidy—will be double losers. They will have to pay for a subsidy program that results in an increase in their rents. A recent survey estimated that more than half the nation's 33 million renters would have to spend more than 30 percent of their income in order to afford the present HUD determined fair market rents in their communities.[3]

In spite of the lengthy and very expensive housing allowance experiment no answer was given regarding the inflationary affect of a large scale program. As John Kain noted,

> Not only did the housing requirement fail to increase the recipient's housing consumption by much, but they seem to have adversely affected participation, especially among household in greatest need.

> Having induced such a small increase in demand, the supply experiment had no perceptible impact on rents. . . .The experiment's finding to date are therefore of little or no help in assessing a national housing allowance program that would use a form of earmarking to induce a significant increase in housing expenditures.[4]

5. What was true yesterday may not be true tomorrow. The combination of liberal tax changes and liberal lending, by banks that are no more, resulted in a rental housing production boom. It produced a glut of housing in some places and high vacancies in most places. The change in the tax laws, and the shift in emphasis of the remaining banks from making loans to collecting on loans may result in a different supply scenario.

Tomorrow arrived in 1991. Fewer than 137,000 apartments were started in multifamily (five or more units) buildings. This is the lowest level since the U.S. Census started tracking the data in 1959. It is less than one sixth of the level in 1972 (906,000) and less than one half of the level recorded during the 1981–1982 recession (288,000).[5]

Some Supply Programs for an Age of Uncertainty

The design of a housing production program, for people who are presently decently housed, in places that we aren't certain need additional housing, changes all the ground rules that HUD has operated under in the past.

1. Unlike prior programs, where the heavy pile of subsidy meant that the developer was insulated from market conditions, the units in this program must make market sense.

2. Unlike prior programs, in which HUD greatly reduced the risk to the developer and expected in return a smaller profit from the developer, the developer's success will be determined by his knowledge and instincts. HUD should have no great expectations about limiting his profit.

3. Unlike prior programs, in which HUD was left holding the bag in the case the developer made a mistake, under these programs, the developers will be left holding their babies.

4. Unlike prior programs, in which the apartment is meant to serve the long term needs of low income tenants, the benefit to the middle income occupant is incidental to the purpose of the program.

5. Unlike prior programs, in which the subsidies were large and long term, the subsidy will be small and short term.

6. Unlike prior programs, the selection of developers will be a clerical task, that even some of the operators in the Pierce Administration would have difficulty abusing.

25-25-25

The major risk the conventional developer takes is the market risk. Is there a market for his product? The program's objective is to get him off the fence if he is unsure. It is a program at the margin. The subsidy is designed to cushion the shock of his entry into the market. But from there on in he is on his own. The key to the subsidy is to allow greater market penetration. To provide him with customers that, but for the subsidy, he could not reach.

The program will be near universal. The modifying "near" refers to those developers who will not want to get near HUD for love or money and those building at the luxury end of the market. For each housing market, HUD would set a market rental for new units taking into account the size of the apartments. The rent would represent the cost of well-designed and well-managed new middle-income units in the locality. The subsidy will be available to *all* developers of new apartments under the fixed rents. The developer, when the units were ready for occupancy, would certify that the rents are at or below the amount set and receive a subsidy commitment.

The subsidy would be equal to 25 percent (no magic in the numbers and HUD could have different percentages for different types of units) of the rent set by HUD and cover 25 percent of the units. In a project, that has a hundred units renting at $600 a month, the landlord would receive a commitment of a monthly subsidy equal to $3,750 (25 [units] x $150 [25% of the rent]). To qualify for the subsidy the tenant must be the *initial tenant*[6] and be paying at least 25 percent of his income. The subsidy would be equal to the difference between the rent and 25 percent of income. A tenant with an income of $1,800 a month ($21,600 a year) would qualify for a $150 subsidy ($600 - $450 [25% of income]).

The subsidy would be based on the HUD set rent. Thus, the efficient developer (or a developer who was being subsidized by a state, local, or community entity) would be at an advantage since the subsidy would represent more than 25 percent of its rent. The developer would be free to distribute the allocation among his units. He could provide the maximum subsidy ($150 in the example) to 25 percent of his units or reduce the rent by $37.50 on all his units or any other combination and permutation. He could use it for his initial units to generate cash flow or save it for his hard to rent units, as long as (1) the subsidy did not exceed $150; (2) the subsidy was used for a unit whose rent was below the HUD fixed rent; and (3) the tenant's contribution represented 25 percent of income.

The landlord would not have to use the commitment. If the market is tight there would be a benefit without a cost to the government. He would be free to rent without the benefit of the subsidy to anyone at any rent. If the tenant graduated out of the subsidy or moved out of the apartment, the subsidy would be forever lost (thereby placing a premium on good management.) Conversely, if the developer builds into a housing glut or misses his market or manages the property poorly, the subsidy is not large enough to save him. He will take the loss rather than HUD.

The advantage of the program is that it involves a minimum of regulation (even income certification can be done on an exception basis—after the initial year tenant income is assumed to rise sufficiently to cut the subsidy by 20 percent unless the tenant can prove otherwise). The program is far cheaper than current programs. Given turnover, the subsidy of $1,800 can be expected to run for five years and cost $9,000— within the range of the *annual* subsidy of some of the Section 8 moderate rehab program. The calculations overstate the cost. Only 25 percent of all renters, in 1989, lived in their units for at least five years. Even among tenants living is private Federally assisted units, 65 percent leave within 5 years. The assumption also assumes that the tenant will qualify for the full subsidy for each of the five years. And, if the subsidy commitment is used in a market that needs the units, there will be little or no cost, since most landlords will not accept a subsidy if it is accompanied by federal regulation if they can find tenants who need no assistance.

There is little risk for the government. The projects don't need insurance as a prerequisite for participation and there are strong incentives for good management. Since everyone is eligible there are almost no opportunities for waste, fraud, and abuse.

The Dutch Auction

A variation of the first program would be subsidizing *all* the units in a project under the 25/25/25 model. The difference would be one of the 25s would represent 25 percent of the developers. Discretion can be eliminated even if the program followed this format. HUD would set out the subsidy amount appropriate for a given area, as in the above case $1,800 per unit (adjusted by size) and select the developer by a Dutch Auction—by low bids. The developer who would be willing to build the units at the lowest subsidy amount would be awarded the commitment. Since the subsidy isn't available until the units are ready for occupancy— there is little danger of the "lowballing" that plagues defense procurement.

At present all the pressure is to receive the highest possible subsidy commitment. The reverse auction reverses the pressure and provides HUD with a firm market basis. There is always a possibility of collusion by the bidders, but the competitive nature of the business minimizes it.

An anonymous housing professional, admittedly without a sense of humor, thought this modest proposal was a satire. However, as Eric Hoffer has noted, "It is the overserious who are truly frivolous." The only in-depth HUD study of the program concluded,

[T]he proposed shallow subsidy rental housing program could be an important incentive to rental housing production as part of a coordinated set of government-backed housing programs which deal with the problem other than those for which the RHPP [Rental Housing Production Program] is designed. Once the program is adopted and structured, by its nature it can be adjusted either at different times or even by regions to encourage greater or lesser production simply by changing the formula for computing the amount of subsidy for each project. Assuming that the program can be adopted in such a way as to retain this flexibility, it should be seriously considered as a partial solution to the housing problems of the country.[8]

And, now on to the assistance part of the problem.

"Choice" in the Marketplace

A World of Fictions

The Section 8 housing voucher format is eminently logical. There is a gap between what poor people can afford and the cost of decent housing and the government bridges the gap with money. The Government is assumed to *know* the right rent-to-income ratio and the right cost of decent housing. It has set the former at 30 percent of income and the latter at the 45th percentile of gross rent (excluding newly constructed units and *substandard* units) of recent movers in the locality (generally a metropolitan area).

The government, unfortunately, is living in a world of fictions. There is absolutely no rational basis for using 30 percent as the right ratio:

Housing expenditures of American families are too diverse to be explained by simple principles. Much of the diversity is real i.e., inherent in consumer behavior. Choice of housing (which necessarily means choice of community and neighborhood) is an extremely complex set of economic, social, and political impulses.[9]

The search for the right ratio has produced absurd results. In the early 1970s, the "right ratio" was 25 percent of income. It served as a maximum in public housing and as a minimum in the Section 236 subsidized rental program. Today, one pays the same percentage of income in a brand new apartment in a pleasant neighborhood as in Tyler House quality housing.

The voucher is premised on the notion of "equality of outcomes" rather than "equality of opportunity." All poor people regardless of their income, age, family situation, or preference are presumed to have a desire to pay 30 percent of their income. The 30 percent standard doesn't even measure housing comfort. Would you want to pay for high-cost housing and sit on fruit cartons or pay for moderate-cost housing and be able to afford comfortable furniture?

In calculating the right rent, HUD uses only standard units of recent movers. If by definition all of the units are standard, why is the number set at the 45th percentile of recent mover's rents? It is actually above the median since recent movers live in newer housing and pay higher rents than nonmovers.* What is the purpose served by the government setting such a high-cost standard given the inverse relationship between the cost of the unit and the number of families served?

To add injury to insult, the program hurts those that it does not help. Most poor rely on the low end of the rental market for their housing. This is the sector that is in deep trouble because of the inability of unsubsidized poor tenants to pay the rents. This results in frequent moves by poor families to avoid the rent collector—the vacancy rate of between 8 and 9 percent in low rent units ($200 - 299) is higher than the rate for all other units on the market except luxury units ($800 or more).[10] The high turnover means additional costs (repainting, protecting the unit against vandalism, and the cost of finding a new tenant) at a time when the building's owner is experiencing a substantial drop in income. In this type of setting it should not come as a surprise that buildings are not in tip-top shape. The voucher by drawing people out of these units and into the middle of the market is also pushing buildings off the market. The result of a weak market is the abandonment of buildings rather than lower rents. For those remaining it leaves the prospect of a smaller number of low rent units.

The mistake is compounded by the structure of the rent voucher program. The subsidy that a tenant receives is equal to the difference between the FMR and 30 percent of income, *no matter what the rent of the unit chosen*. Since this is a back-door income transfer, the only way to earmark the program for housing is to impose a high housing standard. The apartment is, therefore, subjected to the scrutiny of an inspector armed with a twenty-page checklist (backed up by an *Inspection Manual* that runs hundreds of pages). What honest inspector ever got into trouble for being too scrupulous? What landlord wants to be subjected to such a test merely for the honor of serving a poor family? There is no such thing as a free standard. At "best" after repairs the rent goes up to or above the

---

*   If the program were to achieve universal coverage, it would require the non-poor to live in housing with below-average rent.

standard. At worst, in a sea of standard apartments, the participant cannot obtain a drop from the housing subsidy bucket. The average rent burden in the housing voucher program was 34 percent of net income and 39 percent of the applicants could not find a unit which met the standard and, therefore, received no subsidy.[11]

Ironically, in spite of all the money spent on running and reporting on the housing allowance experiment, HUD misread the results. Katherine Bradbury and Anthony Downs in summarizing a conference at the Brookings Institution, that brought together academic specialists and the contractors who ran the experiment for HUD, asked,

> [S]hould society try to impose housing quality standards on *anyone* in the absence of a clearly established relationships between such standards and the quality of human life? . . . Even expert, highly trained housing inspectors did not agree how to classify specific housing units. . . .Even more important, there is almost no evidence that moving to a high quality unit . . . improves the health, incomes, welfare, or happiness of households formerly living in low quality or substandard units. . . . Moreover, when housing standards are used, there will be many cases in which specific houses will be disqualified for what appear trivial reasons, such as having windows that are several square inches too small.[12]

Bernard Frieden, in another forum, after noting that the housing allowance experiment found that there was a higher percentage of families who were "very satisfied" with their housing among those who remained in units that failed to meet the housing standard than among families who moved to standard units, *in spite of the fact that only the latter qualified for the subsidy*, wrote,

> An important question for the next wave of housing programs is: Who should decide how much a family ought to consume and where it ought to live, the family or an administrator who sets the standards? . . . There may conceivably be public benefits involved that would justify overriding the preferences of the poor themselves and require them to pay for better housing than they would otherwise choose to do. If that is so federal officials have a responsibility to present a case for setting aside the wishes of the poor.[13]

A Little Humility and a Multitude of Choices

The new system (Choice) rests on three premises: (1) All Americans should be able to obtain decent housing in a suitable environment without having to sacrifice the other necessities of life (from HUD's point of view people should be able to obtain the necessities of life without sacrificing housing). (2) The more one spends for housing the more likely it is that the housing will be decent. (3) The case has not been made to set aside the housing wishes of the poor. If there is to be discretion (independence) in the housing area let it be in the hands of those who are presently dependent.

The subsidy a household would receive under Choice would be determined by *its* wishes as expressed by the rent burden (rent-to-income ratio) it wishes to bear. The greater the interest in housing the greater the subsidy, with a maximum subsidy at 35 percent of income. The basic subsidy table is set for a 3-4 person household (table 8.1) and varies with the size of the household (table 8.2). There is an additional bonus for families with extremely low income - less than *50 percent of the poverty threshold* (table 8.3).

TABLE 8.1
Basic Subsidy Table
(3–4 Person Household)

Rent Income Ratio	Monthly Assistance
Less than 20%	$ 0
20	20
21	40
22	60
23	80
24	100
25	120
26	138
27	156
28	174
29	192
30	210
31	225
32	240
33	255
34	270
35	285
More than 35	285

TABLE 8.2
Family Size Variations

Family Size	Percent of Basic Amount
1–2	85%
3–4	100
5–6	115
7–8	130
9–10	145

TABLE 8.3
High Needs Bonus

Percent of Poverty Threshold	Bonus
0–10%	20%
10–20	16
20–30	12
30–40	8
40–50	4

The subsidies may be revised to suit political and economic dictates. The choice of the amount is a pragmatic one. It must satisfy two conflicting objectives: it must be high enough to give the poor a choice of decent housing units while spending a moderate amount of their income and low enough so that eventual expansion of the program is acceptable to taxpayers not directly benefiting from the program. There is an additional political principle namely the Avis Principle. No person should be able to obtain better housing than someone with a higher income unless they are trying harder (as evidenced by their rent-to-income ratio).

Although the income limits will vary around the country, the program is predicated on the use of a single set of subsidy amounts for the entire nation. Although this sounds counter intuitive as a general rule areas of high housing costs are high income areas and low housing cost areas are low income areas and the highest subsidies will go to areas in which housing cost is high relative to income (other areas benefit by low ratios).

TABLE 8.4
"Choice" in America

Location	Annual Income*	Monthly Rent*	Monthly Subsidy	Tenant Rent/Income (in percent)
East Coast				
Boston	$13,920	$642	$257	33**
New York	$ 9,720	$405	$177	28
Philadelphia	$10,410	$410	$169	28
Washington	$14,070	$537	$195	29
South				
Atlanta	$10,890	$423	$170	28
Louisville	$10,140	$293	$ 93	24
Miami	$ 9,240	$423	$197	29
New Orleans	$ 9,570	$399	$175	28
Mid-America				
Pittsburgh	$ 9,810	$362	$146	26
Chicago	$11,880	$464	$182	28
Cleveland	$10,500	$316	$104	24
Green Bay	$10,260	$340	$124	25
West Coast				
Los Angeles	$11,490	$547	$240	32
San Francisco	$14,310	$678	$272	34
Honolulu	$10,950	$496	$218	30

* Assumptions: Four person household in a 2 bedroom unit. Income is equal to 60% of very low income level. Rent is equal to 80% of Fair Market Rent level established in March and April of 1988. ** Not exact because of rounding.

There are no free rides in the program. If a family prefers improved housing, it must prove it by bearing a portion of the additional rent. The government should be generous, but should not encourage extravagance. The subsidy table (8.1) is a declining one ($20 for each step between 20-25

percent, $18 between 26-30 percent, and $15 between 31-35 percent) and
the basic maximum subsidy is $385. The program earmarks the assis-
tance for housing. Unlike the housing voucher the amount of assistance
is directly dependent on the beneficiary's desire for housing.

Is there a need for standards? There is no reason to believe the poor
are any less competent in shopping for housing than in shopping for food.
If they are satisfied with lower cost housing both they and the government
benefit by its lower cost. The issue of standards need not be addressed
on a yes-no basis. There are many intermediate positions. For example,
standards could be applied: when there is more than one child involved;
or when the federal subsidy exceeds a certain dollar amount; or the
subsidy could be available only in a unit in a building that has no serious
outstanding code violations.

Will there be collusion between landlords and tenants? There are a
number of factors that minimize the collusion. First, the subsidy is a
declining one so that the tenant pays a higher share of increases and leaves
less subsidy to split. Second, there will be no right rent to shoot at. Every
tenant in the building will have a different subsidy table (see below).
Third, the less-than-friendly relations between the landlord and tenant.
The imposition of standards and fraud prevention can be combined. The
housing inspection, for example, can be required when the federal
subsidy is in excess of, say, $250 a month.

Is the program fair? All things being equal, the poorest person gets the
largest subsidy. If two families, with incomes of $6,000 and $12,000
respectively rent a $360 apartment, the former's subsidy would be about
twice as large ($210 v. $113). On the standard that the poor should not
get better housing unless they try harder, if the two families expend the
same effort, they get the same subsidy and the $12,000 family gets a
better unit. At 30 percent of income, the $12,000 family is able to obtain
a $510 unit and the $6,000 family obtains a $360 unit. The percentage of
rent covered by the subsidy is, nevertheless, much higher for the poor
renter (58% v. 41%).

A major criticism is that the program is old hat. It is merely a "percent
of rent" formula, which was tested in the Housing Allowance Experiment
and proved to be wanting. This would be a devastating critique were it
true. In truth, housing economist's have had as great difficulty categoriz-
ing the Choice approach as taxonomists had with the duck-billed platypus. In a paper done by the Urban Institute, Choice was referred to as a

formula: (1) that was equivalent to the percent of rent formula; (2) that approach[es] a housing gap subsidy by varying its rate of subsidy; and (3) as a hybrid of the percent of rent and housing gaps subsidies."[14]

Choice looks like a duck. For any household the higher the rent, the higher the subsidy (up to the 35 percent limit). Choice, however, neither swims nor quacks like a duck. There are crucial differences between the *percent of rent* and the Choice *percent of rent/income ratio* format. In the case of a $360 apartment, referred to above, under the approach tested in the housing allowance program, both families, in spite of the major difference in income, receive the same subsidy. Under Choice, the lower income family's subsidy is nearly twice as large. In the case, in which the two families have the same percent of income, under the percent of rent formula, the higher income family will receive a *larger subsidy* and the portion of the rent covered by the subsidy will be the same for both families; under Choice the higher income family will receive the same subsidy and the portion of the rent covered by the subsidy will be higher for the poorer family.

At first glance, the program seem to be an administrator's nightmare. The only people who will perhaps understand it are unemployed economists and mathematicians. Tables will have to be scanned and ratios calculated. One of major criticisms of the percent of rent formula used in the experiment was that few of the participants understood the relationship between the rent and what they would have to pay. Even after two years, less than half understood a higher rent meant they would have to pay more.[17] This problem would be *de minimis*, in the Choice program.

HUD would provide, to each administering agency, a floppy diskette. Each beneficiary would receive an individualized table that would tell them the rent they would have to pay at different monthly rents. Table 8.5 illustrates a table with $10 intervals. In an actual program the intervals can drop to a dollar.

All of the decisions will be made in the political sunshine. The system will provide instant feedback. Given the size of the family and the subsidy, the rent burden will be known. If the burden is too high (the subsidies are too low) and additional money is needed, a political decision can be made as to whether to raise the subsidies and limit the number of people assisted or keep the subsidies at the same level and expand the program.

TABLE 8.5
Individualized Choice Table

(Income - $6,933; Family Size - 3)			
Rent	You Pay	Rent	You Pay
$100	100	310	155
110	110	320	158
120	116	330	160
130	116	340	162
140	116	350	165
150	118	360	167
160	121	370	170
170	123	380	172
180	125	390	175
190	128	400	178
200	130	410	180
210	132	420	183
220	134	430	186
230	137	440	189
240	139	450	192
250	141	460	194
260	143	470	197
270	145	480	200
280	148	490	205 [maximum]
290	150	500	215
300	153	510	225

Virtuous Circles

The alternative approach dissolves the bond between production problems and poverty problems. The new framework separates subsidies to facilitate new housing production from subsidies to alleviate the housing problems of the poor. Through these means it is possible to create a harmony of political interests and an economically efficient system. It might even be deemed a virtuous circle. Serving the small housing needs of middle income families has obvious appeal in a middle class society. It also provides large benefits to poor families by allowing existing standard units to "flow down" to lower income families. This in turn makes more politically acceptable forms of assistance to the poor economically viable, thereby resulting in the achievement of both goals—the elimination of poor housing and of housing poverty.

Local Autonomy and Consumer Sovereignty

Choice provides hope for public housing. But first the relationship between the three parties—HUD, PHA, and the residents must be fundamentally altered. The relationship must continue (subsidies are crucial) but it need not be intimate. HUD is not the fount of all wisdom and in the main PHAs are peopled with managers and employees as competent as those at HUD (this might be called "praising with faint damn"). What sets PHAs apart from private managers is that the former operate in a system that lacks a rational pricing mechanism and whose incentives, wrapped in reams of unreadable regulations, are often perverse.

It is time to liberate the tenants and the PHAs from a situation in which they are both captives. The tenants need to be viewed as consumers who are to be offered choices, rather than as supplicants who are assigned spaces. Rents need to reflect the difference in the cost and quality of the unit rather than the tenant's economic situation.

Although PHAs may be rusty, since the books have been consolidated for years, the allocation of costs to the project and unit level is not an insurmountable task. Firms that manage buildings for numerous owners separate costs on buildings and units every day. A PHA may be simple minded and just divide its costs by the number of units and have each unit bear the same rent or a PHA may attempt to set rents that are too high. Mistakes will be self-correcting, since the PHA will be faced with a new breed of tenant. If knowledge is power, the ability to calculate the subsidy that the PHA will be receiving and the cost for alternative accommodations will make the tenant a tough customer.

Choice has some distinct advantages over the Section 8 housing voucher. The notion of fair-market rents (which Choice rejects) is inappropriate in the context of public housing. The FMRs are based on rents in the privately owned stock of housing which may have almost no relation to the age and other features of public housing. To cite one example almost all of the public housing units in Los Angeles predate 1956 (because of the California requirement that the construction of public housing need be approved by a local referendum). There are few people in Los Angeles who would be willing to pay the 1992 fair-market rent of $804 in order to live in a two-bedroom apartment in public housing. If the voucher were to be given to tenants they will march lockstep into private housing. The voucher will have to chained to the project if public housing is to be viable.

The FMR is not based on the reality of public housing. In almost every city it is well in excess of the debt service and operating costs of public housing. The study which Congress in 1990 suggested that HUD look at in studying the funding of public housing noted:

> The crux of the matter is that the system is not based on an estimate of what it costs to run the stock of public housing. Rather it is based on the cost of an alternative program. The market rents used as a proxy for legitimate costs do not necessarily reflect the inherent cost of [public housing].[18]

The Section 8 voucher would also be a leaky delivery bucket. A typical authority would have units of different quality that would rent at different prices. Assume the prices are $300, $400, and $500 in a community in which the fair-market rent was set at $400. If we assume three families with incomes of $6,000 their monthly voucher would equal $250 ($400 – $150 [(30% of $6,000/12]). In the case of the $400 apartment things work out just right. However, in the case of the $300, a $100 of the subsidy would not arrive at the coffers of the PHA. And, in the case of the $500 apartment the tenant would be in dire straits, having to pay 50 percent of his income for housing.

The Choice System would produce a very different result. The family that chose the $300 unit would pay approximately 27 percent of its income and receive a subsidy of $163. The family with the $400 unit would pay 32 percent of its income and receive a subsidy of $240. The family with the $500 unit would pay 43 percent of its income and receive a subsidy of $285. Choice would be cheaper for the Federal government ($688 v. $750) and more generous to the PHA ($688 v.$650) since all the money is earmarked for housing.

How Will PHAs Fare?

If the long waiting lists are true indicators of the attractiveness of public housing most PHAs would have no difficulty in moving comfortably into the new program. Contrary to popular perception, only 41 percent of public housing households contain children (only 3 percent of the units contain five or more children)[19] and on a scale of one to ten (with one being the worst), 65 percent of public housing tenants rate their units at 8 or above and 73 percent rate their units as better than their previous home (although only 44 percent rate the neighborhood as better).[20] If the PHA's can keep their rents in line with private rentals they should be able to run "profitable" operations.

In areas where the waiting list only represents the bargain price of public housing and the tenants have a low opinion of their environment (19 percent of the tenants gave their buildings and 38 percent gave their neighborhoods a five or lower rating), the PHA will have to make a decision. The PHA will have to chose whether it wishes to retain its role as the guardian of dead-end housing or take on the role of gatekeeper of housing opportunity. The PHA will have the opportunity to broaden its role from that of a landlord of a given amount of real estate to that of a facilitator of housing opportunities for low income families. As at present, both the subsidies for private and public housing will flow through the PHA. Until recently, the distinction between public and assisted private housing was so sharp that it required they be placed under different assistant secretaries at HUD. Now that the wall coming is down at the federal level and there is only one provider of subsidies and the PHA is usually the sole distributor, it is time to whittle away at the distinction between public and private housing.

PHAs will have to think and compete like their private counterparts and be accountable for their decisions. Likewise, their residents will have the luxury and the responsibility that goes with choice. Portions of the public housing stock are so far gone that any investment is not in the best interest of the tenants or the PHA. However, if modernization is appropriate the PHA must act as if the money being spent is theirs and be on notice that for the tenants also, the program is not a free ride. Many a tenant will be able to live with a less than new kitchen and bathroom rather than have a modern kitchen at a cost of $27,688 and a bathroom with a price tag of $6,392[21] if these costs necessitate a substantial rent hike.

Blinders must be taken off. A housing crisis can exist amidst a housing surplus. Many private units are on the brink where there is no money for a major repair while simultaneously the tenants are at the end of their income rope. In such a situation, the wise strategy would be the channeling of money to tenants to enable them to afford to pay for the proper upkeep of their present buildings. The best for public housing may be the enemy of the good for low-rent housing.

PHAs will have new opportunities. In low-quality projects, which at present have high vacancy rates there is a possibility of stabilization if tenants are offered low rents. Often, however, the granting of choice will quicken the exodus. The result is the peoples' answer as to whether the project is serving an economic or social purpose. Public housing is not grounded in buildings but in providing decent housing for people.

From Here to There

This conservative revolution can occur gradually. I would envision initially a demonstration at a number of housing authorities.[22] The Choice subsidy will only be available to households on the waiting list of the participating PHAs or present tenants of a PHA who desire to move to another unit in the PHA. The PHA will set the rents on the vacant units offered to holders of Choice certificates on the basis of cost, quality, and location. PHAs will not be bound by any of the rent determination requirements of the basic public housing legislation.

The recipients of the Choice certificates who are on the waiting list will be able to use the certificate in a variety of ways. They can move into public housing. They can remain in their present dwelling or move to private housing units that meet the local housing code requirements. Existing tenants in public housing will only be eligible to receive the certificate, during the demonstration stage, if they move to a vacant public housing unit.

The basic funding will come from the debt service and operating subsidy to the PHA allocated to the units participating in the demonstration. To cover the cases in which the recipients will choose private housing, the participating PHAs will receive funds from the incremental Section 8 housing vouchers. As an historical note, HUD proposed a demonstration program involving a predecessor of the Choice program for Fiscal 1982 involving 15,000 units. OMB rejected the program without comment. The rejection got a "confidential" and curt HUD response that found its way into the *Congressional Record*, "The denial of the . . . demonstration merely proves that the technicians at OMB would rather criticize old programs than examine new ideas." Their argument that a "tight budget year" is the wrong time for innovative ideas shows a good deal about the OMB mentality and the intellectual level of their analysis.[23]

A decade later the presence of an administration concerned with increasing the power of tenants and doing something about public housing, should not mislead the reader into thinking that there is much interest in the Choice alternative. The concern that the last scandal was only the penultimate one doesn't leave much room in the mind for even old new ideas. Public housers still believe that a little better management will get them over the hump—nothing needs radical changing. As Tom Paine noted, "a long habit—of not thinking a thing wrong gives it the superficial appearance of being right." Some are insulted that everybody doesn't think that the housing voucher (the fruit of an investment of over $200 million and much psychic income) isn't the greatest thing since trolleys were put on rails. Finally the fact that Choice is not bedecked with mathematical garb doesn't help. As Irving Kristol, in a similar context, commented:

> [T]he trouble with the thing . . . is that it is too simple, too easy to understand. Accustomed as we are to the increasing complexity of the natural sciences, and the occult jargon of the social sciences, we are inclined to be suspicious of the transparent simplicity, which we are likely to equate with naivete or wishful thinking. The average person, listening to an exposition . . . will nod his head at every point - but after it is done will remain incredulous: if it is that obvious. what is all the fuss and controversy about. The average economist, on the other hand, is only to likely to be indignant, outraged, and contemptuously dismissive: what is the point of his hard-won expertise in sophisticated economic theory if . . . policy can be reduced to such plain terms?[24]

Incrementalism vs. Alternatives

To many HUD is the black hole of management and public housing is the heart of darkness. If we continue to search for incremental fixes, HUD will grope in the gloom and many of those waiting to live in decent housing which they can afford will be dead. What Noel Tichy, a business management professor, has written of American business holds for HUD, "Incremental fixing the old broken bureaucracy just isn't doing the job . . . What's required are quantum ideas . . . " The time has come to change the paradigm. In the words of Paul Goodman, "What stands most in the way of solving our most important problems is the feeling of well-intentioned people that there are no alternatives; all we can do is improve the present methods.[26]

Notes

1. "Testimony of James Treadway, Executive Vice President of PaineWebber," *Lantos Hearings*, part 4, 239.
2. Bureau of Census, Housing Vacancies and Homeownership - Second Quarter 1990, table 3.
3. "Renters Face Growing Affordability Gap," *Housing Affairs Letter*, 27 September 1991, 8-9.
4. "A Universal Housing Allowance" in *Do Housing Allowances Work*, ed. Katherine Bradbury and Anthony Downs, 365 (Washington D.C.: The Brookings Institution, 1981).
5. "NAHB Dims Construction Forecast," *Housing Affairs Letter*, 27 September 1991, 9.
6. This could be modified, for example, to a subsidy in which the maximum dropped on each turnover—$150/$100/$50/$0 or $150/$75/$0.
7. Connie Casey, "Characteristics of HUD-Assisted Renters and Their Unites in 1989," 5 (HUD Office of Policy Development, Division of Housing and Demographic Analysis, September 1991).
8. Sheldon Baskin, *Evaluation of Proposed Shallow Subsidy Rental Housing Production Program*, (prepared for HUD - Team IV Housing Policy Review Task Force, June 1973).
9. Sherman Maisel and Louis Winnick, *Family Housing Expenditures: Elusive Laws and Intrusive Variances* (Berkeley: University of California Press - Real Estate Research Program, 1960).
10. Robert Callis, *Housing Vacancies and Homeownership* Annual Statistics, 1990, 12, table 2. (Bureau of Census Current Housing Reports).
11. Stephen Kennedy and Meryl Finkel, *Report of First Year Freestanding Housing Voucher Experiment*, 3-4. Abt Associated, 26 June 1987).
12. "Conference Discussion" in Bradbury and Downs, *Do Housing Allowances Work?*, 383.
13. "Housing Allowances: An Experiment That Worked," *Public Interest*, Spring 1980, 35.
14. Ozanne, Larry, "Discussion of Irving Welfeld's Proposed Housing Allowance," Urban Institute, 31 March 1972, 2 (unpublished memorandum).
15. Ibid., 8-9.
16. Ibid., 13.
17. Joseph Friedman and Daniel Weinberg, *The Demand for Rental Housing: Evidence from a Percent of Rent Housing Allowance*, (Abt Associates, 1980), 140-42.
18. HUD, *Alternative Operating Subsidy Formulas*, May 1982, 272.
19. Connie Casey, "HUD-Assisted Renters, table 2.
20. Ibid., tables 5 and 7.
21. Robert Guskind and Carol Steinbach, "Sales Resistance," *National Journal*, 6 April 1991, 798, 799. (The reported costs at Kenilworth-Parkside).
22. The Akron Ohio Housing Authority, the only authority that has closely examined the proposal has shown a definite interest in participating in a demonstration program. See Prepared Statement of Paul Messenger (March 7, 1990) in *House Subcommittee on Housing and Community Development Hearings on Public Housing and Section 8 Programs*, 101st Congress, 2d Session, 291, 299-300.
23. 127 *Cong. Rec.*, pt. 22:29776, S. 97th Cong., 1st sess., 1981.
24. "Ideology and Supply-Side Economics," *Commentary*, April 1981, 48.
25. Quoted in Huey, John "Nothing is Impossible," *Fortune*, 23 September 1991, 135.
26. "An Interview with Paul Goodman," *Harvard Review*, Fall 1964, 63.

Bibliography

Books

Bell, Robert. *Culture of Policy Deliberation*. New Brunswick, N.J.: Rutgers University. Press, 1985.

Bernstein, Marver. *The Job of the Federal Executive*. Washington D.C.: Brookings Institution, 1958.

Bradbury, Katherine and Anthony Downs eds. *Do Housing Allowances Work*, Washington DC: Brookings Institution, 1981.

Davies, Richard. *Housing Reform During the Truman Administration*. Columbia, Missouri: University of Missouri Press, 1966.

De Leeuw, Frank. *Operation Costs in Public Housing*. Washington, D.C.: Urban Institute, 1970.

Downs, Anthony. *Summary Report: Federal Housing Subsidies Their Nature and Effectiveness and What We Should Do About Them*. Washington, D.C.: National Assoc. of Home Builders, 1972.

Frieden, Bernard and Lynne Sagalyn. *Downtown Inc. How America Rebuilds Cities*. Cambridge, Mass.: M.I.T. Press, 1989.

Friedman, Joseph and Daniel Weinberg. *The Demand for Rental Housing: Evidence from a Percent of Rent Housing Allowance*. Cambridge, Mass.: Abt Associates, 1980.

Hagman, Donald. "Windfalls and Their Recapture." In Donald Hagman and Dean Misczyinski, *Windfall for Wipeouts*. Chicago: American Society of Planning Officials, 1978.

Kaufman, Herbert, *Red Tape Its Origins Use and Abuse*. Washington, D.C.: Brookings Institution, 1977.

Kennedy, Stephen. *Report of First Year Freestanding Housing Voucher Demonstration*. Cambridge, Mass.: 1987.

Kissinger, Henry. "Bureaucracy and Policymaking: The Effect of Insiders and Outsiders on the Political Process." In Kissinger and Bernard Brodie, *Bureaucracy, Politics, and Strategy*. Los Angeles: University of California Press, 1969.

Maisel, Sherman and Louis Winnick. *Family Housing Expenditures: Elusive Laws and Intrusive Variances*. Berkeley: University of California Press at Berkeley Real Estate Research Program, 1973.

Raw, Charles, Bruce Page and Godfrey Hodgson. *Do You Sincerely Want to be Rich*, New York: Bantam Books, 1987.

Smith, Wallace. *Housing: The Social and Economic Element*. Berkeley: University of California Press, Berkeley, 1970.

Sternlieb, George. *The Tenement Landlord*. New Brunswick, N.J.: Urban Studies Center, Rutgers, 1966.

179

Thompson, Dennis. *Political Ethics and Public Office.* Cambridge, Mass.: Harvard University, 1987.

Touche Ross. *Study of Tax Considerations in Multi-family Investments.* Washington, D.C.: HUD, 1972.

Winnick, Louis, *New People in Old Neighborhoods.* New York: Russell Sage Foundation, 1990.

Public Documents

Callis, Robert. Housing Vacancies and Homeownership: Annual Statistics, 1990. Bureauof Census, Current Housing Report, H 111.

Casey, Connie. Characteristics of HUD-Assisted Renters and their Units in 1989. HUD, Office of Policy Development and Research, Division of Housing and Demographic Analysis, September 1991.

Federal Housing Administration. Sixteenth Annual Report, (1949).

_____. Nineteenth Annual Report, (1952).

General Accounting Office. Rental Housing Inefficiencies From Combining Moderate Rehabilitation and Tax Credits, June 1990.

_____. Serving A Broader Range of Families in Public Housing Could Reduce Operating Subsidies, 1979.

_____. Use of Subsidies, 27 February, 1990.

_____. Assisted Housing: Utility Allowances Often Fall Short of Actual Utility Expenses, March 1991.

Hirsch, Arnold. "The Causes of Racial Segregation: A Historical Perspective." In U.S. Civil Rights Commission, *Issues of Housing Discrimination,* November 1985.

Housing and Home Finance Agency. The Housing Situation: A Factual Background, June 1949.

Housing and Urban Development. Housing in the Seventies: A Report of the National Housing Policy Review, 1974.

_____. Office of Policy Development and Research, Alternative Operating Subsidy Systems for the Public Housing Program, May 1982.

_____. Office of Public Housing. Modernization Approvals Data System (MADS) FY 1988 Reports, July 1989.

Inspector General. Audit of Section 223 (f). Coinsurance Program, 9 December 1988.

_____. Audit of the Section 8 Moderate Rehabilitation Program, 26 April 1989.

Kaiser, Frederick. Past Program Breakdowns in HUD-FHA: Section 608 Multifamily Rental Mortgage Insurance Program of the 1940s. Library of Congress Congressional Research Service, March 1990.

President's Committee on Urban Housing. Report: A Decent Home, 1968.

Parente, Francis. "Housing Management Problem Survey." In Hearings before a Subommittee of a House Committee On Appropriations, Part 8. Subsidized Housing, 95th Cong., 1st sess., 1977.

President of the U.S. Message transmitting to Congress the Third Annual Report on National Housing Goals, House Doc. 92-136, 29 June 1971.

Schefler, Marion. "Study of Legislative History of the Rapid Depreciation Provision." In 120 Congressional Record, pt.4: 4,948, Extension of Remarks, 93rd Cong., 2d sess., 1974.

Schussheim, Morton. The Mission and Management of HUD. Library of Congress, Congressional Research Service, 5 July 1990.

Semer, Milton, Julian Zimmerman, Ashley Foard, and John Frantz. "A Review of Federal Subsidized Housing Programs." In National Housing Policy Review, *Housing in the Seventies Working Papers 1*, Washington, D.C.: HUD, 1976.

Taubman, Paul. "Housing and Income Tax Subsidies." In National Housing Policy Review, *Housing in the Seventies Working Papers 2*, Washington, D.C.: HUD, 1976.

U.S. Bureau of Census. "Housing Vacancies and Homeownership: 2d Quarter, 1990."

U.S. Congress. 95 Congressional Record, part 4: 4808-11, S. 81st Cong., 1st sess., 1949.

_____. 113 Cong. Rec., pt. 1: 163, H., 90th Cong., 1st sess., 1967.

_____. 113 Cong. Rec., pt. 22: 30,351-53, S., 90th Cong, 1st sess. 1967.

_____. 114 Cong. Rec., pt. 15: 20,321 H., 90th Cong., 2d sess., 1968.

_____. 126 Cong. Rec., pt. 24: 31,520, H. 96th Cong., 2d sess., 1980.

_____. 127 Cong. Rec., pt. 22: 29,776, S. 97th Cong., 1st sess., 1981.

U.S. Congress. "Housing Subsidies and Housing Policy." Hearings before the Joint Economic Committee, 92nd Cong., 2nd sess., December 1972.

U.S. Congress, House. "Abuse and Mismanagement at HUD." Twenty Fourth Report by the Committee on Government Operations, 101st Cong. 2d Sess., 1990, H. Report 101-977.

_____. "Abuses in the Administration of the Passaic, NJ Housing Authority." Hearings before the Employment and Housing Subcommittee of the Committee on Government Operations, 101st Cong. 2d sess., 1990.

_____. "Abuses, Favoritism, and Mismanagement in HUD Programs." Parts 1-6, Hearings before the Employment and Housing Subcommittee of the Committee on Government Operations, 101st Cong. 1st and 2d sess., 1989-90.

_____. "Availability and Applicability of Information and Data Relating to Housing and Local Markets." Hearings before the Subcommittee on Policy Research and Insurance of the Committee on Banking, Finance, and Urban Affairs, 101st Cong., 2d sess., 1990.

_____. "Housing and Loan Management Procedures for HUD Assisted Housing." Hearings before the Subcommittee on Housing and Community Development of the Committee on Banking, Finance, and Urban Affairs, 100th Cong., 2d sess. 1988.

_____. "HUD - Independent Agencies Appropriations for 1979." Hearings before a Subcommittee of the Committee of Appropriations, 95th Cong., 2d sess., 1978.

_____. "HUD Investigations." Hearings before the Subcommittee on Housing and Community Development of the Committee on Banking, Finance and Urban Affairs, 101st Cong., 1st sess., 1989.

_____. "HUD-Space-Science-Veterans Appropriations Act of 1973, part 3." Hearings before a Subcommittee of the Committee on Appropriations, 92d Cong., 2d sess., 1972.

_____. "Investigation and Hearing of Abuses in Federal Low-And Moderate-Income Housing, before the Banking and Currency Committee." 92d Congress, 1st sess., 1970.

_____. "Mortgage Servicing and HUD Property Management." Hearings before a Subcommittee of the Committee on Government Operations, 94th Cong., 1st sess., 1975.

_____. "Public Housing and Section 8 Programs." Hearing before the Subcommitteeon Housing and Community Development of the Committee on Banking, Finance and Urban Affairs, 101st Cong., 2d sess., 1990.

_____. "Review of FHA Part 2: Update on FHA Insurance Funds." Subcommittee of the Committee on Government Operations, 93rd Cong., 2d sess., 1974.

U.S. Congress, Senate. "Distressed HUD-Subsidized Multifamily Projects." Hearings before the Banking, Housing, and Urban Affairs Committee, 95th Cong., 1st sess., 1978.

_____. "FHA Investigations," volumes 1-4. Hearings before the Committee on Banking and Currency, 83rd Cong., 2d sess., 1954.

_____. "Final Report and Recommendations: A Report of the HUD/Mod Rehab Investigation Subcommittee of the Committee on Banking, Housing and Urban Affairs." 1990.

_____. "Housing and Urban Development Legislation of 1968." Hearings before the Subcommittee on Housing and Urban Affairs of the Committee on Banking and Currency, 90th Cong., 2d sess., 1968.

_____. "HUD and Certain Agencies 1980 Appropriations." Hearings before the Committee on Appropriations," part 2, 96th Cong., 1st sess., 1979.

_____. "HUD-Independent Agency Appropriations for Fiscal Year, 1988." Subcommittee of Committee on Appropriations, part 2, 100th Cong., 1st sess., 1987.

_____. "Nomination of Deborah Gore Dean." Hearings before the Banking, Finance and Urban Affairs Committee, 100th Cong., 1st sess., 1987.

_____. "Nomination of Samuel R. Pierce, Jr." Hearings before the Banking and Currency Committee, 97th Cong., 1st sess., 1981.

_____. "The Abuse and Mismanagement of HUD," volumes I-II. Hearings before the HUD/Mod Rehab Investigation Subcommittee of the Committee on Banking, Housing and Urban Affairs, 101st Cong., 2d sess., 1990.

_____. "Housing Authorizing Legislation." Senate Banking, Housing and Urban Affairs, 96th Cong. 1st sess., 1979.

_____. "Hearings before the Committee on Appropriations on HUD and Certain Independent Agencies Appropriations." Fiscal Year 1980, Part 2, 96th Cong., 1st sess., 1979.

Magazines, Newspapers and Unpublished Materials

Anonymous. *A Review - Conversion of Non-Profit HUD Multifamily Projects to Limited Distribution Entities,* [undated document submitted to HUD in the late 1970s].

Baskin, Sheldon. "Evaluation of Proposed Shallow Subsidy Rental Housing Production Program." Prepared for Team IV of the National Housing Policy Review Task Force, June, 1973.

Colina Investors, Ltd. "Confidential Private Offering Memorandum, $1,487,500, 35 Limited Partner Interests." 20 March 1981.

"Comp Mod Funding Formula." *Housing Affairs Letter*, 3 May 1991.

DeParle, Jason. "What the Smartest Man in Washington Doesn't Understand. And Why it Will Hurt You." *The Washington Monthly*, November 1989.

"Ex-Housing Secretary Says Aides Were at Fault in Disputed Program." *New York Times*, 26 May 26 1989.

"FHA Impact on the Financing and Design of Apartments." *Architectural Forum*, January 1950.

"FHA Investigation." *Journal of Housing*, May 1954.

"FHA's Five Year-Old Scandal." *House and Home*, 14 May 1954.

Fielding, Byron. "Rozet Bobs and Weaves on Capitol Hill." *Housing Affairs Letter*, 2 March 1990.

_____. "Rozet-Golar Deal Bears Watching," *Housing Affair Letter*, 4 December 1990.

Fitzgerald, Sara and Sandra Sugawara. "Executive Notes," *The Washington Post*, 10 May 1982.

Frieden, Bernard. "Housing Allowances: An Experiment That Worked," *Public Interest*, Summer 1980.

Garth, Jeff. "Regulators say 80s Budget Cuts May Cost U.S. Billions in the 1990s." *New York Times*, 19 December 1989.

Gordon, Michael. "Within the Arms Debate, a 2d Debate." *New York Times*, 9 February 1988.

Guskind, Robert and Carol Steinbach. "Sales Resistance." *National Journal*, 6 April 1991.

Harlan, Christi. "Giant Trammel Crow Finds Texas Slump Only Round One." *Wall Street Journal*, 26 September 1990.

Heilman, John. "Congress's Watch Dog: Mostly It Still Goes for the Capillaries." *Washington Monthly*, November 1989.

Hilzenrath, David. "HUD Curbs Operator of Projects." *The Washington Post*, 2 February 1990.

Hilzenrath, David and Susan Schmidt. "Public Housing's Money Man." *Washington Post*, 24 November 1989.

"The HUD Ripoff." *Newsweek*, 7 August 1989.

Huey, John. "Nothing is Impossible." *Fortune*, April 1981.

ICF. "Final Report - The Characteristics of HUD Processed and Direct Endorsement Mortgages." (HUD Consultant's Report: 18 December 1989).

Jaffee, Harry. "The Rise and Fall of a Real Estate Dynasty - R.I. P. DRG." *Regardie's*, March 1990.

Kahn, Alfred. "Conversation for the 90s—The Deregulation Experience." Harris Bank, May 1990.

"Kemp Favorite Takes Questionable Partner." *Housing Affairs Letter*, 25 October 1991, 5.

Kristol, Irving. "Ideology & Supply Side Economics." *Commentary*, April, 1981.

Kuntz, Phil. "At Least Once in the Reagan Era, HUD Favors Came From the Top." *Congressional Quarterly*, 30 September 1989.

_____. "Killing Mod-Rehab with Kindness." *Congressional Quarterly*, 22 July 1989.

Luttwak, Edward. "Why We Need More Waste, Fraud, And Mismanagement in the Pentagon" *Commentary*, February 1982.

Morain, Dan. "Bank Swindler Named in S&L, HUD Fraud." *Los Angeles Times*, 19 September 1989.

Morain, Dan and Jill Stewart. "HUD Entrepreneur Feels the Heat." *Los Angeles Times*, 25 November 1989.

"NAHB Dims Construction Forecast." *Housing Affairs Letter*, 27 September 1991.

Ozanne, Larry. "Discussion of Irving Welfeld's Proposed Housing Allowance." Urban Institute, 31 March 1972 (unpublished paper submitted to HUD).

Packard, David. "Roundtable on Ethics and the Defense Industry." *The GAO Journal*, Spring 1988.

Payne, James. "The Congressional Brainwashing Machine." *Public Interest*, Summer 1990.

"People. " *National Journal*, 31 October 1981.

Quickel, Stephen. "The Robin Hood Game." *Forbes*, 1 October 1976.

"Renters Face Growing Affordability Gap." *Housing Affairs Letter*, 27 September 1991.

Riley, Michael. "Where Were the Media on HUD." *Time*, 24 July 1989.

Scheer, Robert. "Rehabilitated Housing a Costly Failure." Los Angeles Times, 7 August 1978.

Stegman, Michael. "Excessive Costs of Creative Financing: Growing Ineffiencies in the Production of Low Income Housing." *Housing Policy Debates* 2, 2, 1991.

"The Undoing of Silent Sam Pierce." *U.S. News and World Report*, 18 September 1989.

Uzzell, Lawrence. "The Unsung Hero of the Reagan Revolution: Secretary of Housing and Urban Development Samuel R. Pierce." *National Review*, 9 December 1988.

Wartzman, Rick. "How a Big Financier of Housing Projects Ran Afoul of HUD." *Wall Street Journal*, 31 August 1990.

"Whatever Became of Oversight." *National Journal*, 22 July 1989.

Index

Abrams, Philip, 73, 88, 90–93
"Abuses, Favoritism and Mismanagement in HUD Programs." *See* Lantos Committee.
"Abuses and Mismanagement at HUD," 1, 116
Accelerated Depreciation, *See* Tax Shelter
Accrual Based Accounting, 60, 62
Adams, Judge Arlin, 72
Adams, Inspector General Paul, 84–85, 105, 119–122
"Affordable Buicks," 159
"Affordable Food," 159
"Affordable Housing," 159
African Methodist Episcopal Church (AME), 54, 58–59
Albequerque, NM, 119
American Federation of Labor, 16
Anderson, Jack, 114
Anti-Ballistic Missile Treaty, 88
Anti-Rat Program, 29
Appropriations Act for Fiscal Year 1984, 87
Architectural Forum, 10, 16
Associated Financial Corp. (AFC), 63–64
Association of American Business Bureaus, 18
Atlanta, 6, 169
Audubon Park, 12
Avis Principle, 168

Back-door Income Transfer, 165
Baker, Howard, 119
Baltimore, 20
Bambi, 94
Bankruptcy Laws, 65
Banks, 10, 17, 21–22, 160
Barksdale, Maurice, 79, 98, 102
Barrett, Rep. William, 38
Baskin, Sheldon, 96, 151, 178 fn 8.
Bazarian Jr., Charles, 63, 73
Beachhaven, 1

Bell, Kleiner, 56
Bell, Robert, 145
Belle Glade, FL, 98
Bellerose, NY, 12
Benton Mortgage Co., 90
Biloxi, MS, 90
Black, Manafort & Kelly, 105
Boise-Cascade, 69 fn 11
Boland, Rep. Edward, 54, 73, 93, 130
Boland Amendment, 73
Bonner, Bertram, 11, 13
Boston, MA, 39, 44, 139, 169
Boston Herald, 89
Bradbury, Katherine, 166
Brain Drain, 148
Bridgeport, CT, 139
Briscoe, Leonard, 98, 101–03
Broad Range of Income, 136
Brock, Rep. William, 38
Brooke, Sen. Edward, 44, 94, 121–22, 134–35
Brookings, Bishop H. Hartford, 54, 58–59
Brookings Institution, 149, 166
Brooklyn, NY, 1, 33
Brooklyn Eagle, 1
Brownstein, Asst. Sec. Phillip, 33
Buffalo, NY, 96
Burstein, Joseph, 130
Bush, Fred, 94
Bush, President George, 94–95

California, 63, 146, 174
California Corporations Department, 57
Camden, NJ, 139
Capehart, Sen. Homer, 14
Capitalism, 151
Capone, Al, 67
Cardozo, Judge Benjamin, 98
Carmen, Gerald, 94
Carpenters Union, 58
Carter, President Jimmy, 89
Catholics, 104
"Cats," 103

Ceiling Rents, 134
Chernobyl Limited Partnership, 66–67
Chicago, IL, 6, 59, 139, 169
Chicago Housing Authority, 68
"Choice," across America, 169; adminis-
    tration, 171–72; collusion, 170; fair-
    ness, 170; percent of rent, 170–71;
    percent of rent/income ratio, 167–68;
    political sunshine, 171; poverty
    bonus, 167–68; premises, 166–67;
    public housing, See Choice/Public
    Housing; subsidy tables, 167–68, 172
"Choice"/Public Housing, comparison
    with housing vouchers, 173–74; cus-
    tomers 173; demonstration, 176–77;
    local autonomy, 173; modernization,
    175–76; new role for PHAs, 175–76;
    reasons for the status quo, 177; rela-
    tion to private market, 175–75
Cinderella, 138
Circuit Court of Appeals, 72
Civil Service, 148–50
Clark County, NV, 90–93, 95
Clark County Housing Authority, 91
Cleveland, OH, 95, 139, 169
Cochran, Sen. Thad, 93
Code of Federal Regulations, 86, 89, 90
Coinsurance - Colonial House, 79–81,
    98; Donny De, 78–81; Debbie Dean,
    80–101; defaults, 78, 80–82; DRG,
    78–82, 85, 98–99,101; fees, 77–79,
    84; flaw, 82–84; GNMA, 77, 81–83,
    85; inspector general, 84–85, 120;
    legislation, 76; lenders, 82–84; lob-
    bying, 80–81, 98–99, 102; monitor-
    ing, 83–85, 128; rationale , 76–77;
    Secretary Pierce, 80, 98–99; Title I
    comparison, 82; York Associates, 82;
    volume, 78
Colina Partnership, 60–63, 68
Colonial House. See Coinsurance
Commonwealth United Corporation,
    55–56
Community Development Corporations,
    59, 68
Comprehensive Modernization For-
    mula, 140
Concord, NH,´39
Conference Committee, 37

Congress - Affordable housing, 159; co-
    insurance, 76; Debbie Dean, 100,
    116; interest subsidy programs, 27–
    31, 33, 37–39, 43–46; inspector gen-
    eral, 121–123; oversight, 115–17;
    Rozet, 53, 63–64, 116, 127–28; pub-
    lic housing, 131–140, 174; Section 8
    mod rehab, 87–88, 93, 99–100; Sec-
    tion 608, 6–7, 8–9, 11, 15–17; Samuel
    Pierce, 71–73
Congressional Record, 33, 176
Congressional Research Service, 126
Congress of Industrial Organizations, 16
"Congress's Watch Dog: Mostly It Still
    Goes for the Capillaries," 117
Consolidation of Debt, 21
Consolidation of Contracts, 134
Consolidated Savings, 63
Cornell, 71
Cornfeld, Bernie, 55–56, 60, 65
Cost Certification, 13
Court of Special Sessions, 71
Cowett Edward M., 55–56
Cranston, Sen. Alan, 63–64
Cranston-Gonzalez National Affordable
    Housing Act, 138, 159
Crawford, Carol, 119
Crook Factor, 146
Crow, See Trammel-Crow
Cross-Section-of-Income, 53
Crusade, 33
Crystal Park, 90
C-Span, 115
Cushing, Hunter, 102, 104–105

Dallas TX, 39–40, 160
D'Amato, Sen. Alfonse, 93
Danforth, Sen. John C., III 64
D'Aquila, Anthony, 19–20, 22
Dayton, OH, 20, 81
Dean, Debbie, 1, 80–81, 92–93, 95, 99–
    105, 116, 119, 122, 148
DeBartolomeis, Silvio, 100, 104–05
Deborah Gore Dean, See Debbie Dean
DeConcini, Sen. Dennis, 93
DeFault, Donnie, See Donnie De
DeFranceaux, Donald, See Donnie De
DeFranceaux, George, 57, 78
DelliBovi, Alfred, 83
Demery, Thomas, 81, 102, 105, 120–22

Democrats, 40
Denton, Sen. Jeremiah, 93
Denver, CO, 31, 43
Department of Housing and Urban Administration, *See* HUD
Department of Justice, 22
Department of Transportation, 114
Depreciation, 41–43, 87
Des Moines Field Office, 7
Detroit, MI, 139
DeVito, Danny, 20–21
Diefendorfer, William, 118
Direct Endorsement Program, 83
District of Columbia Field Office, 8
Dole, Sen. Robert, 93
Domenici, Sen. Pete, 119
Downs, Anthony, 46, 166
Donnie De, Initial ventures, 78; coinsurance 78–82; record, 78; DRG, 78–82, 98–99, 101; lobbying, 80–81, 98–99; pedigree, 78; self dealing, 81–82
Drexel, Burnham, Lambert, 65
Dreyfuss, Richard, 20
DRG. *See* Coinsurance
DRG Financial. *See* Coinsurance
DRG Funding. *See* Coinsurance
DRG Insurance. *See* Coinsurance
DRG Ventures. *See* Donnie De.
Duck, 171
Duck-Billed Platypus, 170
Dutch Auction, 163
"Dynamiters," 20

E.F. Hutton, 57
Eckhardt, Rep. Robert, 38
Economic Recovery Tax of 1981, 63, 87
Eisenhower, Pres. Dwight, 5, 71, 115–16
"Ethics and the Defense Industry," 152
Eurobonds, 55
Ewing, NJ, 89
"Executive of the Year," 121

Fair Housing, 73
Fair Market Rents, *See* FMR
Fair Share, 86, 87–88
False Completion Certificates, 21
False Credit Applications, 21
Fannie Mae, 28, 65, 152, 159
Far East, 75

Federal Bureau of Investigation, 5, 22, 81, 116
Federal Deposit Insurance, 76, 83
Federal Housing Administration, *See* FHA
Fenwick, Millicent, 89
Fernandez, Waldo, 64
FHA - Coinsurance, 75–79, 88–83; investigation, 1, 5; Naclerio, 102; rent supplement, 28; section 8 mod rehab, 90–91, 94; Section 221(d)(3), 27–28, 62; Section 223 (e), 30; Section 235, 31–36; Section 236, 38–40, 42–43; Section 608, 6–13, 126; Title I, 17–19, 22–24
FHA Circular, 34–35
"FHA Investigation" (1954), 5
FHA *Minimum Property Requirements for Multi-Family Buildings*, 10
FHA "Mortgage Letter," 35
FHA *Underwriting Manual*, 36
Federal Managers Financial Act, 74
Federal National Mortgage Assoc., *See* Fannie Mae
Fifth Amendment, 72, 101
Flagpoles, 114
Flexible Subsidy, 54
Flushing, NY, 19
FMR, 85–86, 91–92, 95–96, 165, 173–74
Foley, Raymond, 7
Food for Africa, 105, 122
Forbes, 157
Ford administration, 149
Ford Pinto, 37
Forest Oaks, 81
Fort Worth, TX, 101
Fort Worth, Texas Regional Office, 79
Fortune, 143
Franks, Rep. Barney, 105
Free Siding, 21
Frieden, Bernard, 166
Fund of Funds, 55–56

GAO, 2, 91, 96, 117–18, 136, 152, 153
General Accounting Office. *See* GAO
General Counsel. *See* John Knapp
General Electric, 74
General Motors, 159
Geneva Towers, 65

George Mason University, 118
Georgetown Prepatory School, 80
Gilliam, Dubois, 89-90, 98, 99, 119, 147
Ginnie Mae, 28, 77, 81-83, 85, 120
Glen Oaks Village, 12
Golden Fleece Award, 96
Gonzalez, Rep. Henry, 73, 120
Goodman, Paul, 177
Gorbachev, 115
Government National Mortgage Assoc.
    See Ginnie Mae
Grace, Thomas, 8
Grassley, Sen. Charles, 93
Great Society, 29, 33, 51
Green Bay, WI, 169
Gresham's Law, 144
"Gulag of Washington," 113-14
Gulledge, Asst. Sec. Eugene, 31, 40, 43-
    44, 130

Hagerty, James, 5
Hagman, Donald, 13
Hale, Janet, 100
Harrell, Marilyn Louise. *See* Robbin
    HUD
Harris, Sec. Patricia Roberts, 143, 145
Harvard Law School, 41
Hawaii, 56, 61
Hawkins, Sen. Paula, 93
Hayes, Robert, 115
Heaven's Gate, 76
Heclo, H. Hugh, 116, 118
Heileman, John, 117
Heinz, Sen. John, 93
Helmsely, Leona, 127
HHFA, 1, 5, 7, 12, 22
Hills, Sec. Carla, 52, 54, 80, 98-99, 143-
    45
Hindenburg, 84
HIPPLE, 57
Hoboken, NJ, 96
Hoffer, Eric, 163
"Holder in Due Course," 22
Hollyday, Guy, 5
Holmes, Sherlock, 121
Homeownership, 29-31. *See also* Sec-
    tion 235
Honolulu, HI, 145, 169
"Horse and the Swallows," 159
Horton, Willie, 99

Housing Allowance Experiment, 92,
    160, 166, 170
House Appropriations Committee, 54,
    73, 144
House Banking and Currency Commit-
    tee, 31
House Banking, Finance, and Urban Af-
    fairs Committee, 73
House Employment and Housing Sub-
    committee, *See* Lantos Committee
House Government Operations Commit-
    tee, 72, 95, 97, 116, 120
House HUD, Space, Science, and Veter-
    ans Appropriations Subcommittee,
    73
House Judiciary Committee, 72
Housing and Community Development
    Act of 1974, 53, 85, 136
Housing and Home Finance Agency, *See*
    HHFA
Housing and Urban Development Act of
    1965, 129
Housing and Urban Development of
    1968, 37-38
Housing and Urban Development Act of
    1970, 135
Housing in the Seventies: A Report of the
    National Hsing Rev., 13, 130
Housing Partnership Investments Lim-
    ited, *See* HIPPLE
Housing Resources Management Inc.
    (HRM), 59, 65
Housing shortage, 6-7, 157, 159
Housing Vouchers, Affect on low rent
    market, 165; format, 164-65 housing
    gap, 164; housing standards, 165-66;
    opportunity vs. outcome, 164-65;
    public housing, 173-74; right ratio,
    164; right rent, 164-65
Houston, TX, 79
HUD, Choice, 166, 173-74, 176-78; co-
    insurance, 76-8, 80-85; Congress,
    116; crooks, 146-47; Debbie Dean,
    99-100; discretionary programs,
    150-523; flotsam and jetsam, 103-5;
    GAO, 117-18; inspector general, 84-
    85, 105, 119-20; interest subsidy pro-
    grams, 28-34, 37-38, 40, 43-48;
    leadership, 143-46, 148; manage-
    ment, 125-28; media, 113-15; Mur-

phy, Lynda, 80, 102-3; new housing for the poor, 157-58; OMB, 118-19; Pierce, 2, 71-76, 80, 97-99, 146; public housing, 134-40; reform, 150-152; Robbin HUD, 2, 125, 147; Rozet, 54, 56, 58-60, 63-69; 128, 1504; Section 8 existing, 85, 92; Section 8 mod rehab, 87-88, 90-96; Section 23, 128-131; staffing 148-50; Wilson, Lance, 93, 98 101-2, 157
HUD Board of Contract Appeals, 65
Hue, Lois, 61

Income Equities Corp., 56-57
Independent Counsel. See Adams, Judge Arlin
Inspection Manual, 165
Inspector General (other than Paul Adams), 73, 104, 120-121, 126
Inspector General Act of 1978, 85, 121
Investors Overseas Services. See IOS
Internal Revenue Service, 5, 62, 69, 93, 116
IOS, 55

Jackson, Jesse, 52, 64
Jackson, Reggie, 152
Jaffee, Harry, 79
Jersey City, NJ, 12
JOBCO, 146
Johnson, John R., 61
Johnson, Pres. Lyndon, 28
Jose de Diego-Beekman, 45, 56
"Junk Notes," 61-63
Justice Department, 22, 93

Kahn, Alfred, 128
Kain, John, 160
Kaiser Committee, 46
Kalish, Robert, 66
Karem, Michael, 103-04
Kargman, Max, 46
Katz, Lawrence, 36
Kaufman, Herbert, 147
Keating, Frank, 65
Kemp, Sec. Jack, 48, 64-65, 68, 131, 143
Kentucky Reagan for President Committee, 104
Kissinger, Henry, 101, 143-44
Knapp, John, 87-88, 100

Korean War, 11
Kristol, Irving, 177
Kuwait War Resolution, 106

Lampoc Prison, 147
Landrieu, Secretary Moon, 143
Lane, Vince, 68
Lantos, Rep. Tom, 1, 76, 80-81, 125, 144
Lantos Committee, 1, 72, 89, 115, 122, 144, 146-47
Lantos Hearings, See Lantos Committee.
Las Vegas, NV, 90
Leaky Bucket, 174
Leased Housing. See Section 8 Existing or Section 23
Lee, Jack, 19-20
Levitt, Bill, 17
LHA, See PHA
Life Magazine, 20
Limited Distribution Entities, 27, 40-41, 56, 59-63
Limited Partnerships, See Limited Distribution Entities
Loan Management Projects, 53-54
London, 119
Lone Ranger, 84
Long, Sen. Russell, 7, 8, 15
Los Angeles, CA, 6, 65, 169, 174
Los Angeles Times, 56, 122
Long Island, NY, 19
Lott, Sen. Trent, 93
Louisville, KY, 169
"Lowballing," 163
Lubar, Sheldon, 76
Lynn, Sec. James, 143, 145

Maginot Line, 153
Manafort, Paul, 94-95, 105, 106
Management Assistance Group Inc. (MAGI), 61
Maples, Marla, 1
Margugio, Paul, 132
Marshall, Justice Thurgood, 75
"Masters of the Universe," 101-3
Master Workout Agreement, 59
McCain, Sen. John, 93
McCarthy, Sen. Joseph, 133
McGrath, Jack, 74
Meal Ticket Program, 157-58
Media, 1, 113-15

Melbourne, Viscount, 106
Mercury Marauder, 37
Miami, FL, 169
Miller, Budget Director James C. 3rd, 74
Milwaukee Field Office, 36
"Minority Crook of the Year," *See*
    Briscoe, Leonard
Misczynski, Dean, 13
Mississippi, 61, 68, 90
Mitchell, Sen. George, 64
Mitchell, John, 95
Model Cities, 51, 59, 106
Model Homes, 20
Modernization, 138-40, 175
Mondale, Sen. Walter, 33
Montgomery Ward, 23
Monticciolo, Joseph, 146-47
Moore, Sen., 93
Moratorium, 44, 51, 130, 136, 145
Morreale, Vin, 66
Morrison, Rep. Bruce, 88, 121-22
"Mortgaging Out," 13
Moses, Stephen D., 58, 65
Motel Almogordo, 8
Moynihan, Sen. Patrick, 71
Mozambique, 105
Municipal Securities Group, 101
Murphy, Sen. George, 94
Murphy, Lynda, 64, 80-81, 102-3

Naclerio, Alexander, 102, 146
Namath, Joe Willie, 79
National Association of Home Builders,
    16, 40, 46, 98-99
National Association of Housing and Re-
    development Officials, 16
National Association of Housing Manag-
    ers and Owners, 46
National Association of Realtors, 145
National Coalition for the Homeless, 115
National Corporation of Housing Part-
    nerships, 57, 78
National Development Services Corp.
    (NDS), 58, 61
National Investors Development Ser-
    vices Corp. (NIDC), 58-59, 65
Negative Sum Game, 150
Neri, Patrick, 122
Newark, NJ, 139
Newark Field Office, 32, 146

New Coca-Cola, 76
New Haven, CT, 139
Newman, Stanley, 90, 98
New Mexico, 8, 58
New Orleans, LA, 39, 139, 169
New York City, NY, 51, 97, 49, 146, 149,
    169
New York Field Office, 8
New York Regional Office, 146
New York Times, 74, 115, 122, 159
New York Yankees, 126
Nixon, Pres. Richard, II 44, 145
Non profit organizations, 27, 51-54, 58
North American Indemnity Company, 19
Northern California, 23
NYU Law School, 71

Oakland, CA, 20
Office of Economic Opportunity (OEO),
    29, 59
Office of General Counsel, 88
Office of the Inspector General, *See* In-
    spector General
Office of Management and Budget, *See*
    OMB
Office of Policy Development and Re-
    search, 92
Office of the Solicitor General, 93
Oklahoma, 63, 65
Okun, Arthur, 147
Ols, John, 118
Omaha, NE, 6
OMB, 2, 74, 118-19, 147, 176-77
Operating Subsidies, 135
Order of the Garter, 105-06

Packard, David, 152
Paine, Thomas, 177
PaineWebber, 101-02; 149, 157
Passaic, NJ, 132
Paterson Tavern, 32, 115
Paterson, NJ, 32
Paul and Peter, 158
Payne, Sen. Frederick, 11
Payne, John, 118
Penn, Arthur, 68
Pentagon, 2
Pepper, Sen. Clyde, 132-33
Percent-of-Rent-Formula, 170-71
Percy, Sen. Charles, 30

Performance Funding System, See PFS
PFS, 138, 140
PHAs, 11, 86, 88–89, 92, 129–40, 174–77
Philadelphia, PA, 139, 169
Philco, 8
Pierce, Sam, agenda, 72–73; background, 71, 74, 97; Debbie Dean, 92, 97, 99–102, 105; ethical standard, 73, 98; Hills Carla, 80, 98–99; interests, 75; management philosophy, 74–75; media coverage, 72; power, relationship to, 75, 96, 101; selection process, 75, 92–93, 98, 102, 105; Watt, James, 94; Wilson, Lance, 98, 101–2
Pike, Hugh, 57, 65
Pitts, Jon Will, 83
Pittsburgh, PA, 169
Political Ethics and Public Office, 149
Pollack, Michael, 79
Ponzi Scheme, 85
Porkbarrel programs, 85–95
Potomac, 115
Powell, Clyde, 8, 146
Program Ombudsman, 84–85
Protex-Wall, 19
Providence, RI, 139
Proxmire, Sen. William, 45, 95–96, 100
Prudential Insurance Company, 74
Pruitt-Igoe, 115
Public Housing Authorities, See PHAs
Public Housing Decontrol Initiative, 132
Public Housing Program, Brooke amendments, 134–35; capital improvements, 138–40; congressional responses, 133–38, 140; 23; contract consolidation, 134; elderly, 134; federal control/local autonomy, 131–32, 134–38; record, 27, 133–134; initial legislation, 131–32; 1949 redirection, 133–34; management, 131–140; operating subsidies, 133, 134–36, 138; private rental housing, 133, 140; rent policies, 134–35, 137–39; site selection, 134; tenant selection, 132–34, 136–37; vacancy rates, 138, 139–40
Puerto Ricans, 34, 104
PUSH, 52, 65

Queenan, J. Michael, 93–94

Rainbow Coalition, 64
Ramblers, 40
Readers Digest, 8
Reagan administration, 73–74, 88,
Reagan, President Ronald, 72, 89, 159
Realty Investment Associates, *See* RIA
Redlining, 33–34
Red Tape, 114, 147, 153
Regardie's, 79
Rental Housing Production Program, 164
Rent Supplement Program, 28–29
Rent to Income Ratios, 38–39, 47, 134–3, 137–9. *See* also "Choice"
Republicans, 29, 129–31, 133
Reuss, Henry, Rep., 38
Revenue Act of 1913, 41
Rexall, 55
Rhinelander, John, 149
RIA, 57
"Right Ratios," 164
"Right rent," 164
Riot Commission, 134
Rip Van Winkle, 113
Robbin HUD, 2, 115, 125, 147
Robin Hook. *See* A. Bruce Rozet
Robertson, Sen. H. Willis, 43–44
Rogue Elephant, 106
Romney, Sec. George, 31, 36, 40, 136, 143–45
Rozet, A. Bruce, Chernobyl Ltd., 66–67; Commonwealth United 54–56; compensation, 57, 61; Cornfeld, 55, 5, 60, 65; HIPPLE, 57; HRM, 59, 65; HUD management, 59, 66–67, 68; IEC, 56–57, 68; Jackson, Jesse, 52–53, 64; junk notes, 61–63; Kemp, Jack, 64–65, 68; NDS, 58–59; political influence, 63–64; PUSH, 52–53, 65; SEC, 57, 65; tax shelters, 40–42, 46, 56–63
Ruskin, John, 147

Salvation Army, 158
San Antonio, TX, 39, 47
San Francisco, CA, 23, 65, 160, 169
San Francisco Field Office, 23
Savings and Loan, 63, 72, 76,83, 128
Schumer, Rep. Charles, 94
Schussheim, Morton, 126, 128

Seabrook Apartments, 95, 105
Seabrook, NJ, 95
Sears Roebuck, 23
Seattle, WA, 39
Securities and Exchange Committee (SEC), 57, 65
Section 8 Existing, 85–86. *See also* Housing Voucher
Section 8 Moderate Rehabilitation Program audit, 120–22 Dean, 92–93, 97, 99–101, 105; Demery, 102, 105; fair market rents, 85–86, 91–92, 95–96; fair sharing, 85, 87–88; legal opinion, 87–88; Pierce, 74–75, 92, 105; program framework, 86; project selection, 86, 92–95; 105; regulations, 86–90; tax credits, 87, 91, 96; waste, 95–96
Section 8 New Construction and Substantial Rehabilitation, 73, 88–90, 145–46
Section 23, 128–131
Section 221 (d)(2), 30
Section 207, 16
Section 221 (d)(3) Below Market Interest Rate Program, 27–28, 59, 61
Section 223 (e), 30, 35
Section 223 (f), *See* Coinsurance
Section 235, accomplishments, 29; administrative problems, 34–36; condition of properties, 32–34, 36–37; congressional oversight, 31; corruption, 32, 34, 146; history, 29–31; maintenance, 35–36; management, 127; money (lack of), 35–37; Romney, 31, 36, 145; underwriting standards, 30–31, 35
Section 236, accomplishments, 29; aftermath, 44–48; 51–54; income limits, 37–39; legislative history, 37–38; management 40, 127; mortgage processing, 39–40; operating expenses 39–40, 45, 47–49; profit, 40–41; rent-to income ratios, 38–39, 47; reorganization, 40; Romney, 40, 145; tax shelters, 41–42
Section 244, 76. *See* Coinsurance
Section 608, 5, accomplishments, 6, 17; amendments, 9, 11, 12–13; architecture, 10; congressional oversight, 15–

16; construction, 11–12; corruption, 8, 146; fees, 9–12; growth, 6–8; housing shortage 6–7, 16–17; land, 11–14; leaseholds, 12; legislative background, 6, 19–21; management, 126; media coverage, 1, 114; profitability, 9–14; windfalls, 12–14
Secretary's Committee on Waste, Fraud, and Mismanagement, 100
Senate Appropriations Subcommittee, 100, 135
Senate Banking, Housing and Urban Affairs Committee, 63–64, 73, 117
Senate Committee on Banking and Currency (1954), 5–6, 14, 16–7
Senate Investigating Committee, 116–17, 151
Seven Days in May, 2
Sevier, Walter, 79
Shays, Rep. Christopher, 122
Sierra Pointe Apartments, 90–92
Shelby, Richard, 94
Simon, William, 14
Sixteenth Annual Report of the FHA, 17
Sixty Minutes, 31, 115
Smith, Wallace, 14
Soap operas, 75
Socialism, 151
"Social Pork Barrels," 97
Sofaer, Abraham, 88
Sonneblick Goldman, 57
South Bronx, 45, 56
Southmark, 82
Soviet Union, 75
Sowell, David, 98
Sparkman, Sen. John, 43–44
Specter, Sen. Arlen, 93
Springfield-Holyoke, MA, 93
Staff report, 31–32
Stanford Research Institute, 55
"Star Wars," 88
State Department, 88
State Street Development Corp., 121
Stegman, Michael, 152
"Steppin Fetchit," 73
Sternlieb, George, 30, 51
St Germain, Rep. Fernand, 76
Stockman, David, 97
Stokvis, Jack, 96

Straight-Line Depreciation. *See* Tax
  shelter
Strauss, Joe, 93
Suede Shoe Boys, 20, 146
Sum-of-the-Years Digits. *See* Deprecia-
  tion
Sunasco, 55
Sunset Park, 33-34
Supreme Court, 22, 149
Surrey, Stanley, 41
Switzerland, 66
Syndication, 56-63, 91-92, 96

Taft, Sen. Robert, 17
Tampa, FL, 139
"Tar Baby" Projects, 52
Taubman, Paul, 41
Tax Credits, 64, 87, 91-92, 96
Tax Reform, 64, 87
Tax Reform Act of 1986, 87
Tax shelters, 41-43, 46-64, 87, 91-92,
  128
Taylor, William "Bill," 94
Teapot Dome, 72
Texas, 63
The Economist, 119
The Tenement Landlord, 30
*Third Annual Report on National Hous-
  ing Goals*, 44
Thompson, Dennis, 149
Thornburgh, Attorney General Richard,
  72
Thurmond, Sen. Strom, 93
Tichy, Noel, 177
Time, 113
Tin Men, 20-21, 23
Titanic, 127
Title I, 5; government viewpoint, 17-18;
  lack of monitoring, 23; lender's role,
  17, 21-23; management, 126-27;
  scams, 18-21; structural fault, 21-22
Toote, Gloria, 97
Touche Ross, 43
Trammel-Crow, 127
Tribal Potlatch, 106
Truman, President Harry, 7
Trump, Donald, 1
Trump, Frederick, 1, 11, 12, 14
Trump, Ivana, 1
Tulsa, 65

"25-25-25," 161-63
"Two Herds of Horses, Two Stacks of
  Carrots," 158-59
Tyler House, 59, 65, 164

UDAG Program, 74, 89-90, 95-96, 98,
  101-04; 119; 147, 149
Ujima Village, 65
United Airlines, 125
United States Testing Laboratory, 19
U.S. Attorney General, 68
U.S. Bureau of Census, 160
U.S. Housing Act of 1937, 85, 129-130,
  131-133
U.S. News and World Report, 97
U.S. Treasury, 5, 71, 128
Urban Development Action Grants, *See*
  UDAG Program
Urban Institute, 170
Useful Life. *See* Depreciation

van der Voort, Thomas L., 100
Venereal House, 80
Veterans, 6-7
Veterans Administration Housing Pro-
  grams, 7, 13
Veteran's Emergency Act of 1946, *See*
  Section 608
Virgin Islands, 139

Wagner, Sen. Robert, 132
Wallace, Mike, 27, 31
Wall Street, 149
Wall Street Journal, 94, 122
Walsh, Sen.David, 132
Washington D.C., 6, 31, 43, 57, 101, 105,
  139, 169
Washington Monthly, 74
Washington Post, 122, 159
Watts (Los Angeles), 65
Watts, James, 94, 53
Weaver, Sec. Robert, 37, 143
Weinberger, Caspar, 136
Wherry, Sen.Kenneth, 15
"Why We Need More Waste, Fraud, and
  Abuse in the Pentagon," 2
Wilshire Investments Corp., 63
Widnall, Rep. William, 30; 129
Wilson, Lance, 93-94, 98, 101-03, 149,
  157

Wilson, Sen. Pete, 93
Windfalls, 1, 5, 8, 12–14, 91, 150, 157
Windfall for Wipeouts, 13
Winn Group, 93, 47
Winn, Phil, 92–94, 104
Wiseman, Shirley, 98, 104
Wolfe, Thomas, 101
Wood, Sec. Robert, 143
Woodbury, Coleman, 16
Woodlawn Community Development
    Corp., 59, 68

Worcester, MA, 90, 121
World War II, 2, post-war housing condi-
    tions, 6–7, 16
Wrap Around Notes, 61–63

Yale University, 71
Yonkers Housing Authority, 146
York Associates, 82